UNPOPULAR OPINIONS

UNPOPULAR OPINIONS

by

DOROTHY L. SAYERS

LONDON
VICTOR GOLLANCZ LTD
1946

Printed in Great Britain by
The Camelot Press Ltd., London and Southampton

CONTENTS

FOREWORD

I HAVE CALLED THIS COLLECTION of fugitive pieces "Unpopular Opinions," partly, to be sure, because to warn a person off a book is the surest way of getting him to read it, but chiefly because I have evidence that all the opinions expressed have in fact caused a certain amount of annoyance one way and the other. Indeed, the papers called "Christian Morality," "Forgiveness" and "Living to Work" were so unpopular with the persons who commissioned them that they were suppressed before they appeared: the first because American readers would be shocked by what they understood of it; the second because what the Editor of a respectable newspaper wanted (and got) was Christian sanction for undying hatred against the enemy; the third—originally intended for a Sunday evening B.B.C. "Postscript"—on the heterogeneous grounds that it appeared to have political tendencies, and that "our public do not want to be admonished by a woman." With the exception of these, and the paper on "Dr. Watson's Third Marriage," all the items in the collection have either appeared as articles or been delivered as addresses at various times ranging from 1935 to 1945.

Speaking generally, the first section courts unpopularity by founding itself on theology and not on "religion." The second will offend all those who are irritated by England and the English, all those who use and enjoy slatternly forms of speech, all manly men, womanly women, and people who prefer wealth to work. The third will annoy those who cannot bear other people to enjoy themselves in their own way.

Perhaps I should add a word about this third section. The game of applying the methods of the "Higher Criticism" to the Sherlock Holmes canon was begun, many years ago, by Monsignor Ronald Knox, with the aim of showing that, by those methods, one could disintegrate a modern classic as speciously as a certain school of critics have endeavoured to disintegrate the Bible. Since then, the thing has become a hobby among a select set of jesters here and in America. The rule of the game is that it must be played as solemnly as a county cricket match at Lord's: the slightest touch of extravagance or burlesque ruins the atmosphere. The exercise has become a recreation; but those who like their recreations to exert a moral influence may take note of how easy it is for an unscrupulous pseudo-scholarship to extract fantastic and misleading conclusions from a literary text by a series of omissions, emendations and distortions of context. There are a number of literary biographies and works of criticism at present enjoying an undeserved popularity which have been perpetrated by precisely such methods—and not as a game. The final article, on "Aristotle and Detective Fiction" is, on the other hand, quite serious, scholarly and—I will venture to add—sound.

I have not tried to bring my opinions up to date, though where necessary I have added an indication of the time at which they were first uttered. Nor have I altered the rhythm of the spoken word, or expunged the occasional repetitions which are bound to occur in speeches and articles produced on divers occasions on one and the same subject. The gain would not be sufficient to offset the loss of spontaneity.

DOROTHY L. SAYERS.

1946.

CHRISTIAN MORALITY

SETTING ASIDE THE SCANDAL caused by His Messianic claims and His reputation as a political firebrand, only two accusations of personal depravity seem to have been brought against Jesus of Nazareth. First, that He was a Sabbath-breaker. Secondly, that He was "a gluttonous man and a winebibber, a friend of publicans and sinners"—or (to draw aside the veil of Elizabethan English which makes it all sound so much more respectable) that He ate too heartily, drank too freely, and kept very disreputable company, including grafters of the lowest type and ladies who were no better than they should be.

For nineteen and a half centuries, the Christian Churches have laboured, not without success, to remove this unfortunate impression made by their Lord and Master. They have hustled the Magdalens from the Communion-table, founded Total Abstinence Societies in the name of Him who made the water wine, and added improvements of their own, such as various bans and anathemas upon dancing and theatre-going. They have transferred the Sabbath from Saturday to Sunday, and, feeling that the original commandment "thou shalt not work" was rather half-hearted, have added to it a new commandment, "thou shalt not play."

Whether these activities are altogether in the spirit of Christ we need not argue. One thing is certain: that they have produced some very curious effects upon our language. They have, for example, succeeded in placing a strangely restricted interpretation on such words as "virtue," "purity" and "morality." There are a great many people now living in the world who firmly believe that "Christian morals," as distinct from purely secular morality, consist in three things and three things only: Sunday observance, not getting intoxicated, and not practising—well, in fact, not practising "immorality." I do not say that the Churches themselves would agree with this definition; I say only that this is the impression they have contrived to give the world, and that the remarkable thing about it is its extreme unlikeness to the impression produced by Christ.

Now, I do not suggest that the Church does wrong to pay attention to the regulation of bodily appetites and the proper observance of holidays. What I do suggest is that by over-emphasising this side of morality, to the comparative neglect of others, she has not only betrayed her mission but, incidentally, defeated her own aims even about "morality." She has, in fact, made an alliance with Cæsar, and Cæsar, having used her for his own purposes, has now withdrawn his support—for that is Cæsar's pleasant way of behaving. For the last three hundred years or so, Cæsar has been concerned to maintain a public order based upon the rights of private property: consequently, he has had a vested interest in "morality." Strict morals make for the stability of family life and the orderly devolution of property, and Cæsar (namely, the opinion of highly placed and influential people) has been delighted that the Church should do the work of persuading the citizen to behave accordingly. Further, a drunken workman is a bad workman, and thriftless extravagance is bad for business; therefore, Cæsar has welcomed the encouragement of the Church for those qualities which make for self-help in industry. As for Sunday observance, the Church could have that if she liked, so long as it did not interfere with trade. To work all round the week ends in diminishing production; the one day in seven was necessary, and what the Church chose to do with it was no affair of Cæsar's.

Unhappily, however, this alliance for mutual benefit between Church and Cæsar has not lasted. The transfer of property from the private owner to the public trust or limited company enables Cæsar to get on very well without personal morals and domestic stability; the conception that the consumer exists for the sake of production has made extravagance and thriftless consumption a commercial necessity: consequently, Cæsar no longer sees eye to eye with the Church about these matters, and will as soon encourage a prodigal frivolity on Sunday as on any other day of the week. Why not? Business is business. The Church, shocked and horrified, is left feebly protesting against Cæsar's desertion, and denouncing a "relaxation of moral codes," in which the heedless world is heartily aided and abetted by the State. The easy path of condemning what Cæsar condemns or is not concerned to defend has turned out to be like the elusive garden-path in *Through the Looking-Glass*; just when one seemed to be getting somewhere, it gave itself a little shake and one found oneself walking in the opposite direction.

Now, if we look at the Gospels with the firm intention to discover the *emphasis* of Christ's morality, we shall find that it did not lie at all along the lines laid down by the opinion of highly placed and influential people. Disreputable people who knew they were disreputable were gently told to "go and sin no more"; the really unparliamentary language was reserved for those thrifty, respectable, and sabbatarian citizens who enjoyed Cæsar's approval and their own. And the one and only thing that ever seems to have roused the "meek and mild" Son of God to a display of outright physical violence was precisely the assumption that "business was business." The money-changers in Jerusalem drove a very thriving trade, and made as shrewd a profit as any other set of brokers who traffic in foreign exchange; but the only use Christ had for these financiers was to throw their property down the front steps of the Temple.

Perhaps if the Churches had had the courage to lay their emphasis where Christ laid it, we might not have come to this present frame of mind in which it is assumed that the value of all work, and the value of all people, is to be assessed in terms of economics. We might not so readily take for granted that the production of anything (no matter how useless or dangerous) is justified so long as it issues in increased profits and wages; that so long as a man is well paid, it does not matter whether his work is worth-while in itself or good for his soul; that so long as a business deal keeps on the windy side of the law, we need not bother about its ruinous consequences to society or the individual. Or at any rate, now that we have seen the chaos of bloodshed which follows upon economic chaos, we might at least be able to listen with more confidence to the voice of an untainted and undivided Christendom. Doubtless it would have needed courage to turn Dives from the church-door along with Mary Magdalen; (has any prosperously fraudulent banker, I wonder, ever been refused Communion on the grounds that he was, in the words of the English Prayer-book, "an open and notorious evil liver"?) But lack of courage, and appeasement in the face of well-organised iniquity, does nothing to avert catastrophe or to secure respect.

In the list of those Seven Deadly Sins which the Church officially recognises there is the sin which is sometimes called Sloth, and sometimes Accidie. The one name is obscure to us; the other is a little misleading. It does not mean lack of hustle: it means the slow sapping of all the faculties by indifference, and by the sensation that life is pointless and meaningless, and not-worth-while. It is, in fact, the very thing which has been called the Disease of Democracy. It is the child of Covetousness, and the parent of those other two sins which the Church calls Lust and Gluttony. Covetousness breaks down the standards by which we assess our spiritual values, and causes us to look for satisfactions in this world. The next step is the sloth of mind and body, the emptiness of heart, which destroy energy and purpose and issue in that general attitude to the universe which the inter-war jazz musicians aptly named "the Blues." For the cure of the Blues, Cæsar (who has his own axe to grind) prescribes the dreary frivolling which the Churches and respectable people have agreed to call "immorality," and which, in these days, is as far as possible from the rollicking enjoyment of bodily pleasures which, rightly considered, are sinful only by their excess. The mournful and medical aspect assumed by "immorality" in the present age is a sure sign that in trying to cure these particular sins we are patching up the symptoms instead of tackling the disease at its roots.

To these facts it is only fair to say that the Churches are at last waking up. The best Christian minds are making very strenuous efforts to readjust the emphasis and to break the alliance with Cæsar. The chief danger is lest the Churches, having for so long acquiesced in the exploiting of the many by the few, should now think to adjust the balance by helping on the exploitation of the few by the many, instead of attacking the false standards by which everybody, rich and poor alike, has now come to assess the value of life and work. If the Churches make this mistake, they will again be merely following the shift of power from one class of the community to the other and deserting the dying Cæsar to enlist the support of his successor. A more equal distribution of wealth is a good and desirable thing, but it can scarcely be attained, and cannot certainly be maintained unless we get rid of the superstition that acquisitiveness is a virtue and that the value of anything is represented in terms of profit and cost.

The Churches are justifiably shocked when the glamour of a film actress is assessed by the number of her love affairs and divorces; they are less shocked when the glamour of a man, or of a work of art is headlined in dollars. They are shocked when "unfortunates" are reduced to selling their bodies; they are less shocked when journalists are reduced to selling their souls. They are shocked when good food is wasted by riotous living; they are less shocked when good crops are wasted and destroyed because of over-production and under-consumption. Something has gone wrong with the emphasis; and it is becoming very evident that until that emphasis is readjusted, the economic balance-sheet of the world will have to be written in blood.

FORGIVENESS

Forgiveness is a very difficult matter. Many varieties of behaviour go by that name, and not all of them are admirable. There is the kind that says: "I forgive her as a Christian, but I shall never speak to her again." This is adequately dealt with by the caustic definition: "Christian forgiveness, which is no forgiveness at all," and need not be discussed, any more than the self-interest of those who—

> *Drink the champagne that she sends them,*
> *But they never can forget.*

There is also the priggish variety, which greets persecution with the ostentatious announcement, "I forgive you, Jones, and I will pray for you." This, though it can base itself strongly on ethical and Scriptural sanction, shares with pacifism the serious practical disadvantage of so inflaming the evil passions of Jones that if the injured party had malignantly determined to drive Jones to the devil he could scarcely have hit upon a surer way. There is the conditional: "I will forgive you on condition you say you are sorry and never do it again." That has about it something which smacks too much of a legal bargain, and we are forced to remember that no man is so free from trespass himself that he can afford to insist on conditions. Only God is in a position to do that; and we recall the Catholic teaching that confession, contrition and amendment are the necessary conditions of absolution. But if we assert that Divine forgiveness is of this bargaining kind, we meet with a thundering denial from poet and prophet and from God Himself:

> *Doth Jehovah forgive a debt only on condition that it shall*
> *Be payed? Doth he forgive Pollution only on conditions of Purity?*
> *That Debt is not forgiven! That Pollution is not forgiven!*
> *Such is the forgiveness of the gods, the moral virtues of the*
> *Heathen, whose tender mercies are cruelty. But Jehovah's salvation*
> *Is without money and without price, in the continual forgiveness of sins,*
> *In the perpetual mutual sacrifice in great eternity. For behold!*
> *There is none that liveth and sinneth not! And this is the covenant*
> *Of Jehovah. "If you forgive one another, so shall Jehovah forgive you;*
> *That He Himself may dwell among you."*

BLAKE: *Jerusalem.*

13

God's conditions, it appears, are of another kind. There is nothing about demanding repentance and restitution or promises not to offend again: we must forgive unconditionally if we hope to be forgiven ourselves: "as we forgive our debtors"—"unto seventy times seven."

The whole teaching of the New Testament about forgiveness is haunted by paradox and enigma, and cannot be summed up in any phrase about simple kindliness. "Whether is easier: to say *Thy sins be forgiven thee* or to say *Arise and walk*? But that ye may know that the Son of Man hath power on earth to forgive sins (then saith He to the sick of the palsy) Arise, take up thy bed and go." The irony is so profound that we are not certain which way to take it. "Do you think forgiveness is something glib and simple? To be sure —it is just as simple as *this*. Does it seem to you formidably difficult? To be sure, so is *this*—but you see it can be done." Whereat, according to St. Luke, everybody, though pleased, was a little alarmed and thought it a very odd business.

It may be easier to understand what forgiveness is, if we first clear away misconceptions about what it does. It does not wipe out the consequences of the sin. The words and images used for forgiveness in the New Testament frequently have to do with the cancellation of a debt: and it is scarcely necessary to point out that when a debt is cancelled, this does not mean that the money is miraculously restored from nowhere. It means only that the obligation originally due from the borrower is voluntarily discharged by the lender. If I injure you and you mulct me in damages, then I bear the consequences; if you forbear to prosecute, then you bear the consequences. If the injury is irreparable, and you are vindictive, injury is added to injury; if you are forgiving and I am repentant, then we share the consequences and gain a friendship. But in every case the consequences are borne by somebody. The Parable of the Unmerciful Servant adds a further illuminating suggestion: that forgiveness is not merely a mutual act, but a social act. If injuries are not forgiven all round, the grace of pardon is made ineffective, and the inexorable judgment of the Law is forced into operation.

One thing emerges from all this: that forgiveness is not a doing-away of consequences; nor is it primarily a remission of punishment. A child may be forgiven and "let off" punishment, or punished and then forgiven; either way may bring good results. But no good will come of leaving him unpunished and unforgiven. Forgiveness is the re-establishment of a right relationship, in which the parties can genuinely feel and behave as freely with one another as though the unhappy incident had never taken place. But it is impossible to enjoy a right relationship with an offender who, when pardoned, continues to behave in an obdurate and unsocial manner to the injured party and to those whom he has injured, because there is something in him that obstructs the relationship. So that, while God does not, and man dare not, demand repentance as a condition for *bestowing* pardon, repentance remains an essential condition for *receiving* it. Hence the Church's twofold insistence—first that repentance is necessary, and secondly that all sin is pardoned instantly in the mere fact of the sinner's repentance. Nobody has to sit about being humiliated in the outer office while God despatches important business, before condescending to issue a stamped official discharge accompanied by an improving lecture. Like the Father of the Prodigal Son, God can see repentance coming a great way off and is there to meet it, and the repentance *is* the reconciliation.

If God does not stand upon His dignity with penitent sinners, still less, one would suppose, should we. But then, God is not inhibited, as we are, by unrepented sins of His own. It is when the injuries have been mutual that forgiveness becomes so complicated, since, as La Rochefoucauld truly observes, it is very difficult to forgive those whom we have injured. The only fruitful line of thought to follow is, I think, to bear in mind that forgiveness has no necessary concern with payment or non-payment of reparations; its aim is the establishment of a free relationship. This aim is in no way advanced by mutual recrimination, or by the drawing-up of a detailed account to ascertain which side, on balance, is the more aggrieved party. If both were equally and immediately repentant, forgiveness—mutual and instantaneous—would *be* the right relationship.

But are there not crimes which are unforgivable or which we, at any rate, find we cannot bring ourselves to forgive? At the present moment, that is a question which we are bound to ask ourselves. And it is here, especially, that we must make a great effort to clear our minds of clutter. The issue is not really affected by arguments about who began first, or whether bombs or blockade are the more legitimate weapon to use against women and children, or whether a civilian is a military objective; nor need we object that no amount of forgiveness will do away with the consequences of the crimes— since we have already seen that forgiveness is not incompatible with consequence. The real question is this: When the war comes to an end, is there going to be anything in our minds, or in the minds of the enemy, that will prevent the re-establishment of a right relationship? That relationship need not necessarily be one of equal power on either side, and it need not exclude proper preventive measures against a renewal of the conflict—those considerations are again irrelevant. Are there any crimes that in themselves make forgiveness and right relations impossible?

If we again look at the New Testament, we shall find that what some people, with unconscious sarcasm, persist in calling "the simple Gospel" presents us, as usual, with a monstrous and shattering paradox. The most spectacular sin recorded there is the deliberate murder of God; and it is forgiven on the grounds that "they know not what they do." Is ignorance, then, an excuse? Can a man qualify for Heaven by pleading that he cannot tell right from wrong? Is not that the most damning of all disabilities—the final blasphemy that "shall not be forgiven, neither in this world, nor in the world to come"? Here is a distinction drawn like a sword at a point which we can scarcely see on the map.

Or perhaps the dividing line is clear enough, after all. The soldiers who crucified God had not, it is true, the heroic imagination that could see beyond their plain military duty to the eternal verities. But there was nothing in their ignorant hearts impenetrable to light. To such dim glimpses as they had, they seem to have responded. One ran for the hyssop; another said: "Indeed, there was something divine about this criminal." Forgiveness might work here and find no obstruction. But those others—all of them highly respectable people—had seen the healing power of God blaze in their eyes like the sun; they looked it full in the face, and said that it was the devil. This is the ultimate corruption that leaves no place for pardon; "I have so hardened my heart" (said the man in the iron cage) "that I *cannot* repent."

I do not know that we are in any position to judge our neighbours. But let us suppose that we ourselves are free from this corruption (are we?) and that we are ready to greet repentance with open arms and re-establish with our enemies a relationship in which old wrongs are as though they had never been. What are we to do with those who cannot accept pardon when it is offered? And with those who have been corrupted from the cradle? Here, if anywhere, is the unforgivable—not in murdered citizens, ruined homes, broken churches, fire, sword, famine, pestilence, tortures, concentration camps, but in the corruption of a whole generation, brought up to take a devil of destruction for the God of creation and to dedicate their noblest powers to the worship of that savage altar. If for the guilty there remains only the judgment of the millstone and the deep sea, we still have to ask ourselves: What are we to do with these innocents?

For whether is easier: To say, *Thy sins be forgiven thee*?, or to say,

Arise and walk? But that ye may know that the Son of Man hath power on earth to forgive sins (then saith He to the warped mind, the frozen brain, the starved heart, the stunted and paralysed soul) *Arise, take up thy bed and go to thy home.*

No: forgiveness is a difficult matter, and no man living is wholly innocent or wholly guilty. We, as a nation, are not very ready to harbour resentment, and sometimes this means that we forget without forgiving—that is, without ever really understanding either our enemy or ourselves. This time, we feel, forgetfulness will not be possible. If that is so and we make up our minds that no right relationship will ever be possible either, I do not quite see to what end we can look forward.

WHAT DO WE BELIEVE?

(1940)

IN ORDINARY TIMES WE GET ALONG surprisingly well, on the whole, without ever discovering what our faith really is. If, now and again, this remote and academic problem is so unmannerly as to thrust its way into our minds, there are plenty of things we can do to drive the intruder away. We can get the car out, or go to a party or the cinema, or read a detective story, or have a row with the district council, or write a letter to the papers about the habits of the night-jar or Shakespeare's use of nautical metaphor. Thus we build up a defence mechanism against self-questioning, because, to tell the truth, we are very much afraid of ourselves.

When a strong man armed keepeth his palace his goods are in peace. But when a stronger than he shall come upon him . . . he taketh from him all his armour wherein he trusted. So to us in wartime, cut off from mental distractions by restrictions and blackouts, and cowering in a cellar with a gas-mask under threat of imminent death, comes in the stronger fear and sits down beside us.

"What," he demands, rather disagreeably, "do you make of all this? Is there indeed anything you value more than life, or are you making a virtue of necessity? What do you believe? Is your faith a comfort to you under the present circumstances?"

At this point, before he has time to side-track the argument and entangle us in irrelevancies, we shall do well to reply boldly that a faith is not primarily a "comfort," but a truth about ourselves. What we in fact believe is not necessarily the theory we most desire

17

or admire. It is the thing which, consciously or unconsciously, we take for granted and act on. Thus, it is useless to say that we "believe in" the friendly treatment of minorities if, in practice, we habitually bully the office-boy; our actions clearly show that we believe in nothing of the sort. Only when we know what we truly believe can we decide whether it is "comforting." If we are comforted by something we do not really believe, then we had better think again.

Now, there does exist an official statement of Christian belief, and if we examine it with a genuine determination to discover what the words mean, we shall find that it is a very strange one. And whether, as Christians declare, man was made in the image of God or, as the cynic said, man has made God in the image of man, the conclusion is the same—namely, that this strange creed purports to tell us the essential facts, not only about God, but about the true nature of man. And the first important thing it proclaims about that nature is one which we may not always admit in words, though I think we do act upon it more often than we suppose.

I believe in God the Father Almighty, Maker of all things. That is the thundering assertion with which we start: that the great fundamental quality that makes God, and us with Him, what we are is creative activity. After this, we can scarcely pretend that there is anything negative, static, or sedative about the Christian religion. "In the beginning God created"; from everlasting to everlasting, He is God the Father and Maker. And, by implication, man is most godlike and most himself when he is occupied in creation. And by this statement we assert further that the will and power to make is an absolute value, the ultimate good-in-itself, self-justified, and self-explanatory.

How far can we check this assertion as it concerns ourselves? The men who create with their minds and those who create (not merely labour) with their hands will, I think, agree that their periods of creative activity are those in which they feel right with themselves and the world. And those who bring life into the world will tell you the same thing. There is a psychological theory that artistic creation is merely a "compensation" for the frustration of sexual creativeness; but it is more probable that the making of life is only one manifestation of the universal urge to create. Our worst trouble to-day is our feeble hold on creation. To sit down and let ourselves be spoon-fed with the ready-made is to lose grip on our only true life and our only real selves.

And in the only-begotten Son of God, by whom all things were made. He was incarnate; crucified, dead and buried; and rose again. The second statement warns us what to expect when the creative energy is

18

manifested in a world subject to the forces of destruction. It makes things and manifests Itself in time and matter, and can no other, because It is begotten of the creative will. So doing, It suffers through the opposition of other wills, as well as through the dead resistance of inertia. (There is no room here to discuss whether will is "really" free; if we did not, in fact, *believe* it to be free, we could neither act nor live.)

The creative will presses on to Its end, regardless of what It may suffer by the way. It does not choose suffering, but It will not avoid it, and must expect it. We say that It is Love, and "sacrifices" Itself for what It loves; and this is true, provided we understand what we mean by sacrifice. Sacrifice is what it looks like to other people, but to That-which-Loves I think it does not appear so. When one really cares, the self is forgotten, and the sacrifice becomes only a part of the activity. Ask yourself: If there is something you supremely want to do, do you count as "self-sacrifice" the difficulties encountered or the other possible activities cast aside? You do not. The time when you deliberately say, "I must sacrifice this, that, or the other" is when you do not *supremely* desire the end in view. At such times you are doing your duty, and that is admirable, but it is not love. But as soon as your duty becomes your love the "self-sacrifice" is taken for granted, and, whatever the world calls it, you call it so no longer.

Moreover, defeat cannot hold the creative will; it can pass through the grave and rise again. If It cannot go by the path of co-operation, It will go by the path of death and victory. But it does us no credit if we force It to go that way. It is our business to recognise It when It appears and lead It into the city with hosannas. If we betray It or do nothing to assist It, we may earn the unenviable distinction of going down to history with Judas and Pontius Pilate.

I believe in the Holy Ghost, the lord and life-giver. In this odd and difficult phrase the Christian affirms that the life in him proceeds from the eternal creativeness; and that therefore so far as he is moved by that creativeness, and so far only, he is truly alive. The word "ghost" is difficult to us; the alternative word "spirit" is in some ways more difficult still, for it carries with it still more complicated mental associations. The Greek word is *pneuma*, breath: "I believe in the breath of life." And indeed, when we are asked, "What do you value more than life?" the answer can only be, "Life —the right kind of life, the creative and godlike life." And life, of any kind, can only be had if we are ready to lose life altogether— a plain observation of fact which we acknowledge every time a child is born, or, indeed, whenever we plunge into a stream of traffic in the hope of attaining a more desirable life on the other side.

And I believe in one Church and baptism, in the resurrection of the body and the life everlasting. The final clauses define what Christians believe about man and matter. First, that all those who believe in the creative life are members of one another and make up the present body in which that life is manifest. They accept for themselves everything that was affirmed of creative life incarnate, including the love and, if necessary, the crucifixion, death and victory. Looking at what happened to that Life, they will expect to be saved, not *from* danger and suffering, but *in* danger and suffering. And the resurrection of the body means more, I think, than we are accustomed to suppose. It means that, whatever happens, there can be no end to the manifestation of creative life. Whether the life makes its old body again, or an improved body, or a totally new body, it will and must create, since that is its true nature.

"This is the Christian faith, which except a man believe faithfully he cannot be saved." The harsh and much-disputed statement begins to look like a blunt statement of fact; for how can anyone make anything of his life if he does not believe in life? If we truly desire a creative life for ourselves and other people, it is our task to rebuild the world along creative lines; but we must be sure that we desire it enough.

DIVINE COMEDY

I HAVE HEARD IT NOW TWICE OVER—from two independent producers of two separate plays—the exact same warning in almost identical words:

"Well now, ladies and gentlemen, I think there's only one thing I have to say before we start reading through. Although this is a play about—er—angels and God and Christ and so on, you don't want to go extra slow, or put on a special tone of voice or anything. Just treat it as you would an ordinary play. Speak the lines quite naturally and play it straight."

The company nod intelligently, and their drooping spirits revive. They had come prepared to be religious in the usual manner, but if the producer thinks that religion should be "played straight" they are delighted to adapt their ideas to his. Actors are biddable creatures.

The significant thing is that both producers should have taken it for granted, without any prompting from the author of the play, that the warning was urgently necessary. At the name of Jesus, every voice goes plummy, every gesture becomes pontifical, and a fearful creeping paralysis slows down the pace of the dialogue. "So I thought," says the producer, "I'd better jump on that idea from the word go, because I knew if they once got it into their heads they'd never get rid of it."

Most of us never do get rid of it. The Bible is appointed to be read in churches, where the voice struggles helplessly against the handicaps of an Elizabethan vocabulary, a solemn occasion, an overpowering background, a mute assembly, and acoustics with a two-second echo. The more "beautifully and impressively" it is read, the more unreal it sounds. Most unreal of all is the speech of the story's central character—every word a "familiar quotation," pulpit-dissected, sifted, weighed, burdened with a heavy accretion of prophetic and exegetical importance. In a sense not contemplated by the Evangelist, we feel it to be true that never man spake as this man, for by this time the words have lost all likeness to the speech of a living person.

A stern edict of the Censor—probably a very wise one—prohibits the representation on the English stage of the actual person of Christ. This adds to the Apollinarian unreality of New Testament plays. The Humanity is never really there—it is always just coming on, or just going off, or being a light or a shadow or a voice in the wings. If our modern theatre had anything like the freedom of Oberammergau or the medieval stage, I believe one could find no better road to a realistic theology than that of coaching an intelligent actor to play the Leading Part in the world's drama. Nothing so surely probes the inner coherence and vitality of a dramatic "character" as the gruelling test of production. All the puzzles and contrasts which we scarcely notice in a series of readings spread over from day to day are now going to be crammed together into a swift Aristotelian unity, and made visible. If its reality will stand up to that, it will stand up to anything.

The static, the over-simplified will have to go; we shall be forced to make the "bridge" between "gentle Jesus" and the wrath of the Lamb; we shall no longer be able to keep the Godhead and the Manhood in watertight compartments, since the same actor will have to deal with both of them and make the blend convincing.

"Look," we shall find ourselves saying to him, "if you play the first scene in that stained-glass way, there'll be an awful jerk when you have to do a quick come-back on hecklers, and insult the Pharisees, and man-handle the traders out of the Temple. You'll have to plant all those possibilities in the character from the start. You want to be tremendously mobile, never the same from one minute to the next, with a terrific reserve of fire and energy under the crust, so to speak. After all, people wouldn't follow you all round the place if you weren't extraordinarily—what's the word? —vital—dynamic—that sort of thing. . . ."

"Couldn't you make a little more out of that last line—'the dead are raised up, *and the poor have the gospel preached to them*'? It's ironical, isn't it, leading up to that as the biggest miracle of all—but unless you *point* it for them these lads won't notice it and will forget to tell John. They're standing there, all pop-eyed over the signs and wonders, and you've got to put it across to them. . . . No, not too sharply—with just a bit of a twinkle, perhaps . . . and you disciples, you've got to play to that—it's a new idea to you. . . . Right. . . . Now then, disciples off, and you go on and let the crowd have it . . . bird-witted, frivolous, gaping at celebrities, never knowing what they want . . . working up to the big denunciations. And then it all sort of flares away, and you get the meek and lowly side uppermost —if only people will be spontaneous and sincere. . . . Yes, of course, it is most frightfully close-packed. . . ."

"That bit about the gnat and the camel is a *joke*—and, crowd, do try to look as if you hadn't heard it fifty thousand times over on Sundays . . . *act* it for them, dear—fussily filtering out the gnat, and then gulping down that awful great lolloping brute all hair and humps. . . . We want a good guffaw, please, from the stout citizen and a titter from the women . . . the Lawyer mustn't laugh—he probably thinks it dreadfully vulgar, just the sort of thing you would expect from a gluttonous man and a wine-bibber. . . ."

"Oh, yes, I think you're genuinely disappointed about the rich young ruler. . . . I don't think you know everything beforehand in that detailed sort of way—not with your human mind; it would make the whole thing very unreal if you did. . . . Yes, you have a human mind—the Athanasian Creed says so distinctly: 'altogether man, with a rational mind and human body'—so play it quite naturally. . . ."

(Of course, the minute you take Christ as somebody really real, you're landed in theology—but you can't produce acting by arguing about *kenosis* or the monophysite heresy. You've got to translate the thing into terms of life and action—what would the double nature feel like, look like? You can't just say it's a mystery and leave it at that; the real Jesus didn't look like a walking conundrum —He looked like a person.)

"Well, yes, I suppose you do know you're God all the time, but surely not in that rigid, theological sense. I should think it would be more like the way a man knows deep down inside him that he really is a genius. It's the unspoken assumption on which he habitually acts, but it isn't perpetually present to his conscious thought. It's only when something challenges his claim to be true to that interior reality that the knowledge comes surging up to the surface, and he says, with that absolute sense of conviction, I AM . . ."

All very inadequate, of course, but any approach, however small, to a sense of reality would surely be better than no approach at all. We have learnt recently, with agitation and astonishment, that there are many children in this Christian country to whom the whole Christ-story is completely unknown. How, one wonders, is it being presented to these untutored minds? Do they find it interesting? Do they think it exciting? They at least are not stupefied with preconceptions—are we offering it to them as a dramatic reality? or shall we merely succeed in making each of them as stereotyped and dull as ourselves? It is so very difficult to recognise opportunity when it comes in the guise of disaster; but if we are going to offend these little ones by the contamination of our own unimaginative lethargy, it would be better that a millstone were hanged about our necks, and that we were cast into the sea. Are we so shocked at ignorance? There are times when ignorance is a welcome bliss;—what would it be like to go and see *Hamlet* with a perfectly virgin mind?

(NOTE.—Since this was written, the B.B.C. has given me the opportunity of trying the experiment suggested in the text. The reception given to *The Man Born to be King* showed, I think, that the public thought it well worth trying.)

A VOTE OF THANKS TO CYRUS

I OWE A CERTAIN DEBT TO Cyrus the Persian. I made his acquaintance fairly early, for he lived between the pages of a children's magazine, in a series entitled *Tales from Herodotus*, or something of that kind. There was a picture of him being brought up by the herdsman of King Astyages, dressed in a short tunic very like the garment worn by the young Theseus or Perseus in the illustrations to Kingsley's *Heroes*. He belonged quite definitely to "classical times"; did he not overcome Crœsus, that rich king of whom Solon had said, "Call no man happy until he is dead"? The story was half fairy tale—"his mother dreamed," "the oracle spoke" —but half history too: he commanded his soldiers to divert the course of the Euphrates, so that they might march into Babylon along the river-bed; that sounded like practical warfare. Cyrus was pigeon-holed in my mind with the Greeks and Romans.

So for a long time he remained. And then, one day, I realised with a shock as of sacrilege, that on that famous expedition he had marched clean out of Herodotus and slap into the Bible. *Mene, mene, tekel upharsin*—the palace wall had blazed with the exploits of Cyrus, and Belshazzar's feast had broken up in disorder under the stern and warning eye of the prophet Daniel.

But Daniel and Belshazzar did not live in "the classics" at all. They lived in Church, with Adam and Abraham and Elijah, and were dressed like Bible characters, especially Daniel. And here was God—not Zeus or Apollo or any of the Olympian crowd, but the fierce and dishevelled old gentleman from Mount Sinai—bursting into Greek history in a most uncharacteristic way, and taking an interest in events and people that seemed altogether outside His province. It was disconcerting.

And there was Esther. She lived in a book called *Stories from the Old Testament*, and had done very well for God's Chosen People by her diplomatic approach to King Ahasuerus. A good Old-Testament-sounding name, Ahasuerus, reminding one of Ahab and Ahaz and Ahaziah. I cannot remember in what out-of-the-way primer of general knowledge I came across the astonishing equation, thrown out casually in a passing phrase, "Ahasuerus (or Xerxes)." Xerxes!—but one knew all about Xerxes. He was not just "classics," but real history; it was against Xerxes that the Greeks had made their desperate and heroic stand at Thermopylæ. There was none of the fairy-tale atmosphere of Cyrus about *him*—no dreams, no oracles, no faithful herdsman—only the noise and dust of armies tramping through the hard outlines and clear colours of a Grecian landscape, where the sun always shone so much more vividly than it did in the Bible.

I think it was chiefly Cyrus and Ahasuerus who prodded me into the belated conviction that history was all of a piece, and that the Bible was part of it. One might have expected Jesus to provide the link between two worlds—the Cæsars were classical history all right. But Jesus was a special case. One used a particular tone of voice in speaking of Him, and He dressed neither like Bible nor like classics—He dressed like Jesus, in a fashion closely imitated (down to the halo) by His disciples. If He belonged anywhere, it was to Rome, in spite of strenuous prophetic efforts to identify Him with the story of the Bible Jews. Indeed, the Jews themselves had undergone a mysterious change in the blank pages between the Testaments: in the Old, they were "good" people; in the New, they were "bad" people—it seemed doubtful whether they really were the same people. Nevertheless, Old or New, all these people lived in Church and were "Bible characters"—they were not real in the sense that King Alfred was a real person; still less could their conduct be judged by standards that applied to one's own contemporaries.

Most children, I suppose, begin by keeping different bits of history in watertight compartments, of which "Bible" is the tightest and most impenetrable. But some people seem never to grow out of this habit—possibly because of never having really met Cyrus and Ahasuerus (or Xerxes). Bible critics in particular appear to be persons of very leisurely mental growth. Take, for example, the notorious dispute about the Gospel according to St. John.

Into the details of that dispute I do not propose to go. I only want to point out that the arguments used are such as no critic would ever dream of applying to a modern book of memoirs written by one real person about another. The defects imputed to St. John would be virtues in Mr. Jones, and the value and authenticity of Mr. Jones's contribution to literature would be proved by the same arguments that are used to undermine the authenticity of St. John.

Suppose, for example, Mr. Bernard Shaw were now to publish a volume of reminiscences about Mr. William Archer: would anybody object that the account must be received with suspicion because most of Archer's other contemporaries were dead, or because the style of G. B. S. was very unlike that of a *Times* obituary notice, or because the book contained a great many intimate conversations not recorded in previous memoirs, and left out a number of facts that could easily be ascertained by reference to the *Dictionary of National Biography*? Or if Mr. Shaw (being a less vigorous octogenarian than he happily is) had dictated part of his material to a respectable clergyman, who had himself added a special note to say that Shaw was the real author and that readers might rely on the accuracy of the memoirs since, after all, Shaw was a close friend of Archer's and ought to know—should we feel that these two worthy men were thereby revealed as self-confessed liars, and dismiss their joint work as a valueless fabrication? Probably not; but then Mr. Shaw is a real person, and lives, not in the Bible, but in Westminster. The time has not come to doubt him. He is already a legend, but not yet a myth; two thousand years hence, perhaps——

Let us pretend for a moment that Jesus is a "real" person who died within living memory, and that John is a "real" author, producing a "real" book; what sort of announcement shall we look for in the literary page of an ordinary newspaper? Let us put together a brief review, altering some of the names a little, to prevent that "Bible" feeling.

Memoirs of Jesus Christ. By JOHN BAR-ZEBEDEE; edited by the Rev. John Elder, Vicar of St. Faith's, Ephesus. (Kirk. 7s. 6d.)

The general public has had to wait a long time for these intimate personal impressions of a great preacher, though the substance of them has for many years been familiarly known in Church circles. The friends of Mr. Bar-Zebedee have frequently urged the octogenarian divine to commit his early memories to paper; this he has now done, with the assistance and under the careful editorship of the Vicar of St. Faith's. The book fulfils a long-felt want.

Very little has actually been put in print about the striking personality who exercised so great an influence upon the last generation. The little anonymous collections of "Sayings" by "Q" is now, of course, out of print and unobtainable. This is the less regrettable in that the greater part of it has been embodied in Mr. J. Marks's brief obituary study and in the subsequent biographies of Mr. Matthews and Mr. Lucas (who, unhappily, was unable to complete his companion volume of the *Acts of the Apostles*). But hitherto, all these reports have been compiled at second hand. Now for the first time comes the testimony of a close friend of Jesus, and, as we should expect, it offers a wealth of fresh material.

With great good judgment, Mr. Bar-Zebedee has refrained from going over old ground, except for the purpose of tidying up the chronology which, in previous accounts, was conspicuously lacking. Thus, he makes it plain that Jesus paid at least two visits to Jerusalem during the three years of His ministry—a circumstance which clears up a number of confusing points in the narrative of His arrest; and the two examinations in the ecclesiastical courts are at last clearly distinguished. Many new episodes are related; in particular, it has now become possible to reveal the facts about the mysterious affair at Bethany, hitherto discreetly veiled out of consideration for the surviving members of the Lazarus family, whom rumour had subjected to much vulgar curiosity and political embarrassment. But the most interesting and important portions of the book are those devoted to Christ's lectures in the Temple and the theological and philosophical instructions given privately to His followers. These, naturally, differ considerably in matter and manner from the open-air "talks" delivered before a mixed audience, and shed a flood of new light, both on the massive intellectual equipment of the preacher and on the truly astonishing nature of His claim to authority. Mr. Bar-Zebedee interprets and comments upon these remarkable discourses with considerable learning, and with the intimate understanding of one familiar with his Master's habits of thought.

Finally, the author of these memoirs reveals himself as that delightful *rara avis*, a "born writer." He commands a fine economy and precision in the use of dialogue; his character-sketches (as in the delicate comedy of the blind beggar at the Pool of Siloam) are little masterpieces of quiet humour, while his descriptions of the Meal in the Upper Room, the visit of Simon Bar-Jonah and himself to the Sepulchre, and the last uncanny encounter by the Lake of Tiberias are distinguished by an atmospheric quality which places this account of the Nazarene in a category apart.

How reasonable it all sounds, in the journalese jargon to which we have grown accustomed! And how much more readily we may accept discrepancies and additions when once we have rid ourselves of that notion "the earlier, the purer," which, however plausible in the case of folk-lore, is entirely irrelevant when it comes to "real" biography. Indeed, the first "Life" of any celebrity is nowadays accepted as an interim document. For considered appreciation we must wait until many contemporaries have gone to where rumour cannot distress them, until grief and passion have died down, until emotion can be remembered in tranquillity.

It is rather unfortunate that the "Higher Criticism" was first undertaken at a time when all textual criticism tended to be destructive—when the body of Homer was being torn into fragments, the Arthurian romance reduced to its Celtic elements, and the "authority" of manuscripts established by a mechanical system of verbal agreements. The great secular scholars have already recanted and adopted the slogan of the great archæologist Didron: "Preserve all you can; restore seldom; never reconstruct." When it came to the Bible, the spirit of destruction was the more gleefully iconoclastic because of the conservative extravagances of the "verbal inspiration" theory. But the root of the trouble is to be found, I suspect (as usual), in the collapse of dogma. Christ, even for Christians, is not quite "really" real—not altogether human— and the taint of unreality has spread to His disciples and friends and to His biographers: they are not "real" writers, but just "Bible" writers. John and Matthew and Luke and Mark, some or all of them, disagree about the occasion on which a parable was told or an epigram uttered. One or all must be a liar or untrustworthy, because Christ (not being quite real) must have made every remark once and once only. He could not, of course, like a real teacher, have used the same illustration twice, or found it necessary to hammer the same point home twenty times over, as one does when addressing audiences of real people and not of "Bible characters."

Nor (one is led to imagine) did Christ ever use any ordinary behaviour that is not expressly recorded of Him. "We are twice told that He wept, but never that He smiled"—the inference being that He never did smile. Similarly, no doubt, we may infer that He never said "Please" or "Thank you." But perhaps these common courtesies were left unrecorded precisely because they were common, whereas the tears were (so to speak) "news." True, we have lately got into the habit of headlining common courtesies: the newspaper that published the review of St. John's memoirs would probably have announced on a previous occasion:

PROPHET'S SMILE

The Prophet of Nazareth smiled graciously yesterday morning on inviting Himself to lunch with little Mr. Zacchæus, a tax-collector, who had climbed into a sycamore to watch Him pass.

St. Luke, with a better sense of style, merely records that: He looked up and saw him, and said unto him, Zacchæus, make haste and come down; for to-day I must abide in thy house. And he made haste and came down and received Him joyfully.

Politeness would suggest that one does not commandeer other people's hospitality with a morose scowl, and that if one is "received joyfully" it is usually because one has behaved pleasantly. But these considerations would, of course, apply only to "real" people.

"Altogether man, with a rational mind and human body——" It is just as well that from time to time Cyrus should march out of Herodotus into the Bible, for the synthesis of history and the confutation of heresy.

TOWARDS A CHRISTIAN ÆSTHETIC

The essay "Towards a Christian Æsthetic" is included by per-
mission of S.P.C.K., in whose volume Our Culture: Its
Christian Roots and Present Crisis *it also appears as one of*
the Edward Alleyn Lectures, 1944.

> *It will be immediately obvious how deeply this paper is indebted*
> *to R. G. Collingwood's* Principles of Art, *particularly as regards*
> *the disentangling of "Art Proper" (expression and imagination)*
> *from the "pseudo-Arts" of "amusement" and "magic." The only*
> *contribution I have made of my own (exclusive of incidental errors)*
> *has been to suggest, however tentatively, a method of establishing*
> *the principles of "Art Proper" upon that Trinitarian doctrine of*
> *the nature of Creative Mind which does, I think, really underlie*
> *them. On this foundation it might perhaps be possible to develop*
> *a Christian æsthetic which, finding its source and sanction in the*
> *theological centre, would be at once more characteristically Christian*
> *and of more universal application than any æsthetic whose contact*
> *with Christianity is made only at the ethical circumference.*

I AM TO SPEAK TO YOU TO-NIGHT about the Arts in this
country—their roots in Christianity, their present condition, and
the means by which (if we find that they are not flourishing
as they should) their mutilated limbs and withering branches
may be restored by re-grafting into the main trunk of Christian
tradition.

This task is of quite peculiar difficulty, and I may not be able to
carry it out in exactly the terms which have been proposed to me.
And that for a rather strange reason. In such things as politics,
finance, sociology and so on, there really is a philosophy and a
Christian tradition; we do know more or less what the Church has
said and thought about them, how they are related to Christian
dogma, and what they are supposed to *do* in a Christian country.

But oddly enough, we have no Christian æsthetic—no Christian
philosophy of the Arts. The Church as a body has never made up
her mind about the Arts, and it is hardly too much to say that she
has never tried. She has, of course, from time to time puritanically
denounced the Arts as irreligious and mischievous, or tried to exploit

the Arts as a means to the teaching of religion and morals—but I shall hope to show you that both these attitudes are false and degrading, and are founded upon a completely mistaken idea of what Art is supposed to be and do. And there have, of course, been plenty of writers on æsthetics who happened to be Christians, but they have seldom made any consistent attempt to relate their æsthetic to the central Christian dogmas. Indeed, so far as European æsthetic is concerned, one feels that it would probably have developed along precisely the same lines had there never been an Incarnation to reveal the nature of God—that is to say, the nature of all truth. But that is fantastic. If we commit ourselves to saying that the Christian revelation discovers to us the nature of *all* truth, then it must discover to us the nature of the truth about Art among other things. It is absurd to go placidly along explaining Art in terms of a pagan æsthetic, and taking no notice whatever of the complete revolution of our ideas about the nature of things that occurred, or should have occurred, after the first Pentecost. I will go so far as to maintain that the extraordinary confusion of our minds about the nature and function of Art is principally due to the fact that for nearly 2,000 years we have been trying to reconcile a pagan, or at any rate a Unitarian, æsthetic with a Christian— that is, a Trinitarian and Incarnational—theology. Even that makes us out too intelligent. We have not tried to reconcile them. We have merely allowed them to exist side by side in our minds; and where the conflict between them became too noisy to be overlooked, we have tried to silence the clamour by main force, either by brutally subjugating Art to religion, or by shutting them up in separate prison cells and forbidding them to hold any communication with one another.

Now, before we go any further, I want to make it quite clear that what I am talking about now is æsthetic (the philosophy of Art) and not about Art itself as practised by the artists. The great artists carry on with their work on the lines God has laid down for them, quite unaffected by the æsthetic worked out for them by philosophers. Sometimes, of course, artists themselves dabble in æsthetic, and what they have to say is very interesting, but often very misleading. If they really are great and true artists, they make their poem (or whatever it is) first, and then set about reconciling it with the fashionable æsthetic of their time; they do not produce their work to conform to their notions of æsthetic—or, if they do, they are so much the less artists, and the work suffers. Secondly, what artists chatter about to the world and to each other is not as a rule their art but the technique of their art. They will tell you, as critics, how it is they produce certain effects (the poet will talk about assonance, alliteration and metre; the painter about perspective, balance and how he mixes his colours, etc.)—and from that we may get the misleading impression that the technique *is* the art, or that the aim of art is to produce some sort of "effect." But this is not so. We cannot go for a march unless we have learnt, through long practice, how to control the muscles of our legs; but it is not true to say that the muscular control *is* the march. And while it is a fact that certain tricks produce "effects"—like Tennyson's use of vowels and consonants to produce the effect of a sleepy murmuring in "The moan of doves in immemorial elms," or of metallic clashing in "The bare black cliff clanged round him"—it is not true that the poem *is* merely a set of physical, or even of emotional effects. What a work of art really is and does we shall come to later. For the moment I only want to stress the difference between æsthetic and art, and to make it clear that a great artist will produce great art, even though the æsthetic of his time may be hopelessly inadequate to explain it.

For the origins of European æsthetic we shall, of course, turn to Greece; and we are at once brought up against the two famous chapters in which Plato discusses the Arts, and decides that certain kinds of Art, and in particular certain kinds of poetry, ought to be banished from the perfect State. Not all poetry—people often talk as though Plato had said this, but he did not: certain kinds he wished to keep, and this makes his attitude all the more puzzling, because, though he tells us quite clearly why he disapproves of the rejected kinds, he never explains what it is that makes the other kinds valuable. He never gets down to considering, constructively, what true Art is or what it does. He only tells us about what are (in his opinion) the bad results of certain kinds of Art—nor does he ever tackle the question whether the bad moral results of which he complains may not be due to a falseness *in* the Art, i.e. to the work's being pseudo-Art or inartistic Art. He seems to say that certain forms of Art are inherently evil in themselves. His whole handling of the thing seems to us very strange, confused and contradictory; yet his æsthetic has dominated all our critical thinking for many centuries, and has influenced, in particular, the attitude of the Church more than the Church perhaps knows. So it is necessary that we should look at Plato's argument. Many of his conclusions are true—though often, I think, he reaches them from the wrong premisses. Some of them are, I think, demonstrably false. But especially, his whole grasp of the subject is inadequate. That is not Plato's fault. He was one of the greatest thinkers of all time, but he was a pagan; and I am becoming convinced that no pagan philosopher could produce an adequate æsthetic, simply for lack of a right theology. In this respect, the least in the Kingdom of Heaven is greater than John the Baptist.

What does Plato say?

He begins by talking about stories and myths, and after dismissing as beneath consideration the stories and poems which are obviously badly written, he goes on to reject those which are untrue, or which attribute evil and disgusting behaviour to the gods, or which tend to inculcate bad and vulgar passions or anti-social behaviour in the audience. After this (which sounds very much like what moralists and clergymen are always saying nowadays) he leaves the subject-matter and goes on to certain *forms* of poetry and art—those forms which involve *mimesis*—the mimetic arts. Now *mimesis* can be translated "imitation," or "representation"; and we can at once see that certain forms of Art are more mimetic than others: drama, painting and sculpture are, on the whole, mimetic— some natural object or action is represented or imitated (though we may find exceptions in modernist and surrealist paintings which seem to represent nothing in Heaven or earth). Music, on the other hand, is not mimetic—nothing is imitated from the natural world (unless we count certain effects like the noise of drums in a martial piece, or trills and arpeggios representing the song of birds or the falling of water, down to the squeaks, brayings, twitterings and whistlings of cinema organs). In the Third Book of the *Republic*, Plato says he will allow the mimetic arts, provided that the imitation or representation is of something morally edifying, that sets a good example; but he would banish altogether the representation of unworthy objects, such as national heroes wallowing about in floods of tears, and people getting drunk, or using foul language. He thinks this kind of thing bad for the actors and also for the audience. Nor (which seems odd to us) are actors to imitate anything vulgar or base, such as artisans plying their trades, galley-slaves or bos'ns; nor must there be any trivial nonsense about stage-effects and farmyard imitations. Nothing is to be acted or shown except what is worthy to be imitated, the noble actions of wise men—a gallery of good examples.

We may feel that Plato's theatre would be rather on the austere side. But in the Tenth Book he hardens his heart still further. He decides to banish *all* mimetic art—all representation of every kind; and that for two reasons.

The first reason is that imitation is a kind of cheat. An artist who knows nothing about carpentering may yet paint a carpenter so that, if the picture is set up at a distance, children and stupid people may be deceived into thinking that it really is a carpenter. Moreover, in any case, the realities of things exist only in Heaven in an ideal and archetypal form; the visible world is only a pale reflection or bad imitation of the heavenly realities; and the work of art is only a cheating imitation of the visible world: therefore representational art is merely an imitation of an imitation—a deceptive trick which tickles and entertains while turning men's minds away from the contemplation of the eternal realities.

At this point some of you will begin to fidget and say, "Hi! Stop! Surely there is a difference between mimicry intended to deceive and representation. I admit that there are such things as tin biscuit boxes got up to look like the works of Charles Dickens, which may deceive the unwary, and that very simple-minded people in theatres have been known to hiss the villain or leap on the stage to rescue the heroine—but as a rule we know perfectly well that the imitation is only imitation, and not meant to take anyone in. And surely there's a difference between farmyard imitations and John Gielgud playing Hamlet. And besides—even if you get an exact representation of something—say a documentary film about a war, or an exact verbal reproduction of a scene at the Old Bailey—that's not the same thing as *Coriolanus* or the trial scene in *The Merchant of Venice*; the work of art has something different, something more—poetry or a sort of a something . . ." and here you will begin to wave your hands about vaguely.

You are, of course, perfectly right. But let us for the moment just make a note of how Plato's conception of Art is influenced by his theology—the visible world imitating, copying, reflecting a world of eternal changeless forms already existent elsewhere; and the artist, conceived of as a sort of craftsman or artisan engaged in *copying* or imitating something which exists already in the visible world.

Now let us take his second reason for banishing all representational art. He says that even where the action represented is in itself good and noble, the effect on the audience is bad, because it leads them to dissipate the emotions and energies that ought to be used for tackling the problems of life. The feelings of courage, resolution, pity, indignation and so on are worked up in the spectators by the mimic passions on the stage (or in pictures or music) and then frittered away in a debauch of emotion over these unreal shadows, leaving the mind empty and slack, with no appetite except for fresh sensations of an equally artificial sort.

Now, that is a real indictment against a particular kind of art, which we ought to take seriously. In the jargon of modern psychology, Plato is saying that art of this kind leads to phantasy and day-dreaming. Aristotle, coming about fifty years after Plato, defended this kind of art: he said that undesirable passions, such as pity and terror were in this way *sublimated*—you worked them off in the theatre, where they could do no harm. If, he means, you feel an inner urge to murder your wife, you go and see *Othello* or read a good, gory thriller, and satisfy your blood-lust that way; and if we had the last part of his *Poetics*, which dealt with comedy, we should probably find it suggested, in the same way, that an excess of sexual emotion can be worked off by going to a good, dirty farce or vulgar music-hall, and blowing the whole thing away in a loud, bawdy laugh.

Now, people still argue as to whether Plato or Aristotle was right about this. But there are one or two things I want you to notice. The first is that what Plato is really concerned to banish from his perfect state is the kind of art which aims at mere entertainment— the art that dissipates energy instead of directing it into some useful channel. And though Aristotle defends "art for entertainment," it is still the same kind of art he is thinking about.

The second thing is that both Plato and Aristotle—but especially Plato—are concerned with the moral effect of art. Plato would allow representational art so long as he thought that it had the effect of canalising the energies and directing them to virtuous action—he only banishes it, on further consideration, because he has come to the conclusion that *no* representational art of any kind —not even the loftiest tragedy—is successful in bracing the moral constitution. He does not tell us very clearly what poetry he will keep, or why, except that it is to be of what we should call a lyrical kind, and, presumably, bracing and tonic in sentiment, and directly inculcating the love of the good, the beautiful and the true.

Thirdly: Plato lived at the beginning, and Aristotle in the middle of the era which saw the collapse and corruption of the great Greek civilisation. Plato sees the rot setting in, and cries out like a prophet to his people to repent while there is yet time. He sees that the theatre audience is in fact looking to the theatre for nothing but amusement and entertainment, that their energies are, in fact, frittering themselves away in spurious emotion—sob-stuff and sensation, and senseless laughter, phantasy and day-dreaming, and admiration for the merely smart and slick and clever and amusing. And there is an ominous likeness between his age and ours. We too have audiences and critics and newspapers assessing every play and book and novel in terms of its "entertainment value," and a whole generation of young men and women who dream over novels and wallow in day-dreaming at the cinema, and who seemed to be in a fair way of doping themselves into complete irresponsibility over the conduct of life until war came, as it did to Greece, to jerk them back to reality. Greek civilisation was destroyed; ours is not yet destroyed. But it may be well to remember Plato's warning: "If you receive the pleasure-seasoned Muse, pleasure and pain will be kings in your city instead of law and agreed principles."

And there is something else in Plato that seems to strike a familiar note. We seem to know the voice that urges artists to produce works of art "with a high moral tone"—propaganda works, directed to improving young people's minds and rousing them to a sense of their duties, "doing them good," in fact. And at the same time, we find—among artists and critics alike—a tendency to repudiate representational art, in favour of something more austere, primitive and symbolic, as though the trouble lay *there*.

It is as though, in the decline of Greece, and in what is known as the "Decline of the West," both Plato and we agreed in finding something wrong with the arts—a kind of mutual infection, by which the slick, sentimental, hedonistic art corrupts its audience, and the pleasure-loving, emotional audience in turn corrupts the arts by demanding of them nothing but entertainment value. And the same sort of remedy is proposed in both cases—first, to get rid of "representationalism"—which, it is hoped, will take away the pleasure and entertainment and so cure the audience's itch for amusement; secondly, to concentrate on works which provide a direct stimulus to right thinking and right action.

What we have really got here is a sort of division of art into two kinds: *Entertainment-Art*, which dissipates the energies of the audience and pours them down the drain; and another kind of art which canalises energy into a sort of mill-stream to turn the wheel of action—and this we may perhaps call *Spell-binding Art*. But do these two functions comprise the whole of Art? Or are they Art at all? Are they perhaps only accidental effects of Art, or false Art—something masquerading under the name of Art—or menial tasks to which we enslave Art? Is the real nature and end of Art something quite different from either? Is the real trouble something wrong with our æsthetic, so that we do not know what we ought to look for in Art, or how to recognise it when we see it, or how to distinguish the real thing from the spurious imitation?

Suppose we turn from Plato to the actual poets he was writing about—to Æschylus, for instance, the great writer of tragedies.

Drama, certainly, is a representational art, and therefore, according to Plato, pleasure-art, entertainment-art, emotional and relaxing art, sensational art. Let us read the *Agamemnon*. Certainly it is the representation by actors of something—and of something pretty sensational: the murder of a husband by an adulterous wife. But it is scarcely sensational entertainment in the sense that a thriller novel on the same subject is sensational entertainment. A day-dreaming, pleasure-loving audience would hardly call it entertainment at all. It is certainly not relaxing. And I doubt whether it either dissipates our passions in Plato's sense or sublimates them in Aristotle's sense, any more than it canalises them for any particular action, though it may trouble and stir us and plunge us into the mystery of things. We might extract some moral lessons from it; but if we ask ourselves whether the poet wrote that play in order to improve our minds, something inside us will, I think, say "No." Æschylus was trying to tell us something, but nothing quite so simple as that. He is saying something—something important—something enormous— And here we shall be suddenly struck with the inadequacy of the strictures against "representational art." "This," we shall say, "is not the copy or imitation of something bigger and more real than itself. It is bigger and more real than the real-life action that it represents. That a false wife should murder a husband—that might be a paragraph in the *News of the World* or a thriller to read in the train—but when it is shown us like this, by a great poet, it is as though we went behind the triviality of the actual event to the cosmic significance behind it. And, what is more, this is *not* a representation of the actual event at all—if a B.B.C. reporter had been present at the murder with a television set and microphone, what we heard and saw would have been nothing like this. This play is not anything that ever happened in this world —it is something happening in the mind of Æschylus, and it had never happened before."

Now here, I believe, we are getting to something—something that Plato's heathen philosophy was not adequate to explain, but which we can begin to explain by the light of Christian theology. Very likely the heathen poet could not have explained it either— if he had made the attempt, he too would have been entangled in the terms of his philosophy. But we are concerned, not with what he might have said, but with what he did. Being a true poet, he was true in his work—that is, his art was that point of truth in him which was true to the eternal truth, and only to be interpreted in terms of eternal truth.

The true work of art, then, is something *new*—it is not primarily the copy or representation of anything. It may involve representation, but that is not what makes it a work of art. It is not manufactured to specification, as an engineer works to a plan—though it may involve compliance with the accepted rules for dramatic presentation, and may also contain verbal "effects" which can be mechanically accounted for. We know very well, when we compare it with so-called works of art which *are* "turned out to pattern" that in this connection neither circumcision availeth anything nor uncircumcision, but a new creature. Something has been created.

This word—this idea of Art as *creation* is, I believe, the one important contribution that Christianity has made to æsthetics. Unfortunately, we are apt to use the words "creation" and "creativeness" very vaguely and loosely, because we do not relate them properly to our theology. But it is significant that the Greeks had not this word in their æsthetic at all. They looked on a work of art as a kind of *techné*, a manufacture. Neither, for that matter, was the word in their theology—they did not look on history as the continual act of God fulfilling itself in creation.

How do we say that God creates, and how does this compare with the act of creation by an artist? To begin with, of course, we say that God created the universe "out of nothing"—He was bound by no conditions of any kind. Here there can be no comparison: the human artist is *in* the universe and bound by its conditions. He can create only within that framework and out of that material which the universe supplies. Admitting that, let us ask in what way God creates. Christian theology replies that God, who is a Trinity, creates by, or through, His second Person, His Word or Son, who is continually begotten from the First Person, the Father, in an eternal creative activity. And certain theologians have added this very significant comment: the Father, they say, is only known to Himself by beholding His image in His Son.

Does that sound very mysterious? We will come back to the human artist, and see what it means in terms of *his* activity. But first, let us take note of a new word that has crept into the argument by way of Christian theology—the word *Image*. Suppose, having rejected the words "copy," "imitation" and "representation" as inadequate, we substitute the word "image" and say that what the artist is doing is *to image forth* something or the other, and connect that with St. Paul's phrase: "God . . . hath spoken to us by His Son, the brightness of this glory and *express image* of His person." —Something which, by being an image, *expresses* that which it images. Is that getting us a little nearer to something? There is something which is, in the deepest sense of the words, *unimaginable*, known to Itself (and still more, to us) only by the image in which it expresses Itself through creation; and, says Christian theology very emphatically, the Son, who is the express image, is not the copy, or imitation, or representation of the Father, nor yet inferior or subsequent to the Father in any way—in the last resort, in the depths of their mysterious being, the Unimaginable and the Image are *one and the same*.

Now for our poet. We said, when we were talking of the *Agamemnon*, that this work of art seemed to be "something happening in the mind of Æschylus." We may now say, perhaps, more precisely, that the play is the *expression* of this interior happening. But *what*, exactly, was happening?

There is a school of criticism that is always trying to explain, or explain away, a man's works of art by trying to dig out the events of his life and his emotions *outside* the works themselves, and saying "these are the real Æschylus, the real Shakespeare, of which the poems are only faint imitations." But any poet will tell you that this is the wrong way to go to work. It is the old, pagan æsthetic which explains nothing—or which explains all sorts of things about the work *except* what makes it a work of art. The poet will say: "My poem is the expression of my experience." But if you then say, "What experience?" he will say, "I can't tell you anything about it, except what I have said in the poem—the poem *is* the experience." The Son and the Father are *one*: the poet himself did not know what his experience was until he created the poem which revealed his own experience to himself.

To save confusion, let us distinguish between an *event* and an *experience*. An event is something that happens to one—but one does not necessarily experience it. To take an extreme instance: suppose you are hit on the head and get concussion and, as often happens, when you come to, you cannot remember the blow. The blow on the head certainly happened to you, but you did not *experience* it—all you experience is the after-effects. You only experience a thing when you can express it—however haltingly—to your own mind. You may remember the young man in T. S. Eliot's play, *The Family Reunion*, who says to his relations:

> *You are all people*
> *To whom nothing has happened, at most a continual impact*
> *Of external events . . .*

He means that they have got through life without ever really *experiencing* anything, because they have never tried to express to themselves the real nature of what has happened to them.

A poet is a man who not only suffers "the impact of external events," but experiences them. He puts the experience into words in his own mind, and in so doing recognises the experience for what it is. To the extent that we can do that, we are all poets. A "poet" so-called is simply a man like ourselves with an exceptional power of revealing his experience by expressing it, so that not only he, but we ourselves, recognise that experience as our own.

I want to stress the word *recognise*. A poet does not see something —say the full moon—and say: "This is a very beautiful sight—let me set about finding words for the appropriate expression of what people ought to feel about it." That is what the literary artisan does, and it means nothing. What happens is that then, or at some time after, he finds himself saying words in his head and says to himself: "Yes—that is right. *That* is the experience the full moon was to me. I recognise it in expressing it, and now I know what it was." And so, when it is a case of mental or spiritual experience— sin, grief, joy, sorrow, worship—the thing reveals itself to him in words, and so becomes fully experienced for the first time. By thus recognising it in its expression, he makes it his own—integrates it into himself. He no longer feels himself battered passively by the impact of external events—it is no longer something happening *to* him, but something happening *in* him, the reality of the event is communicated to him in activity and power. So that the act of the poet in creation is seen to be threefold—a trinity—experience, expression and recognition; the unknowable reality in the experi- ence; the image of that reality known in its expression; and power in the recognition; the whole making up the single and indivisible act of creative mind.

Now, what the poet does for himself, he can also do for us. When he has imaged forth his experience he can incarnate it, so to speak, in a material body—words, music, painting—the thing we know as a work of art. And since he is a man like the rest of us, we shall expect that our experience will have something in common with his. In the image of *his* experience, we can *recognise* the image of some experience of our own—something that had happened to us, but which we had never understood, never formulated or expressed to ourselves, and therefore never known as a real experience. When we read the poem, or see the play or picture or hear the music, it is as though a light were turned on inside us. We say: "Ah! I recog- nise that! That is something which I obscurely felt to be going on in and about me, but I didn't know what it was and couldn't express it. But now that the artist has made its image—imaged it forth— for me, I can possess and take hold of it and make it my own, and turn it into a source of knowledge and strength." This is the *communication of the image in power*, by which the third person of the poet's trinity brings us, through the incarnate image, into direct knowledge of the in itself unknowable and unimaginable reality. "No man cometh to the Father save by Me," said the incarnate Image; and He added, "but the Spirit of Power will lead you into all truth."

This recognition of the truth that we get in the artist's work comes to us as a revelation of new truth. I want to be clear about that. I am not referring to the sort of patronising recognition we give to a writer by nodding our heads and observing: "Yes, yes, very good, very true—that's just what I'm always saying." I mean the recognition of a truth which tells us something about ourselves that we had *not* been "always saying"—something which puts a new knowledge of ourselves within our grasp. It is new, startling, and perhaps shattering—and yet it comes to us with a sense of familiarity. We did not know it before, but the moment the poet has shown it to us, we know that, somehow or other, we had always really known it.

Very well. But, frankly, is that the sort of thing the average British citizen gets, or expects to get, when he goes to the theatre or reads a book? No, it is not. In the majority of cases, it is not in the least what he expects, or what he wants. What he looks for is not this creative and Christian kind of Art at all. He does not expect or desire to be upset by sudden revelations about himself and the universe. Like the people of Plato's decadent Athens, he has forgotten or repudiated the religious origins of all Art. He wants entertainment, or, if he is a little more serious-minded, he wants something with a moral, or to have some spell or incantation put on him to instigate him to virtuous action.

Now, entertainment and moral spell-binding have their uses, but they are not Art in the proper sense. They may be the incidental effects of good art; but they may also be the very aim and essence of false art. And if we continue to demand of the Arts only these two things, we shall starve and silence the true artist and encourage in his place the false artist, who may become a very sinister force indeed.

Let us take the amusement-art: what does that give us? Generally speaking, what we demand and get from it is the enjoyment of the emotions which usually accompany experience without having had the experience. It does not reveal us to ourselves: it merely projects on to a mental screen a picture of ourselves as we already fancy ourselves to be—only bigger and brighter. The manufacturer of this kind of entertainment is not by any means interpreting and

40

revealing his own experience to himself and us—he is either indulging his own day-dreams, or—still more falsely and venially—he is saying: "What is it the audience think they would like to have experienced? Let us show them that, so that they can wallow in emotion by pretending to have experienced it." This kind of pseudo-art is "wish-fulfilment" or "escape" literature in the worst sense—it is an escape, not from the "impact of external events" into the citadel of experienced reality, but an escape from reality and experience into a world of merely external events—the progressive externalisation of consciousness. For occasional relaxation this is all right; but it can be carried to the point where, not merely art, but the whole universe of phenomena becomes a screen on which we see the magnified projection of our unreal selves, as the object of equally unreal emotions. This brings about the complete corruption of the consciousness, which can no longer recognise reality in experience. When things come to this pass, we have a civilisation which "lives for amusement"—a civilisation without guts, without experience, and out of touch with reality.

Or take the spell-binding kind of art. This at first sight seems better because it spurs us to action; and it also has its uses. But it too is dangerous in excess, because once again it does not reveal reality in experience, but only projects a lying picture of the self. As the amusement-art seeks to produce the *emotions* without the experience, so *this* pseudo-art seeks to produce the *behaviour* without the experience. In the end it is directed to putting the behaviour of the audience beneath the will of the spell-binder, and its true name is not "art," but "art-magic." In its vulgarest form it becomes pure propaganda. It can (as we have reason to know) actually succeed in making its audience into the thing it desires to have them—it can really in the end corrupt the consciousness and destroy experience until the inner selves of its victims are wholly externalised and made the puppets and instruments of their own spurious passions. This is why it is dangerous for anybody—even for the Church —to urge artists to produce works of art for the express purpose of "doing good to people." Let her by all means encourage artists to express their own Christian experience and communicate it to others. That is the true artist saying: "Look! recognise your experience in my own." But "edifying art" may only too often be the pseudo-artist corruptly saying: "This is what you are supposed to believe and feel and do—and I propose to work you into a state of mind in which you will believe and feel and do as you are told." This pseudo-art does not really communicate power to us; it merely exerts power over us.

What is it, then, that these two pseudo-arts—the entertaining and the spell-binding—have in common? And how are they related to true Art? What they have in common is the falsification of the consciousness; and they are to Art as the *idol* is to the Image. The Jews were forbidden to make any image for worship, because before the revelation of the threefold unity in which Image and Unimaginable are one, it was only too fatally easy to substitute the idol for the Image. The Christian revelation set free all the images, by showing that the true Image subsisted within the Godhead Itself —it was neither copy, nor imitation, nor representation, nor inferior, nor subsequent, but the brightness of the glory, and the express image of the Person—the very mirror in which reality knows itself and communicates itself in power.

But the danger still exists; and it always will recur whenever the Christian doctrine of the Image is forgotten. In our æsthetic, that doctrine has never been fully used or understood, and in consequence our whole attitude to the artistic expression of reality has become confused, idolatrous and pagan. We see the Arts degenerating into mere entertainment which corrupts and relaxes our civilisation, and we try in alarm to correct this by demanding a more moralising and bracing kind of Art. But this is only setting up one idol in place of the other. Or we see that Art is becoming idolatrous, and suppose that we can put matters right by getting rid of the representational element in it. But what is wrong is not the representation itself, but the fact that what we are looking at, and what we are looking *for*, is not the Image but an idol. Little children, keep yourselves from idols.

It has become a commonplace to say that the Arts are in a bad way. We are in fact largely given over to the entertainers and the spell-binders; and because we do not understand that these two functions do not represent the true nature of Art, the true artists are, as it were, excommunicate, and have no audience. But there is here not, I think, so much a relapse from a Christian æsthetic as a failure ever to find and examine a real Christian æsthetic, based on dogma and not on ethics. This may not be a bad thing. We have at least a new line of country to explore, that has not been trampled on and built over and fought over by countless generations of quarrelsome critics. What we have to start from is the Trinitarian doctrine of creative mind, and the light which that doctrine throws on the true nature of images.

The great thing, I am sure, is not to be nervous about God— not to try and shut out the Lord Immanuel from *any* sphere of truth. Art is not He—we must not substitute Art for God; yet this also is He, for it is one of His Images and therefore reveals His nature. Here we see in a mirror darkly—we behold only the images; elsewhere we shall see face to face, in the place where Image and Reality are one.

CREATIVE MIND

Address given to the Humanities Club at Reading, February, 1942

THE QUARREL BETWEEN THE SCIENCES and the humanities is chiefly a quarrel of words. And when I say that, I do not mean to suggest that it is a quarrel about nothing. Both parties are setting out to explore reality, each by its own method. But they have only one set of tools between them. And because they use these tools very differently—because they cannot even agree together about the nature and purpose of the tools—the accounts which they present to the world as the result of their explorations are apt to appear mutually unintelligible and violently antagonistic. You would scarcely think they could both be examining the same reality.

Let me say at once that the scientists are working under peculiar difficulties, and deserve our deepest sympathy. For the words—the tools—which the scientist is obliged to use were forged by the other man, and have few or none of the qualities which the scientist desires in an instrument of precision. The modern scientist is chiefly interested in measurable quantities, and is sometimes apt to suppose that nothing is quite real unless it can be measured. But to measure, let us say, the length of anything, he requires a yardstick; and his task will not be an easy one if the yardstick, instead of remaining rigid and uniform, develops a nasty trick of expanding, shrinking, bulging, curling about, or throwing out offshoots in different directions. But this is precisely the way in which language behaves. Words alter their meaning in course of time and in various contexts: to change the metaphor a little, they are like magnets charged with power that affect and deflect all the instruments of precision which come within their field of influence. The desperate attempts of scientists to reduce language to a kind of algebraic formula in which the same symbol has always the same meaning resemble the process of trying to force a large and obstreperous cat into a small basket. As fast as you tuck in the head, the tail comes out, when you have at length confined the hind legs, the fore paws come out and scratch; and when, after a painful struggle, you shut down the lid, the dismal wailings of the imprisoned animal suggest that some essential dignity in the creature has been violated and a wrong done to its nature. Or let us take another image: to make a precise scientific description of reality out of words is like trying to build a rigid structure out of pure quicksilver; it is using language for a purpose that defies the very nature of its being. The whole history of modern scientific terminology is that of a struggle to make language conform to a rule of behaviour which is not its own— a struggle, let me suggest, which has in itself something irrational and unscientific about it, since it is scarcely scientific to endeavour to wrest any substance out of truth to its own nature. Indeed, of late years, scientists have grown more and more inclined to abandon the unequal conflict, and to present their discoveries in terms and formulæ of their own devising, which are not subject to the peculiar mutability which affects human language. They talk to one another in long strings of mathematical symbols, or in those unpronounce-able polysyllabic formulæ which enshrine the nature of new chemical combinations, or in diagrams. The only objection to these symbolic notations is that they communicate nothing except to other scientists in the same line of business. To take the instance I used just now: the substance known as quicksilver. This word, invented by the poet who dwells in every common man, means "living silver." Taken in its literal meaning, it tells the world two things about the substance, both of which are false: it suggests that it is something organic, and that it is a form of the metal called silver. But, taken in its poetic meaning, it tells two other things about it, both of which are true: namely, that its shape is changeable like the shape of a living thing, and that its appearance is metallic, white, and shining like that of silver. Thus the word "quicksilver" conveys to the ordinary man, together with a certain measure of scientific falsehood, an equal amount of poetic truth. To the scientist, how-ever, the poetic truth appears, for his special purposes, irrelevant, and the mixture of falsehood definitely objectionable. The word "quicksilver" is of no assistance to him. Nor is the alternative "mercury" any better. It regrettably recalls the superstitions of the alchemists, by which this metal was associated with the god Mer-cury; and by which the planets were supposed to influence the make-up of the human organism, so that one spoke of a "mercurial" temperament. Words of this kind merely darken scientific counsel. In the hope of getting rid of these unfortunate verbal associations, the chemist falls back upon giving the stuff, not a name, but a symbol. He writes down the letters Hg, and hopes that this time he has finally escaped the influence of the poet. The symbol Hg is (or is intended to be) *pure* symbol. It does not describe, or interpret the substance—it merely stands for the substance; and it has the merit, or the drawback, according to the purpose for which it is used, of conveying absolutely nothing about the substance to anyone who is not previously acquainted with the substance itself.

So far, so good. But in point of fact, the chemist has not got rid of the poet altogether. For one thing, he was careless at the outset in choosing his symbol. The letters Hg are merely the abbreviation of a Greek word—*hydrarguros*—meaning "fluid silver"—a word only one degree less picturesque and inaccurate than the English "quick" or "living" silver. Had the chemist been less lazy, less ready to take the line of least resistance, he could, of course, have avoided this association by selecting some quite arbitrary symbol. The fact that he did not only shows that there is more of the common man and the common poet left hanging about the scientist than he is always willing to admit. But the thing goes deeper than that. Even if the symbol Hg were quite arbitrary and meaningless in origin, it will only remain pure scientific symbol so long as the common poet refrains from tinkering about with it. If it should occur to the poet to lay hands upon it and transfer it to his own poetic vocabulary, it will cease to be scientific formula and will again become language, charged with all the emotional associations, all the mutability, and all the vague magnetic power which belong to the nature of language. If the poet, correctly associating the expression Hg with the substance it denotes, chooses to talk of an Hg temperament in the sense of a mercurial temperament, no bitter outcry from the outraged chemist can prevent him, or disentangle the letters Hg from the literary and emotional accretions that will promptly gather about it. Even if a fortuitous alphabetical similarity should cause popular imagination to see a poetical resemblance between the fluid adaptability of Hg and the activities of the Home Guard, the scientist will be helpless to prevent it. If his symbol is to remain pure, he must be constantly changing it—or else must be at pains to choose a symbol so abstract and unpronounceable that neither he nor anybody else can ever introduce it into ordinary conversation. For anything that can be used in conversation is language, and has to submit to the natural law of language.

It is fascinating to watch the never-ending struggle as language and scientific method develop side by side. The process is always the same. The scientist seizes upon a word originally made by the common poet, and endeavours to restrict it to a single, definite meaning which shall be the same in every context. The physicist, for instance, takes a word like "force" or "energy" and uses it to denote a particular factor in physics that can be mathematically expressed. To his horror, the general public refuses to restrict the word in this manner, and innumerable misunderstandings occur. Not only does the common man continue to use the words in metaphorical meanings which they cannot bear in scientific contexts: he also reads those meanings into the scientist's expositions of physics, deducing from them all kinds of metaphysical conclusions quite foreign to the physicist's intentions. Or, if the scientist does succeed in capturing a word and restricting its meaning, some other word will arrive and take over all the former meanings of the original word; so that the same pair of words may be used in successive centuries to mean totally different things, and may even become substituted for one another, without anybody's noticing what has happened.

Let me give one or two examples of this:—

In the eighteenth century, the word "reason" was taken hold of by scientists, and was used by them to mean something practically identical with the *method of reasoning* which at that time was scoring so great a triumph in the field of scientific discovery. But that was not the meaning of "reason" to a philosopher of the Middle Ages. To *him*, "reason" included very much more—for example, the qualities we now call "intellect," "intuition" and "imagination," as well as the faculties of observation and deductive logic. When a medieval theologian called God the Son "the Divine Reason," he did not mean that the Creator of the world was an inductive process: he meant something much nearer to what the modern Russian theologian Berdyaev meant when he said: "God created the world by imagination." In the Middle Ages, the word "imagination" meant primarily the faculty of producing mental *images*—something more like what we now mean by "visual fancy." But as the word "reason" became more and more identified with "scientific method," the word "imagination" had to take over more and more of the work previously done by the word "reason." The various uses of these words are still found side by side in common speech. When we say contemptuously that a thing is "all imagination," we mean that it is mere fancy—an image corresponding to no reality. But when we say that a scheme of—let us say—post-war construction, displays "real imagination," we mean, not merely that it is seen vivid and complete like an "image" or picture, but that it shows profound insight and intellectual grasp of the whole subject. The two adjectives "imaginary" and "imaginative" correspond to the older and the later use of the word "imagination."

The word "image" itself has different meanings in different contexts: compare, for instance, its meaning in the phrase "to make a graven image" and in the phrase "God made man in His own image" and then compare both of them with the optician's technical use of the word when he says that the appearance formed on a screen by an optical lens is a "true image," whereas that formed in a mirror is not. The optician is using the word in a restricted sense—he is using it, that is, as a technical term—one word, one meaning. When the common man reads a scientific book, he has to learn what is the precise technical use of the terms employed by the scientist. When the scientist reads a work of literature, he has to remember that every word in that book must be interpreted—not absolutely, as though it were a technical term, but relatively to its context.

The possibilities of confusion are very great—especially when one bears in mind that a scientist in one department is himself only a "common poet" in his use and understanding of the technical vocabulary of another department of science. Theology, for example, is a science with a highly technical vocabulary of its own; and when (for example) a biologist ventures (as he frequently does) into criticism of other people's theology, he is apt to tumble into errors quite as grotesque as those made by popular preachers who adorn their sermons with misapplied scraps of biology. I remember reading with fascination and malignant joy a prolonged argument between a distinguished scientist and a theologian on the subject of transubstantiation. It occupied a great deal of paper, and went on for months. But from beginning to end of the correspondence, it never occurred to the scientist to suspect, nor to his opponent to inform him, that the technical theological meaning of the word "substance" was not merely different from its meaning in current contemporary speech, but almost its direct opposite. It could scarcely even be called a quarrel about words—it was a random exchange of words which prevented them from ever discovering what the subject was they had undertaken to quarrel about.

Or take again the case of the word "reality." No word occasions so much ill-directed argument. We are now emerging from a period when people were inclined to use it as though nothing was real unless it could be measured; and some old-fashioned materialists still use it so. But if you go back behind the dictionary meanings—such as "that which has objective existence"—and behind its philosophic history to the derivation of the word, you find that "reality" means "the thing thought." *Reality* is a concept; and a real object is that which corresponds to the concept. In ordinary conversation we still use the word in this way. When we say "those pearls are not real," we do not mean that they cannot be measured; we mean that the measurement of their make-up does not correspond to the concept "pearl," that, regarded as pearls, they are nothing more than an appearance; they are quite actual, but they are not real. *As pearls*, in fact, they have no objective existence. Professor Eddington is much troubled by the words "reality" and "existence"; in his *Philosophy of Physical Science* he can find no use or meaning for the word "existence"—unless, he admits, it is taken to mean "that which is present in the thought of God." That, he thinks, is not the meaning usually given to it. But it is, in fact, the precise meaning, and the only meaning, given to it by the theologian.

I have taken up a lot of your time with this talk about words—which may seem very far removed from the subject of creative mind. But I have two objects in doing so. The first is simply to warn you that my use of words will not always be your use of words, and that the words of the common poet—the creator in words—must never be interpreted absolutely, but only in relation to their context. They must be considered as fields of force, which disturb and are disturbed by their environment. Secondly, I want to place before you this passage from the works of Richard Hard—an eighteenth-century English divine:

"The source of bad criticism, as universally of bad philosophy, is the abuse of terms. A poet they say must follow *nature*: and by nature, we are to suppose, can only be meant the known and experienced course of affairs in this world. Whereas the poet has a world of his own, where experience has less to do than *consistent imagination*."

It was the Royal Society who announced in 1687 that they "exacted from their members a close, naked, *natural* way of speaking . . . bringing all things as near the mathematical plainness as they can." Words, they imply, are not to be metaphorical or allusive or charged with incalculable associations—but to approximate as closely as possible to mathematical symbols: "one word, one meaning." And to this Hard retorts in effect that, for the poet, this use of language is simply not "natural" at all. It is contrary to the nature of language and to the nature of the poet. The poet does not work by the analysis and measurement of observables, but by a "consistent imagination." He creates, we may say, by building up new images, new intellectual concepts, new worlds, if you like, to form new consistent wholes, new unities out of diversity. And I should like to submit to you that this is in fact the way in which all creative mind works—in the sciences as everywhere else—in divine as well as in human creation, so far as we can observe and understand divine methods of creation. That is, that within our experience, creation proceeds by the discovery of new conceptual relations between things, so as to form them into systems having a consistent wholeness corresponding to an image in the mind, and, consequently, possessing real existence.

Let us take a few instances quite at random. The physicists have been exciting us a good deal lately by horrible revelations about the stuff the visible universe is made of. They tell us that it is not "really" full of solid things as we suppose, and that it is not "really" full of the different kinds of things we suppose. Everything (if I understand them rightly) is composed of the same thing—namely (I must go very carefully here for fear of committing them to some too positive statement)—namely, certain items of a more or less electrical nature, moving about (whatever motion may be—or would it be better to say "functioning"?) in a great deal of empty space, whatever that may be. Boiled down to the last proton and neutron, everything in the universe is the same thing. There is no clear-cut dividing line between one thing and another. There is only some kind of related activity and a numerical relation to distinguish the atom of helium from any other of the ninety-two elements, or you and me from the air we breathe. Indeed, there is, in a sense, nothing very much to show where you and I leave off and the rest of the universe begins. When we ponder this too closely, we may begin to wonder whether we possess any reality at all. But (escaping from the hypnotic power of words) we may console ourselves with the thought that the reality of the atom, or of ourselves, consists precisely in the relation that binds us into a recognisable unity. Our behaviour corresponds to a mental concept which sees us as a whole. The atom and ourselves are as it were created out of an undifferentiated universe by an act of consistent imagination which holds us together as one thing. It does not matter for our purpose *whose* imagination is supposed to be involved—the important thing for our reality is that we can be thus imaged into existence.

At what point does the creative imagination of the baby begin to select consistent unities out of the atomic material offered to his observation? The psychologists have not yet told us very much about this. We do know, however, from a study of the history of language, that perception of the unity of "this-tree-here" precedes the perception of the unity of "trees-in-general." There has to be a mental gathering-together of like images before the creation of a great all-embracing image of "the tree" in the abstract. The

49

realisation that this-thing is in many respects like that-thing leads to a concept of a thing-in-itself: the relation in which this-thing and that-thing and all the other like things are bound into a unity. At this point we begin to ask whether the word "tree" denotes any objective reality apart from the separate trees that make up the concept. We can measure individual trees, use them, do things with them; whether we can do anything with tree-in-general, except think about it, is another question. We will not stop to discuss that for the moment—merely noting that the concept "tree" is a great act of creative imagination, which at least enables us to *think* much more usefully about individual trees. We can reason about the concept "tree-in-the-abstract" *as if* it were an actual object, and, having thought about it, we can apply our conclusions to actual, measurable trees.

Note the words "*as if*"—because the moment we say those words we are coming very near to the thing called poetic creation. Let us take another instance. At some point the primitive savage, at some point the individual infant, having perceived a likeness among certain groups of related atoms, begins to make a further relation between these groups—this time a numerical relation: one tree, two trees, twenty trees, a hundred trees. And from the perception of this relation he creates a new concept: number-in-itself.

According to one great mathematician: "God made the integers; all else is the work of man." And, according to many mathematicians, number is, as it were, the fundamental characteristic of the universe. But what *is* number, other than a relation between like things—like groupings of atoms—like unities? We say that we see six eggs (or we said so when eggs were plentiful). Certainly we see egg, egg, egg, egg, egg, egg in a variety of arrangements; but can we see six —apart from the eggs? No man hath seen an integer at any time. There has perhaps never been a greater act of the creative imagination than the creation of the concept of number as a thing-in-itself. Yet, with that concept, the mathematician can work, handling pure number *as if* it possessed independent existence, and producing results applicable to things measurable and observable.

I am trying to suggest to you what are the characteristics of creative imagination—creative mind, reason, intellect, or whatever you like to call it. In this rough survey of creative achievement, we may pick out these phrases: the perception of likenesses, the relating of like things to form a new unity, and the words "as if."

I will now take two instances of a rather different kind of creation —the poet's kind. The poet's imagination creates by metaphor. It perceives a likeness between a number of things that at first sight appear to have no measurable relation, and it builds them into a new kind of unity, a new universe, that can be handled with power *as if* it possessed independent existence, and whose power is operative in the world of things that can be observed and measured.

When I said some time ago that the efforts of the scientist to use language as though it were mathematical symbol resembled those of a man trying to cram a cat into a basket, I was not actually using metaphor. But I was pointing out a series of likenesses from which a metaphorical image might be created. The poet will take this process a step further. He will write a line such as that famous line of Shakespeare's about the honey-bees:

The singing masons building roofs of gold.

Now, the scientist who wants one word, one meaning, may very properly object to almost every word in this line. He will point out that the word "singing" would be better confined to the noise produced by the vibration of the vocal chords; that bees have no vocal chords; that the noise they make is produced by the vibration of their flight apparatus; and that it has no such emotional significance as the idea of "singing" implies. Further, that bees are not, in the strict sense of the word, masons, and that their manipulation of wax in their mandibles to make honey cells is quite unlike the action of masons in a stone-cutter's yard; "building" he might allow; but "roofs" (he will say) is an inaccurate description of a conglomeration of hexagonal cells; while the word "gold" is preposterous, seeing that neither the atomic structure nor even the colour of the product in question is correctly indicated by such a misleading word. He will not, that is, recognise the poet's new unity, constructed from a new set of likenesses, because it does not conform to scientific method. It is a different set of likenesses, not verifiable with a yardstick; and the unity is not one which can be separated from the surrounding universe by any tests which his technique can apply. But if he comes to test it with the technique which he possesses, not as a scientist, but as a common man, he will find that the metaphor behaves exactly like any other unity constructed by the creative imagination: it does establish a likeness; it does behave as a separable whole, and it produces observable effects *as if* it possessed independent existence. It can, for example, produce that observable effect on observable nerve and blood tissues that is known as "making one's heart leap"—it may even produce an observable reaction from the tear-glands, resulting in a measurable quantity of brackish water. A scientific description of the process of cell formation by the worker-bee might produce other observable results, equally important: but it would not produce those.

It will be noticed that the words of that line—

> *The singing masons building roofs of gold*

are far more powerful in combination than they are separately. Yet each word brings with it a little accumulation of power of its own—for each word is itself a separate unity and a separate creative act. "Singing" has the suggestion of a spontaneous expression of joy and physical well-being, and—since the singing creatures are a whole hiveful—it also suggests social rejoicing, a gladness felt in common. "Masons" and "building" bring with them associations of the joy of skilled craftsmanship, the beauty of great buildings, and a further social suggestion, in that buildings are commonly designed to be the homes, or working-places, or shrines for worship of all sorts of people. "Roofs of gold" carries a special reminiscence of the Golden City of the New Jerusalem—together with such romantic names as the Golden City of Manoa and so on; and "gold" has, of course, innumerable rich and glowing suggestions, ranging from the light of the sun to the common association of worldly wealth. All these are welded in one line into the image of the joyful craftsmen singing over their task as they build the golden city; and this, by a metaphor, is identified with the sensation of standing in a sunny garden, hearing the drone of the bees as they pack the honeycomb with sweetness. Two images are fused into a single world of power by a cunning perception of a set of likenesses between unlike things. That is not all: in its context, the line belongs to a passage which welds the fused image again into yet another unity, to present the picture of the perfect State:

> *for so work the honey-bees,*
> *Creatures which by a law in nature teach*
> *The act of order to a peopled kingdom.*

This is not scientist's truth; it is poet's truth, like the truth latent in that unscientific word, "quicksilver." It is the presentation of a unity among like things, producing a visible, measurable effect *as if* the unity were itself measurable.

The creation of a whole work of art proceeds along the same lines. A work of fiction, for example, possesses poetic truth provided that the author has rightly seen which things can be so related as to combine into a convincing unity—provided, as Hard says, the work is an act of *consistent* imagination. If the imagination is consistent, the work will produce effects *as if* it were actually true. If it is not consistent, then the effects produced will be the wrong ones —they will not work out properly—any more than Kepler's circular solar system would work out properly in observation, because it was wrongly imagined. As soon as Kepler had imagined his system consistently, the calculations came out right; it is, of course, open to the relativist to say that Kepler's system with its central sun and elliptical planetary orbits is no more *absolutely* true than any other system, and, indeed, that whether the earth goes round the sun or the sun round the earth is merely a question of how you look at it. That may be perfectly true; but it does not affect the issue. To a relativist, no doubt, the Ptolemaic, earth-centred system with its elaborate epicycles is as relatively true as the Copernican—only, it is much less convenient, much less simple, much less productive of good results in practice; in a word, it is much less powerfully imagined. Similarly, one may say that the most preposterous story in *Peg's Paper* has just as much or little claim to be called scientific-ally *true* as *Hamlet*. Neither set of events ever happened in any verifiable or provable sense of the words. If *Hamlet* has a truth that the *Peg's Paper* novelette has not, it is because it is created by a more consistent imagination, and its measurable effects on humanity are richer and more valuable.

For the next instance of "consistent imagination" I will ask you to wander with me down a very curious little bypath. It was during the last century that the great war was fought between churchmen and men of science over the theory of Evolution. We need not fight afresh every battle in that campaign. The scientists won their victory; chiefly, or at any rate largely, with the help of the palæon-tologists and the biologists. It was made clear that the earlier history of the earth and its inhabitants could be reconstructed from fossil remains surviving in its present, and from vestigial structures remaining in the various plants and animals with which it is now peopled. It was scarcely possible to suppose any longer that God had created each species—to quote the text of *Paradise Lost*— "perfect forms, limb'd and full grown," except on what seemed the extravagant assumption that, when creating the universe, He had at the same time provided it with the evidence of a purely imaginary past which had never had any actual existence. Now, the first thing to be said about this famous quarrel is that the churchmen need never have been perturbed at all about the *method* of creation, if they had remembered that the Book of Genesis was a book of poetical truth, and not intended as a scientific handbook of geology. They got into their difficulty, to a large extent, through having unwit-tingly slipped into accepting the scientist's concept of the use of language, and supposing that a thing could not be true unless it was amenable to quantitative methods of proof. Eventually, and with many slips by the way, they contrived to clamber out of this false position; and to-day no reasonable theologian is at all perturbed by the idea that creation was effected by evolutionary methods. But, if the theologians had *not* lost touch with the nature of language; if they had not insensibly fallen into the eighteenth-century conception of the universe as a mechanism and God as the Great Engineer; if, instead, they had chosen to think of God as a great imaginative artist—then they might have offered a quite different kind of interpretation of the facts, with rather entertaining consequences. They might, in fact, have seriously put forward the explanation I mentioned just now: that *God had at some moment or other created the universe complete with all the vestiges of an imaginary past.*

I have said that this "seemed an extravagant assumption"; so it does, if one thinks of God as a mechanician. But if one thinks of Him as working in the same sort of way as a creative artist, then it no longer seems extravagant, but the most natural thing in the world. *It is the way every novel in the world is written.*

Every serious novelist starts with some or all of his characters "in perfect form and fully grown," *complete with their pasts.* Their present is conditioned by a past which exists, not fully on paper, but fully or partially in the creator's imagination. And as he goes on writing the book, he will—especially if it is a long work, like the *Forsyte Saga* or the "Peter Wimsey" series—plant from time to time in the text of the book allusions to that unwritten past. If his imagination is consistent, then all those allusions, all those, so to speak, planted fossils, will tell a story consistent with one another and consistent with the present and future actions of the characters. That is to say, that past, existing only in the mind of the maker, produces a true and measurable effect upon the written part of the book, precisely as though it had, in fact, "taken place" within the work of art itself.

If you have ever amused yourselves by reading some of the works of "spoof" criticism about Sherlock Holmes (e.g. *Baker Street Studies*, or H. W. Bell's *Sherlock Holmes and Dr. Watson*),[1] you will see just how far pseudo-scientific method can be used to interpret these "fossil remains" scattered about the Sherlock Holmes stories, and what ingenuity can be used to force the indications into an apparent historical consistency. As regards the past of his characters, Conan Doyle's imagination was not, in fact, very consistent; there are lapses and contradictions, as well as lacunæ. But let us suppose

[1] Readers may turn to the four essays at the end of this book.

a novelist with a perfectly consistent imagination, who had conceived his characters with an absolutely complete and flawless past history; and let us suppose, further, that the fossil remains were being examined by one of the characters, who (since his existence is contained wholly within the covers of the book just as ours is contained wholly within the universe) could not get outside the written book to communicate with the author. (This, I know, is difficult, rather like imagining the inhabitants of two-dimensional space, but it can be done.) Now, such a character would be in precisely the same position as a scientist examining the evidence which the universe affords of its own past. The evidence would all be there, it would all point in the same direction, and its effects would be apparent in the whole action of the story itself (that is, in what, for him, would be "real" history). There is no conceivable set of data, no imaginable line of reasoning, by which he could possibly prove whether or not that past had ever gone through the formality of taking place. On the evidence—the fossil remains, the self-consistency of all the data, and the effects observable in himself and his fellow characters—he would, I think, be forced to conclude that it *had* taken place. And, whether or no, he would be obliged to go on behaving *as if* it had taken place. Indeed, he could not by any means behave otherwise, because he had been created by his maker *as a person with those influences in his past.*

I think that if the churchmen had chosen to take up that position, the result would have been entertaining. It would have been a very strong position, because it is one that cannot be upset by scientific proof. Probably, theologians would have been deterred by a vague sense that a God who made His universe like this was not being quite truthful. But that would be because of a too limited notion of "truth." In what sense is the unwritten past of the characters in a book less "true" than their behaviour in it? Or if a prehistory that never happened exercises an effect on history indistinguishable from the effect it would have made by happening, what *real* difference is there between happening and not-happening? If it is deducible from the evidence, self-consistent, and recognisable in its effects, it is quite real, whether or not it ever was actual.

I am not, of course, giving it as my opinion that the world was made yesterday all of a piece, or even that it first came into being at the point where prehistory stops and history begins; I am only saying that if it had, then, provided the imagination were consistent, no difference of any kind would have been made to anything whatever in the universe. Though, of course, if we were willing to accept such a theory, we might find it easier to deal with some of our problems about time. And, by the way, we should then expect a continuous deposit, as time went on into the future, of fresh evidence about the past. That is, new palæological and other records would be discovered from time to time as the author put them there and directed attention to them—much in the same way as evidential allusions to Peter Wimsey's schooldays are apt to make their appearance from time to time as the series of his adventures continues. You will notice that palæological discoveries *are* made from time to time—this proves nothing either way; on either hypothesis they would be bound to occur. All I have tried to do in this piece of fantasy is to show that where you have a consistent imagination at work, the line between scientific and poetic truth may become very hard to draw.

You will probably be tempted, by your habit of mind, to ask—what does all this prove? It does not, in the scientific sense of the word, prove anything. The function of imaginative speech is not to prove, but to create—to discover new similarities, and to arrange them to form new unities, to build new self-consistent worlds out of the universe of undifferentiated mind-stuff.

Every activity has its own technique; the mistake is to suppose that the technique of one activity is suitable for all purposes. In scientific reasoning, for example, the poet's technique of metaphor and analogy is inappropriate and even dangerous—its use leads to conclusions which are false to science, which builds its new unities out of quantitative likenesses, and things which are numerically comparable. The error of the Middle Ages, on the whole, was to use analogical, metaphorical, poetical techniques for the investigation of scientific questions. But increasingly, since the seventeenth century, we have tended to the opposite error—that of using the quantitative methods of science for the investigation of poetic truth. But to build poetic systems of truth, the similarities must be, not quantitative, but qualitative, and the new unity that will emerge will be a world of new values. Here, metaphor and analogy are both appropriate and necessary—for both these processes involve the arranging of things according to some quality that the dissimilars have in common: thus (to go back to my early simile) common language and an infuriated cat, though in quantitative respects very unlike, have in common a certain quality of intractability. And thus, too, the associative values of words, which make them such bad tools for the scientist, make them the right tools for the poet, for they facilitate the establishment of similarities between many widely-differing concepts, and so make easy the task of the creative imagination building up its poetic truths.

Perhaps I ought to add a caution about words. I said that words were, metaphorically, fields of force. May I, in my metaphorical, poetical and unscientific way, press this analogy a little further. It is as dangerous for people unaccustomed to handling words and unacquainted with their technique to tinker about with these heavily-charged nuclei of emotional power as it would be for me to burst into a laboratory and play about with a powerful electro-magnet or other machine highly charged with electrical force. By my clumsy and ignorant handling, I should probably, at the very least, contrive to damage either the machine or myself; at the worst I might blow up the whole place. Similarly the irresponsible use of highly-electric words is very strongly to be deprecated.

At the present time we have a population that is literate, in the sense that everybody is able to read and write; but, owing to the emphasis placed on scientific and technical training at the expense of the humanities, very few of our people have been taught to understand and handle language as an instrument of power. This means that, in this country alone, forty million innocents or thereabouts are wandering inquisitively about the laboratory, enthusiastically pulling handles and pushing buttons, thereby releasing uncontrollable currents of electric speech, with results that astonish themselves and the world. Nothing is more intoxicating than a sense of power: the demagogue who can sway crowds, the journalist who can push up the sales of his paper to the two-million mark, the playwright who can plunge an audience into an orgy of facile emotion, the parliamentary candidate who is carried to the top of the poll on a flood of meaningless rhetoric, the ranting preacher, the advertising salesman of material or spiritual commodities, are all playing perilously and irresponsibly with the power of words, and are equally dangerous whether they are cynically unscrupulous or (as frequently happens) have fallen under the spell of their own eloquence and become the victims of their own propaganda. For the great majority of those whom they are addressing have no skill in assessing the value of words, and are as helpless under verbal attack as were the citizens of Rotterdam against assault from the air. When we first began to realise the way in which the common sense of Europe had been undermined and battered down by Nazi propaganda, we were astonished as well as horrified; yet there was nothing astonishing about it. It was simply another exhibition of ruthless force: the employment of a very powerful weapon by experts who understood it perfectly against people who were not armed to resist it, and had never really understood that it was a weapon at all. And the defence against the misuse of words is not flight, nor yet the random setting off of verbal fireworks, but the wary determination to understand the potentialities of language, and to use it with resolution and skill.

It is right that the scientists should come to terms with the humanities; for in daily life scientists also are common men, and the flight from language will never avail to carry them out of its field of power. They must learn to handle that instrument, as they handle other instruments, with a full comprehension of what it is, and what it does, and in so doing they will come to recognise it as a source of delight as well as of danger. The language of the imagination can never be inert: as with every other living force, you must learn to handle it or it will handle you. "The question is," said Humpty Dumpty, "which is to be master—that's all."

POLITICAL

THE GULF STREAM AND THE CHANNEL

(1943)

"When Britain first at Heaven's command
Arose from out the azure main . . ."

her guardian angels did not content themselves with merely singing
a strain or so to celebrate the occasion. They took practical measures
—or at any rate they perpetrated two practical jokes—whereby
they ensured that Britain and her inhabitants should remain a sort
of standing practical joke to the end of time. Everybody—even the
British themselves—must have noticed the effect produced by this
country upon the more staid and serious peoples of the European
continent—and, indeed, of any continent: it is precisely that mixture
of startled recoil, affronted dignity, nervous irritation, reluctant
amusement, and apprehension about what is going to happen next
which characterises the person who has walked through a harmless-
looking door and received a bucket of water on his head. There
is something about the British which is felt to be unwelcoming,
freakish and irresponsible; they are solemn on the outside and
frivolous at heart, and behind their most decorous appearances
there lurks a schoolboy grin; they are not unsuccessful in statesmanship, trade, or warfare, yet about their politics, economics and
military organisation there is always an air of improvisation, as
though they did not take the future seriously; above all, you never
know where to have them, they do not fit handily into any pigeon-
hole, they display an almost morbid reluctance to be *gleichgeschaltet*
—a thing offensive to any tidy mind. Of the three nations which
make up Great Britain all share these characteristics to some extent,
but the English are the worst.

When Neptune shouldered Britain out of the sea, he did not make
a neat engineering job of it. Characteristically, Britain came up
skew-wiff, with one edge thick and hard and the other soft and
thin, like a slice of wedding-cake. The guardian angels, observing
that her more vulnerable side was precisely that which lay nearer

to Europe and was consequently the more open to attack, did their best to square matters up. They arranged that the twenty-two miles separating the Kentish coast from the mainland should be filled with a stretch of water so disagreeable that, without very weighty reasons indeed, nobody in his senses would have any stomach for crossing it. So far, so good; a sensible, but dull precaution. If nobody even attempted to cross the Narrow Seas, where would be the fun? The island must be made desirable—then indeed the joke of making it so near yet so inaccessible would acquire a rich flavour. With coal and iron it was already well stocked; but make it also fertile, and there it would hang, a veritable fruit of Tantalus, bobbing at the mouth of hungry adventurers. The latitude in which the place stood was unfavourable; but the resources of celestial plumbing were not exhausted. The guardian angels, with a chuckle, turned on the hot-water tap off the distant shores of Panama and released the Gulf Stream into the English Channel. By those two geographical jokes—the Gulf Stream and the Channel—everything that appears remarkable in the temperament and history of the British can be sensibly and satisfactorily accounted for.

The effect of the Channel, first and foremost, is to make it difficult and unpleasant to get into this country, and equally difficult and unpleasant to get out. Consequently, Britain has never been a pleasure resort. The only people who cross the Channel in large numbers for pleasure are the British themselves, who, having no other road by which to go anywhere, have in desperation hardened themselves to the idea, and have even come to take a perverse pride and pleasure in the asperities of the Dover-Calais passage. In Tudor times, sturdy Englishmen were actually known to undertake the ordeal as a medicinal measure, "to scour the stomach," as prudent persons will from time to time take a treatment or a course of liver pills. But foreigners have never taken kindly to the idea of rattling backwards and forwards across the Narrow Seas for the sake of the trip. When foreigners came to England, they were apt to stay. The whole history of Britain up to and including the Conquest is a history of invasions. Roman, Phœnician, Angle, Saxon, Dane, one after another they faced the water-jump—gritting their teeth at the prospect, but lured by the promise of tin, or oysters, or fertile territory—arriving green in the face, and determined that, whatever happened, they would not go back. The men of Norway, whose passage was colder and longer, but on the whole less nauseating, alone preferred raiding to settling; but even they sometimes found it more convenient to stay than to go. With each fresh invasion, the older inhabitants were pushed back towards the north and west; and with each fresh invasion, the southern and eastern parts of Britain became steadily more mongrel and polyglot. Lastly came William the Norman, and, like a catalyst, precipitated the unstable mixture that was the south-eastern portion of Britain into that solid and rock-like deposit which we call England. A score of Celtic and Nordic dialects fused with the Romance languages to make the English tongue. A new England, looking with new eyes at the Channel which she had seen all her life, suddenly discovered what it was for. There were no more invasions.

From the moment that England became Channel-conscious she became Channel-minded, and has remained so ever since. Bedded in her historic memory is the recollection of her first duty: to keep herself to herself. The phrase itself is characteristic of her people; I think I have never met an English working man or woman who did not boast of keeping the neighbours at arm's length; to be ignorant of other people's affairs and to cast a veil of impenetrable secrecy about one's own is, to the average English person, the primary mark of respectability. The boast is usually quite un-justified, but that is not the point: what we like to think ourselves is often more revealing than what we actually are. The immediate reaction of all English people to a foreign invader or a foreign idea is to make access as difficult as possible. The Celtic fringes some-times claim to be more open-minded than the English and better mixers; that is because of the many centuries during which they had little occasion to stare apprehensively across the Straits of Dover.

For anyone of English blood there is no more agreeable pastime than to watch the people of cosmopolitan mind trying to induce the British people to toe the line of simplification and standardisa-tion. They are always so naïve, earnest and plausible, and they invariably use all the wrong arguments. At one time it was the Channel Tunnel, which would make it so much easier for foreigners to get to England. At another time it is a proposal to establish casinos in all the South Coast towns so as to attract foreign money. Periodically it is suggested that we should abolish an old-fashioned coinage and a chaotic system of weights and measures, so that foreigners need no longer waste time and energy and qualify for the madhouse by attempting to work out half-crowns in terms of centimes, or reduce square yards (by bundles of $30\frac{1}{4}$) to perches, roods and square miles and thence to square kilometres. And from time to time persons with much feeling for business facilities and none for literary history, implore us to get rid of our English spelling in favour of something which it would be easier for foreigners to understand and remember. The British listen politely to all the arguments and do nothing about anything, and the cosmopolitan cries out in despair against their lack of logic. To no purpose. The British are not so illogical as all that. They understand perfectly that these reforms would make things easier all round. But they do not want things made easier; they want, instinctively and passionately and inarticulately want, everything to be kept difficult. Behind the barrier of the rod, pole, or perch, and the barbed entanglement of the letters OUGH they retire as into a fortress. To make things too easy is to ask for an invasion, even if it is only an invasion of privacy. It is useless to tell the Briton that if the serried ranks of iron railings were removed, his house and grounds, to say nothing of his public parks, would look nicer and be more get-at-able; the very idea of being "got at" makes him uncomfortable. The only thing that will inspire him to tear up his railings is the conviction that they are needed to defend his moat against a still more serious invasion. Unconsciously in peace, consciously in war, the Channel is the magnetic axis about which the British mind rotates.

Now, if the Channel had been filled with the stuff you would expect from its position on the map, the English national temperament, thus conditioned by its chilly environment, would probably have been rigid, narrow, morose, repulsive (in Jane Austen's, if not in the modern sense of the word) and monomaniac. The more engaging and exasperating absurdities of the British arise from the circumstance that the waters which run through the Channel are those of the Gulf Stream and no other. Because of the Gulf Stream the invaders came; because of the Channel they stayed here and turned into Englishmen. The British, even now, do not really object to the arrival of foreigners, provided they come in assimilable numbers and turn into islanders. What is disliked is the inquisitiveness of the tripper and the acquisitiveness of the conqueror. So long as the intention is not hostile, and the new arrivals do not, cuckoo-like, oust the established inhabitants from the nest, the more the merrier. It all adds to the rich confusion of the English language and the glorious jumble of racial types which give flavour to the national hodge-podge. Variety, individuality, peculiarity, eccentricity and indeed crankiness are agreeable to the British mind; they make life more interesting. It is a failure to understand this passion for variety which reduces to despair the people who want to introduce uniform systems of education and neat plans for laying out model townships—or other things, as witness the testimony of the author of *A Canuck in England*:

"Being invited to people's bathrooms is a popular idea, for you really get to know people when you have used their bathrooms a few times. Not the least of the factors which contribute to intimacy is the fact that English plumbing is still worked by a chain. Every chain has its own little idiosyncrasies. Many of them simply defy the uninitiated to manage them properly. Consequently, dignified hostesses, when showing you where the bathroom is and which towel is for you, have also to give a lesson in managing the chain."

Quite so. The British do not at all mind their institutions being so inconvenient and even inefficient, provided they are all as different as possible. You have only to look at a hundred specimens of British handwriting selected at random and compare them with a hundred specimens from Germany or France or Italy. The general impression you gather is that all the foreigners have used, not only the same copybook, but the same pen. And you would be quite right. It is the pen that the British keep in post offices. It is kept in post offices precisely because it is the only pen the British can be relied on not to take a predatory fancy to; it is the pen that makes all handwriting alike. Even if you try to make all British schoolchildren write the same hand (and baffled educators have almost abandoned the attempt), before they have reached man's estate their calligraphy will rebelliously break away and blossom into a rank luxuriance of individualism—the bold, the squinny, the flourishy, the curly, the microscopic, the spidery, the cramped, the sprawling, and, above all, the hieroglyphic, the cryptic, and the triumphantly illegible. And note: that of the whole document the most indecipherable hieroglyph will be the signature. That is the one part which can be made secure even from random guess-work. With the secretiveness of a savage who fears that to give away his name is to assign a magic power over his person, the British correspondent spins an inky cocoon of protection about his identity. Thus Gulf Stream and Channel co-operate—the one to produce an entertaining variety, and the other to make things difficult—in the formation of the British character.

Wherever you turn in this island, you meet the same phenomenon —a proliferating diversity which, impenetrable as a lush jungle, impedes the advance of the foreign explorer. A fine example is the English Common Law, which has no code and scarcely any statutes. It is all case law, an intricate cat's cradle of precedents. It appears to know nothing of right and wrong, but only of rights and wrongs established by long custom, and to base its authority on no general principle, but only upon an endless series of improvisations—such-and-such a decision, made by a particular judge in a particular year between two particular men about a particular goose, insult or party wall. Learned foreigners come and watch British Law in operation; they observe that it works; they even admire its justice; but the trick of it is not communicable. Reforming zealots look at it with the eye of an irritated housewife confronted with the spidery chaos of a scholar's den; they long to take dustpan and broom to it—clear out the old junk and reduce it to a spring-cleaned order. But that would not do; the magic is in the disorder—clear it up, destroy the bewildering old documents, codify the result and set it out neatly upon the shelves as in a public library, and we should find that we could no longer lay hand on those things that we call our liberties: for the easier you make the law, the more readily can you drive a coach and horses through it. Oppression strides over code law as an invading army marches down an arterial road, but the Common Law of England is a maze, baffling and secure; to march through it you would have to hew it down and root it up completely.

Or consider the Church of England. And, having considered it in all its rich ambiguity, consider how you would explain it to an intelligent Latin, who supposes that in matters of faith you must be *either* a Catholic, a Protestant or an atheist, and must hold your particular view with a fierce and rational passion which hews chasms of partisan cleavage through your entire political and social outlook. Then you will suddenly see why the foreigner, struggling to make himself at home in the Englishman's castle, feels as though he had been enticed into an exceptionally well-made apple-pie bed—a bed filled with a surprising assortment of inappropriate things and bristling with difficulties. And when at last you have deciphered British handwriting, interpreted the Common Law, and explained the Church of England, you will perhaps be in a position to make clear to others why the British Empire holds together without visible means of support, and how it is that in the British mind the word "Empire" is understood to be a synonym for "liberty." For the Empire too is a collection of individual decisions, improvised together into a constitution which is both highly idiosyncratic and altogether inscrutable.

But perhaps it is not really necessary to undertake all these specialised studies. Life is short; and for the ordinary observer the quickest and surest way to an understanding of British peculiarities is to purchase a mackintosh and a sun-bathing outfit, come to Britain, and there experience the practical jocularity of the

Channel and the Gulf Stream in its most intimate and pervasive form.

It has, I believe, been said that Britain possesses no climate, only weather. The weather of this country has been much abused—by foreigners, with some justice; by ourselves, with no justice at all, unless we are prepared to hate ourselves; for our weather is our character and has made us what we are.

All British institutions have an air of improvisation; and seem allergic to long-term planning. Indeed, what else can you expect in a country where it is impossible to predict, from one hour to another, whether it will be hot or cold, wet or dry, windy or still —where every arrangement for an outdoor sport or public function may have to be altered at the last minute owing to uncontrollable causes? "Rain stopped play," "If wet, in the Parish Hall," "Weather permitting"—such phrases punctuate the whole rhythm of our communal life, and compel a general attitude to things which is at once sceptical, stoical, speculative and flexible in the last degree. You may plan an agricultural economy, for instance, with a reason-able certainty that any one season will be favourable for wheat *or* potatoes—but, without a miracle, not for both; yet the miracle may occur, like any other anomaly in this unaccountable country, so you must leave a corner of the mind open to miracle. You may have thunder in February, snow in May, hail in July and a heat-wave in November; these conditions naturally discourage any tendency to fixed opinions and a doctrinaire outlook. The Briton is an incorrigible traveller: he will cheerfully pack up his things at short notice for a round trip to Honolulu and the Arctic Circle; why not? he need only take much the same outfit that he requires for a week-end in Cornwall or Kirkcudbright. He can survive in Siberia, the Sahara, Tibet, Calcutta or the Gold Coast as readily as in Mexico, Mandalay, Alaska or the island of Juan Fernandez; why not? he has been inoculated against every conceivable climate, as against so many diseases, by small protective doses of the appro-priate weather; it is the Gulf Stream that built the Empire. The whole aim and object of British weather is to make everything difficult and nothing impossible; and if the Briton is too much in the habit of muddling through it is because he is meteorologically conditioned to the idea that he can reckon on absolutely nothing in his journey except his eventual arrival. For though he may be impeded by gales, floods, blizzards, fogs, snow-drifts, sun-strokes, land-slides, spring tides or the Severn Bore, it is seldom indeed that he is bodily whirled away by a tidal wave, tornado, or cataract, frozen to death, struck lifeless by heat or thunderbolts, smothered in sand-storms, buried by an earthquake or an avalanche, or over-whelmed by the sudden eruption of a volcano.

I have dwelt upon all these things, not to make the Briton appear more lovable, for the Channel has taught him to expect—nay, to desire—astonishment rather than affection, but by way of explaining why it is so difficult to commit him to hard and fast plans for an improved and standardised society. Before you can make him behave like other people, you must fill up the Channel and divert the Gulf Stream; till then, he will always confront you with the impish incalculability of his own weather—a downpour to the west, bright sunshine to the east, and fog in the Straits of Dover.

THE MYSTERIOUS ENGLISH

A Speech delivered in London, 1940

I HAVE COME TO-DAY, taking my life in my hands, to say what I can about the English people, a subject which always pro-vokes much feeling. I think no more perilous undertaking could be imagined, especially as, from time to time, my candour may compel me to praise the English. This will distress both my Celtic hearers, who will think it offensive, and my English hearers, who will think it very bad taste. Still, I will try because, although people disagree a great deal about the English, the one thing they do seem to agree about is that the English are utterly and impenetrably mysterious.

For centuries foreigners have proclaimed that we were mad. *Verrückte Engländer* was always the German word for us. Even M. André Maurois, who knows and likes us, feels it necessary to warn the French visitor to England: "In thirty years you will begin to understand this simple, *mysterious* and noble country." I have read books about the English by Frenchmen, Chinese, Czechs, Dutchmen, Scots, and, of course, Mr. Bernard Shaw, who is Irish. They earnestly explain us with more or less irritation and more or less ingenuity, and nearly always they succeed in missing the obvious. Americans, who have what I can only call the advantage of having started life as Englishmen, usually misunderstand us with that extra thoroughness that waits on family misunderstandings. The English themselves do not as a rule bother to explain them-selves, though occasionally a J. B. Priestley comes along to shed a little light on us, and G. K. Chesterton has done his gallant best, and he is never, never wrong about his own countrymen.

Our refusal to explain is due, partly to our rooted and maddening conviction that it does not matter much what outsiders think, and also to a reasonable doubt whether explanations do not merely darken counsel. However, as there seems to be a general feeling that the English character is becoming a matter of some importance in the present world crisis, I shall do my best to peg down the elusive creature at a few salient points for better examination.

The first, most important thing to notice, and the one which gives the clue to all the rest, is that the English are mongrels; and that, alone of all nations upon earth, they pride themselves upon being mongrels. If ever you hear a man boast of his pure English blood, he may be a Bostonian, he may be a Jew; but whatever he is, he is not English. When Queen Elizabeth said that she was "mere English," she meant that she had a Welsh surname, though she was a Londoner on the distaff side; when I say I am English, I mean that my mother's family came from Hampshire, and that I have one Scotch and one Irish grandparent.

Ask a man of real English descent whether his people came over with William the Conqueror, and he will probably reply: "Good Heavens, no! We're Saxon; there were Budgeries in the Manor of Budge when Billy the Conk arrived. Of course," he will add, and all his subsequent qualifications will begin with "of course"—"of course, a good deal of Norman blood came into the family afterwards. We're a pretty mixed lot, really. There's a legend that old Sir Gilbert brought back a Saracen bride after the third Crusade. And there was Captain John Budgery, the one that sailed with Hawkins—he married a Red Indian—sort of Pocahontas business, you know. And, of course, there's a lot of Scotch and Irish in me, though my mother's grandfather was pure Huguenot. And I've sometimes fancied there might be a dash of the tar-brush somewhere—there was Robert Budgery who turned up as the missing heir from South America in the eighteenth century, nobody ever knew where his mother came from. The Cornish branch, of course, have a strong Spanish streak in them; the Armada, you know, and all that." So he rambles on, unrolling the history of England along with his family tree, and getting more and more mongrel, and more and more pleased with himself, at every word.

We may disbelieve the legend about old Sir Gilbert and the Pocahontas romance; the important thing is that that is what the Englishman likes to believe about himself. And one thing we must remember: that before the Conquest there was no such thing as an

Englishman. There were Angles and Saxons, Danes, various kinds of British Celt, and probably some people with traces of Roman descent, but the strange compound we call an Englishman had not yet appeared, any more than the English language. The basic Englishman is the compound of Anglo-Saxon and Norman-French; and though he contains elements from both those main sources, his characteristic Englishry is neither of them, but the blend of the two.

In this, he is exactly like his own English language. The Anglo-Saxon Chronicle is not written in English: it is written in Anglo-Saxon; the *Tristan* of Thomas is not written in English: it is written in Anglo-French. But the romances written in England in the twelfth and thirteenth centuries are written in what, though antiquated and difficult, is quite definitely and increasingly recognisable as the English speech of to-day; and by the time we get to Chaucer, we are reading something that cannot possibly be called a variety of French or of Anglo-Saxon. It is English; a language in its own right, with its roots in two civilisations, and the most various, flexible, rich and expressive instrument of human speech since the days of Pericles. The well-meaning people who used to implore us to "return to our native Anglo-Saxon tongue"—to call an omnibus a folk-wain and remorse of conscience the againbite of inwit—were really asking us to abandon our English heritage altogether. English is rich and flexible because it is double-rooted; the whole business of the English writer is to know when to use his Saxon and when to use his French, and therefore his Latin, vocabulary; for the Latin runs readily along with the Saxon because the French words are there to give it passage. Look at this:

> *This my hand will rather*
> *The multitudinous seas incarnadine,*
> *Making the green one red.*

It is the thunder of the Latin polysyllables that makes the Saxon monosyllables so ominous and so terrific. As the language, so the nation. The strength of the English, their adaptability, their strange talent for improvisation, their disconcerting mixture of the practical and the visionary are the virtues of their mongrel breeding. It is not surprising that the English are dubious about Nordic blood and racial purity. In small and peaceable peoples they consider claims to purity of blood to be harmless and pretty, but rather childish and absurd; in large and ferocious peoples they consider them to be ugly and dangerous, but none the less childish and absurd. (For you will notice that the English, with their misguided

68

and frivolous sense of humour, which is the despair of all earnest peoples, think a thing none the less funny because it may be dangerous; this is one of the things about them which earnest foreigners find misleading and tiresome.)

A direct result of the mongrel nature of the English, and a thing very noticeable about them, is that they have never in their lives been what the Germans still are, that is, a *Volk*. From the first beginnings of their Englishry, they have been, not a race, but a nation. The comparative absence of folk-music and folk-customs from England is remarkable, compared with their energetic survival in, say, the Highlands of Scotland; and the English have never had a folk-costume at all. The thing that ties them together is not a consciousness of common blood so much as a common law, a common culture, and a very long memory of national consciousness. The law, generally speaking, is Saxon; the culture, generally speaking, is continental.

This at once makes a distinction between us and, say, the Scots, whose law is, generally speaking, Roman, while their culture was, for a long time, largely racial. The English, on the whole, got their constitutional teething over remarkably early. They were already nationally conscious when, in Henry II's reign, they objected to interference by the Pope, not on religious grounds, but because he was a foreign sovereign putting his finger in the English political pie. The Englishman's offensive feeling of superiority over aliens is largely due to the recollection that England was a nation before other peoples had grown out of being tribes, or clans, or bits and pieces of the Roman Empire. The fact that, only the other day, an arrested man was required to be produced under Habeas Corpus, on the ground that his detention was "contrary to the Great Charter," is the sort of thing that reminds the Englishman just how far his rights as a national go back. England is a nation; in essentials she has never, since the time that she could properly be called England, been anything else.

As a result of this, the arrogance and insolence of English people became proverbial at a surprisingly early date. Already somewhere about the fourteenth century, visiting observers are heard to remark plaintively that the English "do not like foreigners"; and somewhere about Queen Elizabeth's time we hear the characteristic English compliment that so-and-so is "almost like an Englishman." The national consciousness is fully established. I doubt whether any other nation uses the word "foreigner" and "alien" with such offensive intonations as the English. As a French observer has remarked: in France, the most thriving hotel in a town is often called: "Hôtel des Étrangers." What English establishment could hope to do business under the title: "Aliens' Hotel"?

Another result of this is the focusing of the political life of the Three Kingdoms about England. It is perfectly true that, ever since the Union, and, indeed, long before that, great posts in the executive and in the services have frequently been held by Scots, Irishmen, Welshmen and Jews. The Celtic members of the community continually point this out, and with very great justice. But the framework in which these men function is the English framework. Foreigners, especially enemy foreigners, make no mistake about this. "*Gott strafe* England," they say, and the legendary Scotsman who laboriously altered this to "*Gott strafe* Britain" correctly recognised the compliment implied. It is England who is the object of hymns of hate: "Wir fahren gegen England." The real enemy is England, and that peculiar English conception of the State which the rest of Britain has assimilated, and to which it so magnificently works.

The distinctive characteristic of this conception has been pointed out by Dr. Wingfield-Stratford. It is the quite peculiar notion of justice and liberty derived from Saxon Law, which has influenced English political thought since the time of King Alfred. English Law has never been codified; it is all case-law. It does not deal with right in the abstract, but with "my rights"; it is not concerned with "liberty," but only with "our liberties." The French Republic had as its motto (and will have again, please God) three abstract words: Liberty, Equality, Fraternity. The framers of the Declaration of Independence committed themselves to a general proposition: "We take these things to be self-evident; that all men are born free and equal."

English Law does not appear to be interested in any such philosophical speculations. Its characteristic utterance is that of the Great Charter: "To no man (i.e. to no individual Tom, Dick or Harry, never mind the rights of man in general) will we (the particular government in power at the time) deny, sell, or delay justice" (which, from the context, means clearly, not *égalité* as such, but an equitable decision in the courts as between man and man). The English Law is concerned with the rights of the individual man as against the State and as against his neighbour. Its aims are no more lofty than that; but it is quite determined that the rights and liberties of the individual shall not be obscured by, or subjected to, any doctrinaire notions about State machinery.

The common Englishman understands this perfectly. If you notice, you will never hear him coming into the courts clamouring for "justice"; what he wants is "my rights," and he will claim them against all comers, including, and indeed, most of all, against the government. And, let us be clear about this, he claims them, not as an Englishman, the member of a superior race, but as an English subject, the member of a superior nation. He will, except at moments when his natural balance is disturbed by spy scares, or by an excessively high rate of unemployment, claim them just as fiercely for the naturalised stranger in his midst. If a person is an English citizen he "did ought to have" his English rights as an individual. The concept of race subdues the individual to one element, one unit, in a super-organism. The concept of nation encourages individual liberties, and the separate importance of the man, the family, the parish, the county. Above all, it encourages that separation of the judicature from the legislature which is the safeguard of the English courts and of the rights of the commoner against being bribed or browbeaten by the State. The violent opposition of Parliament to the attempt to set up special courts for political offences was a declaration that, even in a national emergency of the very gravest kind, the Englishman will not surrender that which he rightly looks upon as the corner-stone of his liberties.

Of course, this strong sense of national solidarity was only able to establish itself so early and develop itself so powerfully because of the English Channel. So long as the Scots could be kept from opening the back door to the Continent, the English could get along with their constitutional experiments without the disturbance caused by foreign invasion, and without anything like the same pressure from foreign influence that was exerted upon European countries with land frontiers. There were plenty of bad scares. Up to 1588 it was still possible that England might lose her individuality, and become a mere part of that Holy Roman Empire to which she had always paid, at any rate, a nominal allegiance (though it is true to say that all through those early years the English had rather taken the view that while, of course, they were part of the Roman Empire, they need not allow that consideration to influence their practical politics).

Still, in theory she was part of the Empire. I suppose that one might say that the conclusive proof that England had achieved full nationality was given when Philip of Spain, setting forth with the Pope's blessing to reconquer England for Rome, was faced by the English fleet sailing under a Catholic Admiral. Whatever we may think about the Reformation, that was an omen that could not be mistaken. From that time, the world knew that England was a nation. But one man had known it earlier. Henry VIII, the most powerful despot that ever sat on the English throne, made his will and, like any feudal over-lord, left his kingdom, as his personal property, to his three children in succession. But, unlike any feudal over-lord, he knew that his was not the final word; he brought his will into the House of Commons, and had it ratified by the English Parliament. "This realm of England," he said, "is an Empire." By this he meant, not an empire in the modern sense of the word, but an Imperium—what we mean to-day when we speak of a Sovereign State.

And when Wolsey, with an instinct less sure than his to detect the changes in the wind of time, urged him to take certain measures, secure in an authority super-nationally derived, Henry found the retort which was to make English history: "We cannot do it; the Commons would not allow it." England was a nation; and he knew it.

This sense of national solidarity, this sense of superiority and security, and this concentration on an island with a sea front worked, together with the mongrelism of the English, to produce that very thing which the foreigner finds so contradictory and inexplicable; the fact that along with the strong insularity of the English there goes the English passion for the exotic, the adventurous and the romantic, and the curious dreamy imagination which seems to go so strangely with the practical executive ability of the English. It is the assurance of one's own position that promotes free expansion. The duke and the dustman can get on together far more easily than either can get on with the climber, because each of them knows where he stands and has nothing to lose. So the English, more and more secure in their internal solidarity and their insular position, could afford to encourage any fancies for adventure both of the mind and of the spirit. We are not a military nation, as has sometimes been said; and I doubt whether it is correct to call us a martial race; but we are an adventurous people. We are the magpies of Europe. We love to decorate ourselves with foreign spoils, mental and spiritual as well as material. We feel we are in no danger of losing our own individuality by decking ourselves in these borrowed plumes. Insecurity tends to turn the soul inwards upon itself, so that it keeps on reckoning itself up to see that it is all there, like M. Perrichon with his parcels; but security looks outward.

So the sea throughout our history has been not only our moat defensive, but also the high-road to adventure.

We run to the far ends of the earth collecting this and that, and are delighted with the strange things we can bring home to adorn our doggedly insular and obstinately English firesides. I do not know anything more characteristically English than the little house I visited a short time ago in the Isle of Wight. It was stuffy and Victorian to a degree, and its staple furniture was quite unbelievably insular and ugly; and it was so crowded with odd treasures that you could scarcely move without tripping over something rich and strange from some far quarter of the world. Pewter and silver, fossils, fragments of lost ships, exquisite pieces of china, musical-boxes, a pair of recorders, a bag of gold angels picked up on the shore, a whole drawer stuffed with the records and the flotsam and jetsam of ships wrecked off the Needles. All jumbled together without any attempt at artistic display, but with a kind of eccentric order quite intelligible to its owner.

England is an adventurer and a collector of unconsidered trifles. It would be true to say that she did not conquer her Empire; she did not even very deliberately acquire it in the interests of her trade; the fact is that she collected it casually, and almost accidentally, in a spirit of lighthearted adventure, as a sailor will collect monkeys and parrots, and, like the sailor, found herself committed to looking after the creature. The English, though they have done a good deal of conquering in this random kind of way, have never considered themselves to be a nation of conquerors, in the sense that Hitler understands the word, or even as a Cæsar would have understood it. We do not see ourselves as invaders of conquered territory. It is true that if you turn out the Englishman's luggage you will find it full of bits of land of alien origin; but the possessor will explain, with perfect sincerity, and more truth than you might suppose, that he never had any idea of foreign conquest. He was just roving about the world doing a little business, when he came across something, the Elgin Marbles, or Cleopatra's Needle, or an island or so, or possibly half a continent that nobody seemed to be looking after, and he just slipped it into his pocket to take care of it.

What is more, he does take care of it. Like the sailor with the parrot, he feels it his duty to feed it, make it comfortable, and teach it the English language, and will go to a surprising amount of trouble and expense to do the right thing by it. Incidentally, you will notice that, just as the Englishman thinks more of his rights and liberties than of right and liberty in the abstract, so with regard to his obligations. He does not, as more earnest people do, undertake to lay down the Whole Duty of Man; but he has, on the whole, a fairly clear notion of "my duties." And he is sure that, having acquired any strange, outlandish thing, such as a parrot or an Empire, he has a duty to perform to it. But his aim is not, and never really has been, conquest. He is an explorer, an adventurer, a romantic, and above all, an individualist. Nearly all his acquisitions have been the result of some private adventure or other, tobacco planting in the West Indies, John Company in India, trapping in Hudson Bay. If you call him an invader, he will be both puzzled and shocked; but there is one opprobrious name you may call him that he will understand and rather like. You may call him pirate. When British sailors swarmed aboard the *Altmark*, crying: "The Navy's here!" German propagandists looked round for an insult that would really infuriate the English . . . something even more offensive than usual. At the tops of their voices they yelled "Pirates!" The common Englishman was complimented beyond measure and went off to drink the healths of the modern descendants of Drake and Hawkins, convinced that all was well with the Fleet.

It is not surprising that the European should suspect a certain hypocrisy in this apparent contradiction between the Englishman's repudiation of the idea of conquest and the plain fact that he has succeeded in laying hands on so much of the earth's surface. Yet there is really no hypocrisy, and no true contradiction. Both things spring from the same root: the powerful sense of national solidarity which results from his being an island mongrel. His outward security has made it easy for him to go roaming about the world; his mixed blood has made a roaming life agreeable to him. Like Kipling's cat, he walks in the wild woods, waving his wild tail, and all places are alike to him. By a happy physical accident, with which mongrel blood may have something to do, he can live anywhere. And his rovings are of the mind as well as the body. He is a handyman, as sailors and roving men are. He is a magpie of other men's customs. He will let his native Yule-log fall into disuse, while he picks up and appropriates Christmas Trees from Germany. He waits while other people make alarming experiments in political revolution, picks up useful tips for himself, and introduces them into his own social scheme, without caring whether they look appropriate, or consistent, so long as he can make them work.

While he is roving about, his imagination roves also. He is least great in the cosmopolitan arts, such as painting and music; he is most great—indeed, he is almost unsurpassed—in the most individual art of all, in lyric poetry and the lyric drama. He has few first-class theologians and few first-class philosophers, but in that strange borderland where religion and philosophy meet and mingle with the lyric imagination he is supreme. Here, two things stand him in good stead: his double tongue, and his passion for the concrete thing, that acquisitive love of colourful bits and pieces which belongs to his sea-going heritage.

This is not the time for a long discourse on English poetry; but here is a thing to notice, the peculiar quality given to it by the use of what I will call "the distinguished epithet." English poetry is weakest, I suppose, where French poetry, for example, is strongest —in what the *Week-End Book* classifies as "State Poetry," that is, formal verses upon generalised subjects of public, as distinct from personal interest. But, when you do get a good poem of this kind written in English, it gains a curiously individual quality from the use of adjectives which no Frenchman would ever have thought of using in that context.

> *The glories of our blood and state*
> *Are shadows, not substantial things;*
> *There is no armour against fate;*
> *Death lays his icy hand on kings;*
> *Sceptre and crown*
> *Must tumble down,*

So far, any Frenchman of the classical period might have written it, though he might hesitate over "tumble" and prefer a "nobler" word.

> *And in the dust be equal made*
> *With the poor crooked scythe and spade.*

There we part company with Latin Europe. A Frenchman, for whom I once translated this into French verse, paused over the equivalent of "crooked scythe." "An odd adjective," he said, "but then, of course, it's an odd word in the original." Among all the abstracts and generalisations, glory, blood and state, shadow, substance, death, icy hand, kings, fate, armour, sceptre, crown, the splendid and sonorous commonplaces of State poetry, came the sudden vivid, concrete, village picture of the actual shape of the scythe, "the poor crooked scythe." The Frenchman recognised instantly that this was a thing insular and apart, the English lyric touch, the assertion of the concrete thing, the right of the poor crooked scythe and spade, and of the odd crooked word, to its individual personality and liberties.

To that we must come back. It is the key to the English mind. Here is another contradiction which it resolves. The English, the most arrogantly insular of all people in their conscious superiority to foreigners are, at the same time, the most astonishingly courteous to them. Sometimes, it is true, this suggests the maddening courtesy of God Almighty condescending to a blackbeetle, but that is not by any means the whole explanation. The Englishman does genuinely like people to be different from himself. He admires them for it, and if his admiration is tinged with compassion for a weaker vessel, at least one has to admit that he treats foreigners no worse in this respect than he treats his wife. He will painstakingly go out of his way to respect their feelings. The proper English word for a native of China is "Chinaman"; but if the Chinaman has taken a dislike to this perfectly correct form of speech, the Englishman will be at great trouble to avoid it, and to refer to him, in his presence, as "a Chinese," though this is as much a mutilation of the English language as it would be to speak of a Dutch or a Spanish. "China" is, in fact, the ancient adjective, as you can see by "China teapot" or "all Lombard Street to a China orange"; but at all costs the Englishman will be polite. Similarly, in Scotland he will be particular to say "Scot" or "Scottish," forms for which the inhabitants of that country have a wholly inexplicable preference, though "Scotch" is good Southern English, and has no necessary connection with whisky. On the other hand, though the spine of the average Englishman curls at being called a "Britisher," he usually accepts this revolting act of mayhem upon his native tongue without protest.

He accepts also, not merely without protest, but with enthusiasm, the malformations of English accent and syntax indulged in by foreigners. You will never see on his face the expression of ill-suppressed anguish with which an Italian, for example, endures the efforts of the English to speak the Italian language. He thinks a French accent charming, he speaks of a pretty Irish brogue and finds it quaint and attractive of the Irish to use Erse syntactical constructions in the speaking of English. He will even listen patiently while people assure him that he cannot speak his own language, and will politely agree that the best English is spoken in Edinburgh or Dublin. He will adopt American expressions if he thinks them energetic and expressive; he is true to his mongrel strain, and is quite ready to believe that there is good to be got from all sources, however unlikely. He will join with sympathy and appreciation in other people's national rejoicings, and do honour to their songs and emblems, even when the sole aim and object of them is to affront him in every possible way. He will read with interest accounts of the celebration of Independence Day in America. He will applaud while Scotsmen sing "Scots wha hae" or "Wi' a hundred pipers and a' and a' We'll gi'e the English a bla' a bla'." When Irishmen perform "The Wearing of the Green" in the street he will hang out of the window and throw them coppers. I know English people who take great pains to present their Celtic friends with shamrocks on St. Patrick's Day and to turn on the wireless for them on St. Andrew's night; but I must say I have never heard of a Celt who sought for the smallest rosebud for his English friends wherewith to celebrate the Feast of St. George. I am not complaining about this; I had not, in fact, noticed it until my attention was drawn to it in connection with this paper. I only mention it as a fact.

The English are also, and notoriously, tolerant of other people's criticism. They are quite ready to agree that everything is ordered better in France, or any other country. It is true that they do not always believe this; but they are seldom offended at hearing it. They are also quite extraordinarily ready to criticise themselves; indeed, they spend most of their time doing it. This habit is misleading, and often leads to misunderstanding. It is taken either as a sign of weakness or of pure hypocrisy.

Actually, it is a sign, if not of strength, at least of colossal self-confidence. It is thus a danger to other nations, who are apt to take the criticisms at their face-value, and to proceed upon the assumption that England must be effete, degenerate, and at odds with herself, because the English are continually saying so. The fact that England has been saying so for some three centuries, without impairing her own powers of defence to any noticeable degree ought to warn them; but it does not.

The danger to ourselves is, that if we not only say these things, but begin really to take notice of other people's comments and criticisms, a thing we never used to do, we may begin to doubt ourselves. Symptoms of this kind of thing have been observable among the semi-intellectuals recently, that curious little cosmopolitan crowd who have lost their English roots and wish to persuade us that Englishry is the last infirmity of Blimpish mind. However, these people have been singularly quiet since fighting started in earnest. It cannot be said of them that:

> *Their voice is heard through rolling drums*
> *That beat to battle where they stand.*

Some of them, indeed, made no attempt to stand, but fled to the States while the going was good, where no doubt they are informing the trustful Americans that they have nothing to hope for from the British Navy.[1]

[1] This was said in 1940. Happily, it would seem, their voice was *not* heard. No doubt the drums were too much for them.

Another danger to others from this English tolerance of rude criticism is that it is apt to mislead them about the peculiar quality of English patience. That patience, being rooted in self-confidence, will go a long time without breaking, but when it breaks, it does so without warning and completely. The Celt is much more swift to wrath than the Englishman, but, with him, the row starts simultaneously with the offence, and you know where you are. The Englishman will at all costs avoid the row. He will put up with cheating and insult for years. Then, without a word of explanation, he will suddenly sever all relations. Consider, for example, the way of the Scot and the way of the Englishman with a cheating shopkeeper. The Scot, at the first sign of something wrong with the bill, will go to the shop and complain. There will be a sumptuous uproar. Epithets will be exchanged. The family histories of both clans will be inquired into. The town will take sides, and the clash of battle will resound in every close. Eventually the shopkeeper will give way, the bill will be adjusted, and normal relations will be resumed, all the more cordially that each side respects the other's strength. The Englishman, on the other hand, will say lazily: "Of course, I know So-and-so is an old scoundrel, and he's probably cheating me at every turn, but I don't want a row with him." One day, however, he will exert himself to look into the matter, and if he is sufficiently annoyed by what he finds, he will pay the bill and silently transfer his custom elsewhere. Nobody will ever know why. No opportunity will be given for explanation or adjustment, and the shopkeeper will wonder what in the world has become of his most profitable customer, who seemed to be good for any amount.

The Englishman does not like rows. It is almost impossible to get him to disturb himself, unless you are fool enough to make him both afraid and angry. Because of his long historical security, his fear and his anger are very hard to rouse, but when they are roused, he is implacable. You will notice that Dr. Goebbels has found it necessary to change his tone since the defeat of France. Before, he laid stress upon the hopeless inefficiency and slackness of this rotten democracy; now, we are "the most obstinate of all opponents." That means that even he has realised that the English have been seriously frightened, and are now very angry indeed. It is clear from *Mein Kampf* that Hitler did not want to frighten the English. His idea was to calm them with offers of friendship. He was to manage the east, while we were to have control over the west of Europe. England did not, of course, want the west of Europe. She is a coloniser, not a conqueror. But Hitler has never understood this. And he failed, as usual, and as our opponents have failed time and again, to understand what are the limits of English patience.

To understand the point at which the English patience breaks, we have only, I think, to remind ourselves what is the phrase most often heard in the English home. And that is: "Leave it alone!" "Tommy, leave the cat alone." "Leave your little sister alone, can't you." "Oh, leave the boy alone; he'll grow out of it." "Leave the young people alone to fight their own battles." And then: "Curse these government departments, why can't they leave us alone?" And so, with rising irritation, as the Englishman looks at the world: "Here, you, leave those wretched Jews alone." "Leave the Poles alone, I tell you." And, finally, in quite unmistakable tones: "Now then, you blue-pencil bastard, you bloody well leave ME alone, or I'll knock your bleeding block off."

The Englishman will interfere in the administration of the world, he will have his finger in every trade pie, he will collect countries as he collects junk, but he cannot bear to see things chivvied about, and he will not tolerate being chivvied himself. Leave the situation alone, don't let's have a revolution; it will probably work itself out to its own natural solution. Keep our domestic policy non-catastrophic; leave things alone. We, who are the least racial of all nations, who care least about folk-customs, are the most attached to tradition and old laws. Don't chivvy things. I know only one constant exception to the rule against chivvying. The English people have always, incessantly and unmercifully, chivvied their governments: and for a very good reason. A government must be either servant or master. If you do not chivvy it, it may chivvy you. So the English chivvy the State as a bustling housewife chivvies her domestic staff. "Get on with your work, you slut," says England to her government, "or take a week's notice. And no back-answers, if you please." "These people," she confides to her neighbours, "if you aren't everlastingly after them they get so lazy and uppish there's no bearing with them." The neighbours, hearing the sharp, scolding voice, go away and say that English housekeeping is clearly in the last stage of confusion, and surrender themselves more and more abjectly to the domination of their own footmen.

From all this, we may begin to see the outlines of the English brand of patriotism. It is the greatest possible mistake to suppose that it does not exist, merely because of the politeness extended to the patriotism of other nations, or because it is not vocal in times of prosperity, or because the English criticise themselves and their government and affect to admire the way things are done else-where; still more, to imagine that it depends upon vast extensions of the British Empire. The romantic love of extension from the centre depends upon the sanctity and security of that centre itself. When the Englishman says "England," he does not think of armies and domination; he thinks of a lane, of a field, of a line of cliffs fronting the sea, of the ships sailing from Bristol Town and coming home to an English port. The word Britain stirs his pride, but it is the word England that stirs his heart. There is his real history, and there is his abiding home. It is useless for people to complain that the words "island fortress" show a merely "defensive spirit." They are the words that move us. They take the English back over the long years of her history. England will never fight heartily or with conviction unless she feels the threat to English soil, English continuity, English things: "My rights, my liberties, my island, my church, my back garden, my back yard, my window-box." The people who try to force England into some doctrinaire mould of continental theory are, I think, mistaken. They are perverting the course of history. England has never had but two doctrinaire rulers; she broke the heart of poor Mary Tudor; she brought Charles I to the block. She can govern an Empire, but only on condition that she may leave it alone to govern itself. She will never be at her best if she sets out to curry favour by conforming to alien doctrines, for she will do it with a bad grace, and her policy will be fumbling and uncertain. She does not want to be liked; she wants to be left alone. She is an individualist; she hates uniformity; the effort to unify her religious practice ended by producing 365 religions and an Establishment with a more bewildering variety of use than any in Christendom. Her attachments are local. In the day of the Armada, the men of Devon refused to aid in the defence of Tilbury, even to look after the Queen, who was down there addressing the troops; their duty, they said, was to their own Devon soil. The English have never cared for being foreign mercenaries, and never cared much about sending big armies abroad; but they will fight like death and hell for Devon and the Cinque Ports, for London or York, for the dullest suburb or the little pub on the corner.

Here is the England of 1914. It is taken from a letter written by Rupert Brooke about a friend of his.

"As he thought of 'England and Germany' the word England seemed to flash like a line of foam. With a sudden tightening of his heart he realized that there might be a raid on the English coast. He didn't imagine any possibility of it succeeding, but only of enemies and warfare on English soil. The idea sickened him. He was immensely surprised to perceive that the actual earth of England held for him a quality, which . . . if he'd ever been sentimental enough to use the word, he'd have called holiness."

And here is the England of 1940. It is from the account of an airman speaking about the battle of Dover:

"When I and the fellows in my Spitfire squadron see bombs being dropped on our own country it seems to give us an entirely different feeling from that we had over Dunkirk. It is not that we did not do our best in France but simply that now the bombs are falling on our own land. That makes all the difference. One becomes conscious of something like a new hatred for the enemy, and it expresses itself in our attack."

That, clumsy but sincere, is the voice of the English anger, and it is the voice, not of world empire, but of a little, isolated, intensely individual country, the mongrel guarding his own door. Let the world have every liberty, so long as it leaves my liberties alone:

Take my drum to England, hang et by the shore,
Strike et when your powder's runnin' low;
If the Dons sight Devon,
I'll quit the port o' Heaven,
An' drum them up the Channel as we drumm'd them long ago.

PLAIN ENGLISH

LIKE MOST PEOPLE OF MY generation, I once had a maiden aunt. Poverty prompted her to send postcards rather than letters and letters rather than telegrams; and when forced to the extravagance of a telegram, she expressed herself with such parsimony that it was difficult to make out her meaning.

There is a kind of English fashionable in the popular Press to-day[1] which powerfully reminds me of her. Indeed, there is one weekly newsprint that appears to be written throughout by maiden aunts in the last stage of destitution. This style has been called, hideously but appropriately, "telegraphese"; and I am sure that, as with my aunt's telegrams, its cause is poverty and its effect obscurity.

It is claimed for "telegraphese" that it is (1) modern (2) clear

[1] This article was written before the War. "Telegraphese" is less fashionable than it was, but the nasty thing is only scotched, not killed.

and concise (3) vigorous (4) economical of space; that it is, in fact, "Plain English." Plain it is, in the sense of ugly; but I think in no other. English it is not; nor is it any of the other things. Let us look at a few random specimens:

"Before they walked past the King a hook was fastened on their dresses. On this, King George hung the insignia, smiled, shook hands."

The trick here is to omit all the conjunctions. This is nothing new; it is older even than my aunt's telegrams, as anybody knows who has ever been to church:

"He suffered for our salvation, descended into hell, rose again the third day from the dead."

As usual, the sixteenth century has got there before the twentieth. But there is a difference. In the quotation from the Creed there is no possible doubt about who did what. In the other passage, we are invited to suppose that the present King smiled and shook hands upon a hook. Of the two writers, even the most cautious agnostic would probably find it easier to believe St. Athanasius.

A passage is not plain English—still less is it good English—if we are obliged to read it twice to find out what it means. Here is another specimen from the same publication as before:

"Leftists are notoriously hungry for reading matter about their favourite subjects as gardeners or film fans, but, etc."

At a first swift perusal of this missing-word problem, we are tempted to supply the word "such"; "as" for "such as" is grammatical and traditional, though archaic: "a prelat, as an abbott or a priour," says Wyclif. It seems, however, unlikely that leftists (i.e. persons of extreme Communist opinions) should be notoriously hungry for news about film fans and gardeners. We must, therefore, conclude that the missing word is "as," and use our own judgment upon the delicate question whether it is to be inserted before or after "notoriously." Its place in the sentence, while making little alteration in the meaning, may be used to convey a subtle distinction of emphasis; but subtlety is outside the scope of telegraphese. What I object to is not so much the loss of subtlety, as the loss of my valuable time. It would be well worth the expense of two extra letters to have the sentence comprehensible at the first glance.

The rigid parsimony of the telegraphist here is the more remarkable, because in other places he wastes space by the unnecessary repetition of adjectival nouns. Thus, in discussing a book, he mentions that Mr. Owen and Mr. Thompson are its joint authors, and goes on to make this clear by referring in the next sentence to "Authors Owen and Thompson." By this time it should be plain that Messrs. Owen and Thompson wrote the book, and are, severally and jointly, its authors. The writer goes on to say:

> "It was a safe bet that where the tone was raised in anger it was the voice of Author Owen, where the writing was deliberate and exact they saw the hand of Author Thompson."

A plain, old-fashioned, economical writer like myself would have thought the identities of the authors sufficiently established by this time to warrant the use of "Owen" and "Thompson" without prefix (a saving of twelve letters); courtesy might even dictate "Mr. Owen" and "Mr. Thompson," and still save eight letters. When, later, we are told that "Assistant Editor Thompson" is a newspaper man, we are not really surprised to find the next sentence beginning "Newspaperman Thompson," although this insult to our intelligence again demands the monstrous expenditure of no fewer than twelve wholly unnecessary letters. After this, the reappearance of "Author Thompson," "authors Owen and Thompson," "Authors Owen and Thompson" four or five times over, with no variation save in the use or non-use of a capital A, loses even such vigour as it once had, and is revealed as a mere monotonous parrot-trick, anything but economical of space.

Not that telegraphese ever does, or ever could, in fact, save space; because one of the rules of this kind of writing is that every sentence has to have a fresh paragraph all to itself. Thus any room saved by leaving out "and" and "as" is wasted in blank spaces at the ends of lines, and in "leading" between paragraphs. This breathless paragraphing presumably symbolises vigour; and it is true that it leaves the reader with the sensation of having been vigorously bumped down a steep flight of steps. During his jerky progress he is unable to give very much attention to the individual steps, and this is perhaps just as well; otherwise he might wonder why, in the paragraph quoted above, the telegraphist should be unable to carry out either the imaginative contrast or the antithetical construction which he so vigorously undertook. Let us make the imagery consistent and the construction a true parallel:

> "It was a safe bet that where the tone was raised in anger, it was the voice of Owen; where the statement was deliberate and exact, it was the voice of Thompson."

Thus we avoid the distracting picture of poor Author Thompson writing to a vocal obbligato by Author Owen, and incidentally tidy up the involved syntax.

Oddly enough, the telegraphist revels in involved syntax. He has a peculiar passion for strange, inverted, participial constructions which, suitable enough for Latin, Greek or any other inflected language, become incomprehensible in the uninflected English. Here is a handsome specimen of its type:

> "This week at the Aldwych Theatre, finalist Academy students nervously stepped on to the stage to give annual matinée performances before judges Irene Vanbrugh, Athene Seyler, Leon Quartermaine, and Nicholas Hannen, knew there might be hawk-eyed producers, theatre managers lurking behind the footlights amongst newspaper critics.
>
> "Judged the best performance of the long nervy afternoon was that of student Kathleen Laurie who etc."

Stepping (like the students) nervously through the first paragraph, we resist the temptation to put in a full-stop after "judges" and so make Irene Vanbrugh and her colleagues the subject of "knew." Consideration tells us that "judges" is here a noun used adjectivally, and that it was the students who stepped nervously because they knew, and so forth. There follows the irresistible temptation to make the students the subject also of "judged"— a construction truly in accordance with the telegraphic style. But, we reflect, the students cannot have judged the performances, for that was the job of the distinguished actors already mentioned. With an incredulous and almost religious awe we see looming up out of this syntactical fog a whacking great participial construction, of the kind that used to terrify us when we did Latin in the fourth form, with the participle at the beginning, the verb in the middle and the subject at the end, but with, unhappily, no merciful Latin inflection to warn us that "judged" is here *judicatus* and not *judicaverunt*. This may be vigorous—it is certainly startling and even shocking—but it is not English. Neither is it modern, nor clear, nor economical. It is a cumbersome, antiquated, outlandish, obfuscating, verbose bore and nuisance. Here is another horrid verbal inversion:

> "Announcing his retirement from music this week was foremost viola-player 60-year-old Lionel Tertis."

And here, another—further embellished by a needlessly incorrect comma and a false metaphor:

"Revealed last week by the Washington Immigration Committee, was a new seam in U.S. gangster activity."

(A seam may occur in a garment or in a mine, but not in an activity.)

One might at least expect of the telegraphist that he would eschew the languid periphrases used by the ordinary journalist to avoid a plain English word. Far from it.

"The monks say they never wanted this particular Abbot, accepted him in the belief that it was the divine will that he should rule over them.

"Now, they declare that Heaven has decreed his removal and the will of the Almighty must be obeyed."

"God" is an excellent little three-letter word; was it worth while to get rid of "and" on the swings, to make up "divine," "Heaven" and "the Almighty" on the roundabouts?

By now the method of the telegraphist is manifest: it is to cut out the short word in favour of the long, the simple in favour of the complicated, the modern in favour of the obsolete, the English in favour of the Latin, the precise in favour of the confused. It is also clear why he prefers the brief sentence, for see what happens to him when he embarks upon a long one:

"He found Parliament boring, the work futile, except in its more stormy moments to which he contributed twice by threatening the House to keep them sitting all night, including the Thursday before one Easter recess when legislators were anxious to get their trains out of London, holiday bound."

There is a poor, tottering collection of broken-winded clauses if you like, each clinging with a gasp to the one before it like a chain of exhausted wanderers trying to haul themselves out of a quicksand.

He found Parliament boring, the work futile (puff, pant) except in its more stormy moments (puff) to which he contributed twice (puff) by threatening the House to keep them sitting all night (heave-ho!) including the Thursday before one Easter recess (pant) when legislators were anxious to get their trains out of London (puff, puff) holiday bound (whew! safe at last! and what a scramble it was!)

Observe that the second clause is wrongly linked up, since this gentleman's obstruction cannot have made the work less futile, though it may have made Parliament less boring. In the fourth clause there is an unnecessary pronoun. In the fifth, the participle "including" is attached to nothing in particular. In the sixth, "get" is ambiguous: the legislators were not anxious to "get" their trains out of London, at any rate, not in the sense in which they were doubtless anxious to "get" themselves and their tormentor out of the House. And why "out of London"? From what other place could the trains go? In the last clauses, a great chance is missed of using the telegraphist's favourite adjectival noun. Let us try to mend this confusion a little:

> He found Parliament futile, and was bored with it, except in its stormier moments. He twice contributed to these by threatening to keep the House sitting all night—once on the Thursday before Easter when members wanted to catch their holiday trains.

That is not beautiful English; but it is plain English; it is also six words shorter than the original.

Here (if you can bear it) is another passage of telegraphese:

> Taking her art very seriously Edna Manley steeped herself in Jamaica, got (*that word-of-all-work*) an encouraging reception at an exhibition in Kingston, where 800 people came to see her work, bought 200 guineas' worth of carvings.

Problem for home-work: Who bought the carvings? Apparently, sculptress Edna Manley; but since she *is* a sculptress, I have a suspicion that the 800 people really did the buying. To be poor, like my aunt, is to be obscure, like my aunt; and the telegraphic writers' disease is poverty—poverty of invention, poverty of vocabulary, poverty of intellect, poverty of imagination. He is deficient in two of his senses, for he can neither visualise a metaphor nor hear any distinction between one word and another. His style is a monotony of flabby lumps, like tapioca pudding. To read many pages of him on end is to slumber in a bad train, shaken by convulsive nods as you jerk uneasily over the points.

Economy and vigour of style are attained, not by leaving out conjunctions and pronouns, but by seeing to it that no word is used which does not add something to the picture. Here is an observation by Lord Chesterfield—a master of style if ever there was one:

> "A constant smirk upon the face and a whiffling activity of body are strong indications of futility."

If you come to think of it, those are the very characteristics of telegraphese—the constant smirk and the whiffling activity. Masters of style waste no time in antics and grimaces; they make everything tell. Here is Chesterfield again:

"Our prejudices are our mistresses; reason is at best our wife, very often heard indeed, but seldom minded."

"At best"—"very often heard"—there is a brief, cynical commentary on marriages as well as on minds.

Here is a piece of inspired reporting:

"When we could endure no more upon the water, we to a little ale-house on the Bankside, over against the Three Cranes, and there staid till it was dark almost, and saw the fire grow; and as it grew darker, appeared more and more, and in corners, and upon steeples, and between churches and houses, as far as we could see up the hill of the City, in a most horrid malicious bloody flame, not like the fine flame of an ordinary fire."

See with what precision the flames are outlined against the darkening background—"in corners and upon steeples"; and how surely Pepys chooses the one right, significant adjective, "a most horrid, *malicious* bloody flame."

Here is Horace Walpole, describing the execution of Admiral Byng, who was court-martialled for his failure to relieve Minorca in 1757:

"He desired to be shot on the quarter-deck, not where common malefactors are; came out at twelve, sat down on a chair, for he would not kneel, and refused to have his face covered, that his countenance might show whether he feared death; but being told that it might frighten his executioners, he submitted, gave the signal at once, received one shot through the head, another through the heart, and fell. Do cowards live or die thus?"

To drop anything out of that could only damage the rhythm without increasing the swiftness; though in these days, when words have become so much defaced by rough usage, it may be necessary to note that "countenance" is not an elegant periphrasis for "face," but is here used in its proper sense of "bearing."

There are stylists in the twentieth century, as well as in the eighteenth, who know how to describe swift action:

"We went round one turning, two turnings, three turnings, four turnings, five. Then I lifted myself slowly up from the gutter where I had been shot half senseless, and was beaten down again by living men crashing on top of me, and the world was full of roaring, and big men rolling about like ninepins."

Here, something has indeed been dropped out: not the necessary links in the syntax, but the unnecessary link in the action. As the narrator has just remarked, "When something happens, it happens first, and you see it afterwards." What *happened* was that the marching column of men was cut in two by an attack on both sides from a cross-street; but G. K. Chesterton leaves out the cause and presents us only with the effect as his narrator felt it. That is, he writes with his eye on the picture; and that is the way to write.

Here is a modern piece of satirical commentary, which achieves a smile but adroitly avoids the smirk:

"Her [Queen Elizabeth's] boasted virginity was a principal instrument of policy as well as a pass-key to her character. Before half her reign was over it had become one of the most venerable of insular institutions, vying in age and importance with the Royal Navy and the Church of England"—*Milton Waldman.*

And lastly, here is English in which those very conjunctions, so mishandled by the telegraphist, are distributed and juggled with, till the sentence runs like a melody:

"Had God company enough of himself? Was he satisfied in the Three Persons? We see that he proceeded further; he came to a Creation. And as soon as he had made light (which was his first creature) he took pleasure in it; he said it was good; he was glad of it; glad of the sea, glad of the earth, glad of the sun, and moon, and stars, and he said of every one, It is good."

Well, that was John Donne, who spoke with the tongue of angels, and we cannot expect Newspapermen Tom, Dick and Harry to speak like that. But they might at least try to speak like men. Language that issues in a series of inarticulate bawlings betrays itself with a dreadful sureness; it is the speech of the weak-gutted, making defiant pretence of a vigour that does not exist. Language should and must change naturally with the years, but it ought not to be emasculated; if the change makes for power and precision, it is good; if for weakness and confusion, it is bad.

The test of good writing is a simple one. If a sentence puzzles or startles you, pull it to pieces. If it is good writing, then the harder you pull, the more tightly you will discover it to be woven together, and the more closely you examine it, the more meaning it will yield. But if it tumbles to bits easily—if you find its syntax dislocated, its epithets imprecise, its meaning vague or contradictory—then it is bad, and should be quickly thrown into the dustbin of oblivion; one should not keep rubbish lying about in the house of the mind.

THE ENGLISH LANGUAGE

(1936)

Esau, it has been observed, was a gentleman. He was, in fact, an amiable, manly fellow, who addled his wits with outdoor sports and attached small importance to his spiritual heritage—very like an English gentleman indeed. And he sold his birthright for a sodden mess.

The birthright of the English is the richest, noblest, most flexible and sensitive language ever written or spoken since the age of Pericles. Every day sees it sold, not only to Brother Jock and Brother Paddy, and young Brother Jonathan, but to the sob-sisters of Fleet Street, to the aged and doddering Mother of Parliaments, to the wicked Uncles of the B.B.C., to the governors, teachers, spiritual pastors and masters of the Board of Education, and to all the myopic old women of both sexes who cannot tell a purposeful hawk from an ill-regulated handsaw. And a nice mess they make of it among them; which mess we greedily and gratefully gulp down.

Like Esau, we think that it does not matter. This is the sin that the Church calls Sloth. Incidentally, the sloth, like Esau, has his hide all covered with hair, and to resemble him does us no credit.

The English language has a deceptive air of simplicity: so have some little frocks; but they are not the kind that any fool can run up in half an hour with a machine. Compared with such highly-inflected languages as Greek, Latin, Russian and German, English appears to present no grammatical difficulties at all; but it would be truer to say that nothing in English is easy but the accidence. It is rich, noble, flexible and sensitive because it combines an enormous vocabulary of mixed origin with a superlatively civilised and almost wholly analytical syntax. This means that we have not merely to learn a great number of words with their subtle distinctions of meaning and association, but to put them together in an order determined only by a logical process of thought. There can be no good English without clear thinking, and (as some cynic has justly observed) "most people would die sooner than think, and most of them do."

Most languages begin by being synthetic—that is, inflected—becoming gradually analytic as men learn to co-ordinate abstract ideas. But the primitive structure still underlies and explains the visible contours as the ancient and enduring bone underlies and explains the flesh. It is therefore easy to come, as our ancestors did, from the study of Latin to the study of English, because that is the natural order of development. But the wisdom of modern educators has freed our children from the shackles of a classical training, and this is about as sensible as freeing young draughtsmen from the study of anatomy. The result in either case is the same: a drawing and an English alike spineless, nerveless, slack-sinewed, ugly, lumpy and meaningless.

If anybody doubts that this country is still engaged in the export of wool, let him examine the utterances of our statesmen in the House of Commons and elsewhere. Here is a passage from a speech made by the Prime Minister[1] about the Economic Conference (*Times* Report, June 28th, 1933):

> "What he could say of the Conference was that every representative there, knowing his difficulties, was determined to come to no arrangement which meant that his difficulties were simply to be treated as though they did not exist, but was determined at the same time to come to an accommodation where accommodation was possible and to bend every ounce of resource that he could in order to get agreement. That was the temper and determination of the Conference."

This is pulling the wool over our eyes with a vengeance. The intention is to define the temper and determination of the Conference in terms that no one could possibly take amiss. (Alas! the very timidity of the definition informs us that the temper was uncertain and the determination obstinate.) To say bluntly, "Since our various interests conflict, every nation will have to give up something" would be dangerous; somebody might retort, provocatively, "Very well: you begin"; or, affrontedly, "What, me? Not bloody likely!" To say bluntly that there were some things no nation could be expected to give up would be dangerous too; because those were the very things other nations would want given up, and the answer might be: "Then what is the good of the Conference?" Some formula was required to give each representative

[1] Mr. Ramsay MacDonald.

the flattering assurance that, though he was notoriously a most accommodating fellow, no important sacrifice could possibly be required of him. The formula when found is (naturally) rather obscure: even when we have succeeded in bending every ounce of resource in interpreting it, we may still be excused for thinking that it means, "Every representative is determined to get his own way, but to be otherwise as obliging as possible." Perhaps it did mean exactly that. At any rate, the Conference was not a success.

Might a more courageous declaration actually have induced a more malleable temper and a less immovable determination? Bold words do not always make wars. When the French Ambassador told Queen Elizabeth that France would not permit her to keep Mary Queen of Scots prisoner in England, Elizabeth replied:

> "Her friends have given shelter to the English rebels, and with her aid and connivance they levied war on me with fire and sword. No sovereign in Europe will sit down under such provocation, and I would count myself unworthy of realm, crown and name of Queen if I endured it."

There was no mistaking a temper and determination like that. Mary remained a prisoner, while the Prince of France sought Elizabeth's hand in marriage.

But whatever excuse politicians may have for prostituting language to the concealment of thought, there can be none for us. And as a rule we offer none; our dishevelment is sheer sluttishness. We think that correctness and comeliness do not matter, provided we say what we mean; unaware that without correctness and comeliness we cannot say what we mean, but often say more, or less, or the precise opposite. "She was one of those actresses who had left the stage on her marriage," says a novelist, careless of syntax. Surely, this is more than was meant; or what kind of actress is this whose marriage sweeps her fellow players from the stage? "It was one of the worst moments he had ever experienced," says another, careless of diction, "sending many of his awkward moments 'abroad' into the limber of insignificant things." The "limber" is part of a gun-carriage—did the author mean only to send the bad moment "abroad" on a gun-carriage? I think he meant to send it further: to the limbo where all such nonsense should go and be forgotten. "Known to all the world as the man responsible for the *Arrow's* meteoric rise," says a third, careless of metaphor. So he gives himself the lie; for a meteor cannot rise, and in fact is a meteor only in virtue of its fall.

It is well, then, to know what we mean and to learn how to say it in English. And by English I mean English, and not any other tongue. In a day when the British Broadcasting Corporation imports its language committee from Ireland and Scotland, and when Fleet Street swarms with Scots, Irish and Americans, it is well to remember that all these persons are foreigners; that the Scots and the Irish were so from the beginning and that the Americans have become so; that they speak our language as foreigners; and that while it is childlike and charming in us to enjoy their sing-song speech and their quaint foreign barbarisms, to imitate these things is childishness and folly. It is true that a language thrives by piracy: it will do us no harm to adopt a striking word of slang or a vivid turn of expression. We must not, however, give our pure gold for cowrie-shells or abandon our beautiful and useful grammatical tools because these barbarians do not know how to handle them.

Let us take as our example that famous distinction which we English alone in all the world know how to make: the distinction between "shall" and "will." "The mere Englishman," says Mr. H. W. Fowler, "if he reflects upon the matter at all, is convinced that his *shall and will* endows his speech with a delicate precision that could not be attained without it, and serves more important purposes than that of a race-label." (Mark, in passing, how slyly the scholar is here laughing in his sleeve at those to whom one word is as good as another. "Mere Englishman," says he, knowing that this will be taken for mock humility. But he knows, too, that *merus* means "pure," and that when Queen Elizabeth called herself "mere English" she meant it for a boast.) Indeed, the distinction is no empty one: "I will do it" (with reluctance, but you force me); "I shall do it" (and God and His angels have no power to stay me).

Consider this sentence, taken from a short novel which contains no fewer than forty-three incorrect uses of "will" and "would":

"I am also thinking about getting some work. It should be easy, because I won't be pushed by necessity."

It looks like a failure of logic. If the speaker is determined not to be pushed by his necessity into whatever work shall offer itself, then, one would say, a man so necessitous and so obstinate will not easily find work before he perishes of his necessities. But the context shows that the author does not mean this. He means: "I shall not be pushed by necessity (because I have plenty of money), and can therefore afford to take a job with small pay; and that should be easy to find."

Is this a trifling matter, not worth making clear? Then see how you can destroy the most beautiful parable in Scripture by using the one word for the other:

"I shall arise and go to my father and shall say unto him . . ."

How jaunty the words are now; how cocksure; how hypocritical; how they compel the sneering comment, "and the poor old blighter will fall for the sob-stuff again."[1]

Remember, too, how the late Lord Oxford, who was a stylist, refused on a famous occasion to surrender the hammer-stroke of "shall," even when faced by a conglomeration of sibilants that might have daunted the most courageous orator:

"We shall not sheathe the sword that we have not lightly drawn . . ."

Not promise; but prophecy.

Does anybody, possessing a tool that will do such delicate work so easily, really desire to abandon it? It is being abandoned. We are letting "shall" and "should" drift out of our hands while we labour to do their work, crudely and coarsely, with "will" and "would." Even so correct and elegant a writer as Mr. Robert Graves is losing his English ear and writing: "I would like to," and "I would prefer to." Here the use is redundant and not ambiguous; but if we do not trouble to distinguish we shall soon lose the power of distinguishing. Moreover, if we use "will" or "would" wrongly nine times, and the tenth time intend it rightly, who, the tenth time, will give us credit for good intentions? The gentleman with the forty-three wrong uses has perhaps a dozen right uses as well; but amid so great a herd of goats his few innocent lambs look like strays.

Is it not worth while also to stretch out a helping hand to the rapidly perishing gerund? The fused participle is usurping its seat and soon will have its life. Here is the perpetrator of the forty-three "wills-and-woulds" happily engaged in fusing the participle:

"There was every excuse for a young man not wishing to be too precise."

Very good: but for what are we to excuse him? Is this a general free pardon to imprecise young men? A not-wishing-to-be-too-precise young man, says the participle, has every excuse—for

[1] In Wycliffe's Bible, the passage actually stands: "I shal aryse"; but the makers of the Authorised Version, with their more developed feeling for the right word, would have none of it."

93

(presumably) murder, arson, larceny, rape or any other crime he cares to commit. But no. The author means only that a desire for imprecision is excusable in a young man. Then let the young man lay claim to the gerund of his desire with a bold possessive. It is *his* desire, "a young man's not wishing," that is excusable. There is little excuse for an author's not wishing to be precise, however readily he may excuse his characters.

Here is a fine pair of specimens from a novel:

> "In history he had come across so many instances of victory being turned into defeat through the winning side underrating the other side's strength."

There is no ambiguity here; it may pass, you think. But make a similar sentence where the substantives are replaced by pronouns, and the hideousness of the structure smites you in the eye:

> "He had come across many instances of us being defeated through me underrating the enemy's strength."

Would the clumsiest boor that ever set pen to paper not hesitate to write such a sentence? Yet in every newspaper written in the English language and in half the books, the gerund is murdered a hundred times a day.

Let us choose one more offender against syntax for summary execution. Let us pick that vile fellow the hanging participle, who, if he would but hang all his employers, would perform the one useful act of his mean existence. Here he stands, hand in hand with his vulgar associate, the unattached infinitive:

> "And though one might avoid the margins his lobby was too tiny not to step on the paint when crossing it."

Who stepped on the paint? The lobby? Who crossed? The lobby? Crossed what? Did the lobby, in an access of religious fervour, cross itself? It cannot be "one" who stepped or crossed, for "one" is marooned in a parenthesis and, having successfully avoided the margins, can trip no further. Nor is it easy to see why, if "one" could grammatically be the crosser, he should not avoid the paint; for, if the lobby was too small to be cleared at a stride, then the larger the lobby the shorter the crossing; which is ridiculous. Clearly it was the little lobby whose infant strides were too short to cross the paint without doing damage.

Lest anyone should go mad in endeavouring to solve the problem of the lobby, let us give the explanation at once. What the writer was trying to say was this: "In the large rooms, one might avoid the (freshly-painted) margins; but the lobby, being small, had been painted all over, so that one could not cross it without stepping on the paint." Is there any reason why that should not be said in good, plain English? Is anything gained by bad and obscure English?

There is the test: is anything gained? Language must develop, and in developing must move from closer to freer constructions. We must not be pedants, but let us ask, before abandoning a nice distinction of words or a delicate syntactical construction: Do we gain anything by the change? If so, let us adopt it. Does the change, at any rate, do no harm? If so, let it run: it will prove its worth if it has any. Do we lose anything by the change? If so, let us resist it at all costs—even at the cost of a little thought and trouble; for, once lost, it is lost for ever.

There are pedants, God mend their ears, who, having read some cheap-jack, rule-of-thumb, cramp-wit folly in a sixpenny text-book, would like to break our free idiom to the bit of an alien fashion. These are not the Latinists (who know better), but the Latinisers; they remember the Latin bones of language, and will have them dry bones. These are the pinching misers, who will hoard their gold, but will not put it out to gain. Of such are the dreary little men who write to the papers protesting—in the teeth of Chaucer, Bacon, Spenser, Shakespeare, Jonson, the English Bible, Milton, Burton, Congreve, Swift, Burke, Peacock, Ruskin, Arnold and the whole tradition of English letters—that a sentence must not end with a preposition. This is no matter of syntax; it is a matter of idiom; and the freedom to handle our prepositions is among the most glorious in our charter of liberties. Here are a few sentences which let these pedagogues take and re-write after their own crabbed fashion, and then ask themselves whether what they have written is English:

Is any song worth singing? That depends on what language it is written in, what music it is sung to and what the song is about.

England is a land worth living in, worth singing of, worth fighting and dying for, and to betray her is a sin such as the sun might fear to look upon.

Let us have as many defenders as are ready to come and the ranks have room for, since so great a menace is not to be trifled with.

Finally, after the politicians, the foreigners, the slovens and the pedants, let us look at the makers of jargon, who are the wireless announcers, the newspaper reporters, the jurors and committee-men, the business-letter-writers, the framers of by-laws and all those who think in abstract nouns and windy periphrases. A single example, taken at random, must do for them. Here is what the *Daily Express* calls a "strongly-worded protest," addressed by the Swansea and District Sunday Schools Union to the B.B.C., under the impression that it was a piece of plain speaking:

> "Having regard to the fact that the homes of many thousands of listeners are otherwise free from such pollution, its introduction into the family circle by means of wireless broadcast is deeply regretted and strongly resented as being liable to pollute the minds of the young people whom we are trying to keep pure."

Look at that great rambling circumlocution at the start, with its hanging participle and redundant abstractions! Look at the flabby impersonality whereby the homes remain passively free from an abstract pollution! Look at the still flabbier impersonality of the "introduction" and the "regret" and even of the "resentment"! Look at the timidity of the phrase "liable to pollute"! Not until the last relative clause is any living person made responsible for anything. "Strongly worded," indeed! If the Swansea and District Sunday Schools Union had the courage to say what they mean, we might believe that they meant what they said:

> "Since thousands of listeners take pains to keep such dirty stuff out of their homes, they deeply regret and strongly resent your thrusting it upon them by wireless; because they fear it may corrupt the young people they are trying to keep pure."

That is personal; that is concrete; that, if you like, is plain speaking; it is also much better English.

But what do we care after all? "What profit shall this birthright do to me?" If our English is not good our speech will be neither beautiful nor intelligible; but does that matter a straw? Have words any power in themselves? We began by contrasting Mr. Ramsay MacDonald with Queen Elizabeth: let us contrast them once again. Here is the Prime Minister speaking to the Commons of England:

> "Schemes must be devised, policies must be devised if it is humanly possible to take that section [of the unemployed] and to regard them not as wastrels, not as hopeless people, but as people for whom occupation must be provided somehow or other, and that occupation, although it may not be in the regular factory or in organised large-scale industrial groups, nevertheless will be

quite as effective for themselves mentally, morally, spiritually and physically than, perhaps, if they were included in this enormous mechanism of humanity which is not always producing the best result, and which, to a very large extent, fails in producing the good results that so many of us expect to see from a higher civilisation based on national wealth."

Do you like it? Or do you prefer this, which is a speech of Queen Elizabeth to the judges?

"Have a care over my people. You have my people—do you that which I ought to do. They are *my* people. Every man oppresseth them and spoileth them without mercy; they cannot revenge their quarrel, nor help themselves. See unto them, see unto them, for they are my charge. I charge you, even as God hath charged me."

I know little enough about social problems, in this age or in that; but I know which speech fills me with the more passionate pity of the poor man at odds with the tyranny of the world.

THEY TRIED TO BE GOOD

(1943)

WE ARE BEING DRENCHED WITH BOOKS and pamphlets about the British people—in particular, about the collapse of national morale between the wars and the astonishing recovery after Dunkirk. Denunciations of our policy and politicians between 1918 and 1940—their stupidity, timidity, hypocrisy and vacillation—are severe, and on the whole justified. These things caused bewilderment at home and abroad. Nobody understands why, after being so far gone, we did not go altogether. Still less does anybody understand why, having betrayed Europe and ourselves, we should look for respect or confidence from anybody. Yet the explanation is not really far-fetched or obscure. It depends upon one plain fact which has been stated over and over again, but which nobody takes seriously.

The staggeringly, quite childishly simple thing about the British people is that they want to be good.

Duo

I do not mean that they are all Platonic philosophers, cherishing a lofty ideal of Abstract Perfection. Most of them are not interested in philosophy at all; and they all detest the Abstract. But they want to be good, in the most naïve and nursery sense of the word. They want to feel that their conduct is such that Our Father in Heaven can be pleased with it. If they can be assured of this parental approval, they do not greatly care what the next-door neighbours think of them. But if they feel themselves to be naughty and in disgrace, they lose self-confidence and develop inferiority psychoses; everything they do goes wrong. The more they try to be good, the more hot water they seem to get into. There are days like that in the nursery, when, inexplicably, nothing one does can please the grown-ups. The Twenty-Years' Armistice was just one of those days. We tried to do as we were told, and blundered from one catastrophe to another.

When I think back to that time, I seem to hear, shrill above the mutter and growl of the troubles brewing up in Central Europe, a loud, monotonous and angry voice, perpetually admonishing and scolding. The voice spoke through many mouths, but it was recognisably one voice. I shall call it the Voice of Enlightenment—for indeed most of the doctrine it preached was the outcome of that era of "Enlightenment," technically so called, which is the source of so many present-day heresies and denials. It is true that for twenty years Britain was false to herself, false to her faith, false to her friends, false to her trust. But it is only fair to remember that, throughout that time, the Voice of Enlightenment never ceased dinning into her ears that everything she had believed in, everything she had been accustomed to do, everything that for her own sake and the world's she needed to do, was *naughty*.

Take, for instance, the whole question of war. Britain has never liked war, but she had always supposed that war in a just cause was right and seemly. Now, at the victorious conclusion of the most exhausting struggle in her history, the Voice of Enlightenment informed her that the whole thing had been, not merely useless ("War settles nothing"), but *naughty*. A just war was as wicked as an unjust war. War itself must be outlawed and abolished. So said the Voice, reinforcing itself with all the numinous authority of the Sermon on the Mount and all the persuasive reasonableness of Progressive Humanism. Britain listened, and tried to be good.

She had a dim feeling that, in a world full of conflicting interests and jarring ambitions, power might be needed to keep the peace. But power in itself was naughty. Her own power of intervention, and indeed her very existence, depended upon the Navy which she proudly loved; but Navies were naughty. She had a great Empire, girt together physically by the sea-routes and spiritually by strangely tangled bonds of sentiment, self-interest, and a sense of duty to one's belongings; but Empire was naughty, belongings of every kind were naughty, self-interest was naughty—the Voice of Enlightenment taught her to be ashamed of her Empire. As for sentiment, Enlightenment poured scorn on all that: to be sentimental was naughty.

Then there was the whole business of the Peace Terms and of Britain's relations with Germany. The last time Britain had made peace had been in South Africa. On that occasion, she had been told that her war was a naughty war—not because it was war, but because the cause was unjust. Thinking it over, the British came to the conclusion that it had not been altogether just; they made a peace remarkable for its generosity, took the vanquished into an equal partnership, and found that this worked very well. The peace made with Germany was of another kind. The issues were confused, but eventually two voices made themselves heard. One said that the vanquished had been insufficiently crushed and that the elaborate network of armed restraints by which it was sought to enclose them was insufficiently powerful for security. The other said that the terms had been too harsh and that it was time to bring the vanquished into partnership with the victors. Listening to them, one could scarcely help coming to the conclusion that the second of the two was the Voice of Enlightenment, for it was saying all the enlightened things. For once, it appeared, Enlightenment and British experience were in agreement. Restraints imposed by power sounded too much like power-politics and the "balance of power in Europe"—things which Enlightenment had been earnest in condemning. Free and equal partnership and co-operation was precisely the thing that Enlightenment most approved. Besides, it had worked before.

Of course, when one takes a former foe into partnership, it is because one is convinced that he, too, "wants to be good." Germany, it now seems, did not want to be good, and Britain ought to have known it. But all the good and intellectual people who preached Progressive Humanism had been proclaiming for years that nobody ever wants to be naughty. There were no sinful men; indeed, there was no such thing as sin. There were only fundamentally good and perfectible men thwarted by oppressive circumstances. Take away the unfavourable environment, and everybody would at once be good and co-operate for the happiness of all. And it cannot be doubted that defeat, impoverishment, and a strong coalition to keep one in that state, form an unfavourable environment for any nation. The British were undoubtedly credulous, but according to their rights they genuinely tried to be good. Their error was in not seeing through Progressive Humanism and the Perfectibility of Man. They should have used more intelligence; but since Enlightenment had been engaged for some time in leading the Flight from Reason and stigmatising intelligence as highbrow, one should not, perhaps, blame them too much.

A period of great confusion followed. The enlightened principle which the British had thoroughly absorbed was that war of any kind was naughty. Armaments, as constituting both a cause and a recognition of war, were supremely naughty. On the other hand, it became clear that Japan in China and Italy in Abyssinia were doing naughty things, and that there was a sad outbreak of naughtiness in Spain. The same wise adults who proclaimed that armaments were naughty were also raising an enlightened voice urging Britain to interfere and prevent these wicked goings-on. Socialist Auntie exhorted her to stop bad Benito and atrocious Adolf from pulling the cat's tail, while Pacifist Mamma took away her stick and told her that ladies didn't use their fists. Britannia could only scream and scold while Benito cocked snoots at the whole family and nasty rough Adolf proceeded to catch the Jewish cat and skin it alive. Enlightenment then suggested that poor Adolf had a complex, because naughty Britannia had taken away his kittens and added them to her family of Imperial lion-cubs. Perhaps he would feel better and kinder if she presented him with the whole litter. Britannia was stubborn about this, and was universally called a selfish little girl. In her defence, she could only protest that her cubs had grown attached to her and didn't want to go.

And here again there was a difficulty. The enlightened spirit which had brooded upon the Ark of the Covenant had revealed, as a Divine Law, the doctrine of self-determination for small nationalities; great trouble had been taken to parcel out territory in such a way that people in Europe who spoke the same language and shared the same ideas should be made independent of rulers with other languages and ideas. The British Empire was, of course, a horrid example of disobedience to this Law. Nobody was quite ready to coerce Britain into giving away her colonies, dependencies and scattered strong-points; they only nagged and sneered, and made her feel naughty about them, so that she became tearful and apologetic and did not like to administer or defend her possessions properly. There was, for example, Ireland. Eire demanded self-determination, and Enlightenment said she ought to have it. But

Northern Ireland also wanted self-determination, and was determined to remain with England. Accordingly, the two bits of Ireland were allowed to determine themselves along the lines adopted in settling Europe. Eire was annoyed, and it was uncomfortable for everybody; but the stubborn fact remained that for England to coerce Eire, or for Eire to coerce Northern Ireland, would have been equally unenlightened. A problem of a similar kind, but more complicated, arose in India. History and tradition made Britain hold on—but fumblingly, because the perpetual cries of "Naughty, naughty!" were unnerving. So, in one sphere after another, action stultified itself.

And then Hitler started.

It has never, I think, been shown quite clearly enough just how Hitler's demands presented themselves to a Britain who was trying to be good, and had already obediently accepted the propositions that nothing was so naughty as war, and that the way to cure the psychosis of the defeated was to indulge the patient. For Hitler founded his demands upon the enlightened principles laid down by the League of Nations. He said that his German-speaking minorities all over the world had the right to self-determination, even if this meant breaking up political and territorial units such as Czecho-Slovakia. An older and less enlightened Britain would have said instantly that to concede this would break down defensive frontiers and upset the Balance of Power. But clearly, since war was naughty, frontiers were naughty—and as for the Balance of Power, there were no words for its naughtiness. She had been made to feel that to defend either of these things was to defend the indefensible. Everybody has demanded indignantly why Britain sacrificed Czecho-Slovakia and then boggled over Poland. The answer, I think, is quite simply that so long as Hitler was demanding the German-speaking Austrians and the Sudeten Germans, he was demanding something to which Enlightenment had taught her he had a right. She was uneasy—her whole historic tradition urged her to oppose these proceedings. But when Hitler went further and demanded peoples and places that by no stretch of imagination could be said to be German, or even to want to be German, then Britain came to the conclusion that—Humanism or no Humanism—Germany was really being wicked. It followed—there was no help for it—that she must be wicked too and declare war.

The war, says Miss Odette Keun,[1] "had a most peculiar effect on England. Contrary to its usual rule of provoking activity, it sent her straight from a twenty-years' sleep into what was, considering

[1] *And Hell Followed*, p. 85.

101

the circumstances, a catalepsy of seven months." Miss Keun appears to be surprised, but that is because she, like other Continental critics, has never understood the mind of England during those twenty years. She sees it as an inexplicable lethargy of the public conscience, accompanied by orgies of perversity and deliberate betrayal by the people at the top. Actually, it was a period of that anguished and meticulous heart-searching which is known to experienced priests as "scrupulosity"; when every action, from the most important to the most trivial, appears to the sufferer to be so infected by sin that no decision can be fully endorsed by the conscience. To do anything at all produces an intolerable conviction of guilt; action is inhibited at the source; and if something does not intervene to break up this unnatural condition, the end may be religious melancholia.

Britain went to war feeling herself in disgrace. Not to wage war was wicked; to wage war was more wicked still; the sacrifice she was called on to make was not redemptive, for the theology of Enlightenment has no doctrine of redemption. Never must she forget that she was committed to the unforgivable sin. No trumpets, no flags, no parades, no martial music were permitted by enlightened opinion; she must crawl into battle in a white sheet. Nor might she tell the world that she thought herself worth fighting for; that would be propaganda, and propaganda was naughty—besides, she was expected to confess that her constitution was rotten, her way of life unsound, her Empire an outrage, her social services contemptible. War aims and peace aims she must declare, but they must be the war and peace aims dictated by the Voice of Enlightenment, not those that were native to her tradition. Tradition, indeed! What had Progressive Humanism to do with tradition, or with history, if it came to that? The apostle of get-on-or-get-out had proclaimed that history was bunk. The cosmopolitan intelligentsia had laid down that English History was a jingoist and hypocritical lie, and that all Britain's past stank like a cesspool. Colonel Blimp, Jerry Mander, Captain Kidd, Mr. Gradgrind and Mr. Stiggins were the only real figures in her spiritual ancestry. English history had been debunked, and the less said about it the better.

What was the English tradition? "Grab," said a voice from the land of the Almighty Dollar; "England and France had their backs to the wall like two old gentlemen defending their money-bags." "English policy," said the voice from Germany (and the quisling governments echoed it in turn) "has always been to prevent the unification of Europe. What else is she doing now? And why does she do it?" To which England might have replied, in the tradition, "Because the unification of Europe always means in practice a tyranny like yours." Which would have been all very well, had not the Voice of Enlightenment insisted that Europe *must* be unified, and that the Peace Aims of Britain should include a European federation under a centralised and authoritarian control. There was nothing to say.

Nagged and scolded from all sides, deprived of arms and self-confidence, Britain slunk into war, with her tail between her legs, ground down by a vivid sense of her irredeemable naughtiness, forbidden to explain herself, forbidden even to look cheerful about it, and (because all talk about armaments had been banished from enlightened conversation as a solecism) entirely unaware of what she was up against.

Things went badly, and she was scolded again. Why did she scuttle out of Norway? Why did she not send men and planes to Poland? To Finland? Why did she not immediately drop bombs on Germany instead of leaflets? She was not properly equipped? Not fully mobilised? Disgraceful! Why not? And why did she not know that Hitler was about to invade Norway? Denmark? Holland? Belgium, without excuse or warning? Had she been asleep or merely selfish and complacent? Why?

The British, if they had not by now been rendered almost speechless by self-consciousness, might well have replied: "Because we tried to be good. We made no arms, because Enlightenment said it was naughty. Our conscription was too little and too late because Labour rigidly opposed it, and we had been carefully taught that Labour was Enlightened and the working man always right. We didn't drop bombs because we might have hurt some civilians, and everybody would have said it was naughty and that we had only ourselves to blame if there were reprisals. And we couldn't believe that Hitler was really wicked (in spite of what some people said) because we had become too enlightened to believe in sin."

When I look back, I do not wonder that Britain was "cataleptic." I only wonder that she had not become blind, deaf, dumb, paralytic and imbecile, without hope of recovery. Fortunately, she has not a hysterical temperament. But the mainspring of her action had been left unwound, and the effect was exactly as though it had been broken.

Then the miracle happened. Hitler scooped up Norway, swallowed Denmark alive, bombed and blazed his path across Holland, battered Belgium to a mummy, tossed the British Army into the sea, blew France to fragments and smashed through to the Channel

Ports. The world stood still. And Britain, stripped naked in the arena to await the pounce of the beast, was aware of a strange quality in the silence. *The scolding had stopped.*

Nobody who is not British or, being British, was not in Britain at that time, can quite understand the enormous sense of relief, the uplifting of spirits, that we then experienced. True, we were terrified —whoever says we were not is a boaster and a fool. But we need no longer obey enlightened and incomprehensible orders. We need no longer rush round commending ourselves by apologies for our existence. There was no more barracking. The amphitheatre was holding its breath, and for the first time in twenty years our performance had the sympathy of the house. Indeed, a few onlookers were already snuffling into their handkerchiefs over the prospect of our imminent decease—a gesture we thought rather silly, since we did not intend to die. (Though we may have had the defiant feeling—very familiar in the nursery—that if we *did* die, then perhaps the grown-ups would be sorry.) But anyhow, there it was; nobody was scolding us—we were not naughty any more.

"In that enormous silence, tiny and——" No, "tiny" is scarcely the word; but "unafraid" is right. Another voice addressed us. It was as though a peevish new-fangled and semi-educated governess had departed and we had been left in charge of Old Nurse—tart, solid, bustling and comfortable—who knew our family ways. When half-gods go, the gods arrive.

There was nothing vaguely ideological about the new voice: it came attached to a corporeal and particular person. Winston Churchill had always been obstinately unenlightened. He was English and aristocratic, and had the bad taste not to be ashamed of his origins. His theology (though by no means elaborate) was coarse and Christian enough to allow for sin and the devil, and sufficiently Pelagian (in the English manner) to admit the possibility of salvation by works. He had always stubbornly affirmed that some things were worse than war. He thought the Empire a good thing, and said so; as good as—perhaps even better than—other people's empires, to which, for some reason, Enlightened Opinion had never seen fit to object. He believed in History—even English history. He affronted the highbrows with vulgar outmoded virtues, such as patriotism, courage, honour, loyalty, cheerfulness and high spirits; he defied the plain, practical low-brows by using the sort of language which a Raleigh would not have thought unbecoming. He not only was, in a symbolic and spiritual manner, a bulldog; by one of those extravagant pieces of luck so frequently showered upon the undeserving English, he *looked* like a bulldog—

the cartoonist's delight, an endearing mascot. He contrived to present the war, not as a cold, passionless, punitive measure to be meted out sad-eyed, to the refrain of "this hurts me more than it hurts you" (which at the time it only too obviously did), but as an adventure combining the exaltation of martyrdom with the thrill of a gorilla-hunt. He lived in the present, according to the Gospel of St. Matthew, instead of in the next era but two, according to the Gospel of St. Marx. He was unregenerate; he was unenlightened; he was England. And he never scolded. He did not tell us that we were as good as gold; he assumed it. Indeed, I cannot for the moment recollect that he told us anything at all; he merely took it for granted that we were all his sort of person, and told the Axis so.

Now I should not dream of asserting that we were, are, or ever shall be as good as gold. All men are sinners, and the British are no exception. But I do say that we tried to be good. Our worst betrayals, our most flagrant stupidities resulted from our efforts to obey the contradictory orders of the silliest nursery governess ever foisted on a well-meaning bunch of children. I have no use whatever for Enlightened Opinion, whose science is obsolete, its psychology superficial, its theology beneath contempt and its history nowhere; besides, it is a craven thing. When it saw what the results of its mischief-making were likely to be, it packed up its loud-speaker and hared for cover. When the storm seemed to be over, out it popped again, talking more briskly than ever. I hope we shall pay no attention to it.

But the future is not now my concern. I am concerned only to interpret the riddle of the English during the decades of disaster. The answer is, I think, that we wanted to be good and tried to be good, but that the sincerest efforts after virtue produce only chaos if they are directed by a ramshackle and incoherent philosophy. We were persuaded that God hated us, and that we ought to go into the garden and eat worms. If a nation is well-meaning and not very clear-headed, it is easily persuaded of these things by people who talk as though they had God in their pocket. I warn these people that if they start tinkering again (as they will undoubtedly try, so soon as Britain seems sufficiently secure to be envied), they may really succeed next time in breaking the mainspring. If that happens, it will be useless to scuttle for shelter behind the uncovenanted virtues of the British. They must look to their Enlightened God to help them, God help them.

ARE WOMEN HUMAN?

Address given to a Women's Society, 1938

WHEN I WAS ASKED TO COME and speak to you, your Secretary made the suggestion that she thought I must be interested in the feminist movement. I replied—a little irritably, I am afraid —that I was not sure I wanted to "identify myself," as the phrase goes, with feminism, and that the time for "feminism," in the old-fashioned sense of the word, had gone past. In fact, I think I went so far as to say that, under present conditions, an aggressive feminism might do more harm than good. As a result I was, perhaps not unnaturally, invited to explain myself.

I do not know that it is very easy to explain, without offence or risk of misunderstanding, exactly what I do mean, but I will try.

The question of "sex-equality" is, like all questions affecting human relationships, delicate and complicated. It cannot be settled by loud slogans or hard-and-fast assertions like "a woman is as good as a man"—or "woman's place is the home"—or "women ought not to take men's jobs." The minute one makes such assertions, one finds one has to qualify them. "A woman is as good as a man" is as meaningless as to say, "a Kaffir is as good as a Frenchman" or "a poet is as good as an engineer" or "an elephant is as good as a racehorse"—it means nothing whatever until you add: "at doing what?" In a religious sense, no doubt, the Kaffir is as valuable in the eyes of God as a Frenchman—but the average Kaffir is probably less skilled in literary criticism than the average Frenchman, and the average Frenchman less skilled than the average Kaffir in tracing the spoor of big game. There might be exceptions on either side: it is largely a matter of heredity and education. When we balance the poet against the engineer, we are faced with a fundamental difference of temperament—so that here our question is complicated by the enormous social problem whether poetry or engineering is "better" for the State, or for humanity in general. There may be people who would like a world that was all engineers or all poets —but most of us would like to have a certain number of each; though here again, we should all differ about the desirable proportion of engineering to poetry. The only proviso we should make is that people with dreaming and poetical temperaments should not entangle themselves in engines, and that mechanically-minded persons should not issue booklets of bad verse. When we come to the elephant and the racehorse, we come down to bed-rock physical differences—the elephant would make a poor showing in the Derby, and the unbeaten Eclipse himself would be speedily eclipsed by an elephant when it came to hauling logs.

That is so obvious that it hardly seems worth saying. But it is the mark of all movements, however well-intentioned, that their pioneers tend, by much lashing of themselves into excitement, to lose sight of the obvious. In reaction against the age-old slogan, "woman is the weaker vessel," or the still more offensive, "woman is a divine creature," we have, I think, allowed ourselves to drift into asserting that "a woman is as good as a man," without always pausing to think what exactly we mean by that. What, I feel, we ought to mean is something so obvious that it is apt to escape attention altogether, viz: not that every woman is, in virtue of her sex, as strong, clever, artistic, level-headed, industrious and so forth as any man that can be mentioned; but, that a woman is just as much an ordinary human being as a man, with the same individual preferences, and with just as much right to the tastes and preferences of an individual. What is repugnant to every human being is to be reckoned always as a member of a class and not as an individual person. A certain amount of classification is, of course, necessary for practical purposes: there is no harm in saying that women, as a class, have smaller bones than men, wear lighter clothing, have more hair on their heads and less on their faces, go more pertinaciously to church or the cinema, or have more patience with small and noisy babies. In the same way, we may say that stout people of both sexes are commonly better-tempered than thin ones, or that university dons of both sexes are more pedantic in their speech than agricultural labourers, or that Communists of both sexes are more ferocious than Fascists—or the other way round. What is unreasonable and irritating is to assume that *all* one's tastes and preferences have to be conditioned by the class to which one belongs. That has been the very common error into which men have frequently fallen about women—and it is the error into which feminist women are, perhaps, a little inclined to fall into about themselves.

Take, for example, the very usual reproach that women nowadays always want to "copy what men do." In that reproach there is a great deal of truth and a great deal of sheer, unmitigated and indeed quite wicked nonsense. There are a number of jobs and pleasures which men have in times past cornered for themselves. At one time, for instance, men had a monopoly of classical education. When the pioneers of university training for women demanded that women should be admitted to the universities, the cry went up at once: "Why should women want to know about Aristotle?" The answer is NOT that *all* women would be the better for knowing about Aristotle—still less, as Lord Tennyson seemed to think, that they would be more companionable wives for their husbands if they did know about Aristotle—but simply: "What women want as a class is irrelevant. *I* want to know about Aristotle. It is true that most women care nothing about him, and a great many male undergraduates turn pale and faint at the thought of him—but I, eccentric individual that I am, do want to know about Aristotle, and I submit that there is nothing in my shape or bodily functions which need prevent my knowing about him."

That battle was won, and rightly won, for women. But there is a sillier side to the university education of women. I have noticed lately, and with regret, a tendency on the part of the women's colleges to "copy the men" on the side of their failings and absurdities, and this is not so good. Because the constitution of the men's colleges is autocratic, old-fashioned and in many respects inefficient, the women are rather inclined to try and cramp their own collegiate constitutions—which were mapped out on freer democratic lines—into the mediæval mould of the men's—and that is unsound. It contributes nothing to the university and it loses what might have been a very good thing. The women students, too, have a foolish trick of imitating and outdoing the absurdities of male undergraduates. To climb in drunk after hours and get gated is silly and harmless if done out of pure high spirits; if it is done "because the men do it," it is worse than silly, because it is not spontaneous and not even amusing.

Let me give one simple illustration of the difference between the right and the wrong kind of feminism. Let us take this terrible business—so distressing to the minds of bishops—of the women who go about in trousers. We are asked: "Why do you want to go about in trousers? They are extremely unbecoming to most of you. You only do it to copy the men." To this we may very properly reply: "It is true that they are unbecoming. Even on men they are remarkably unattractive. But, as you men have discovered for yourselves, they are comfortable, they do not get in the way of one's activities like skirts and they protect the wearer from draughts about the ankles. As a human being, I like comfort and dislike draughts. If the trousers do not attract you, so much the worse; for the moment

I do not want to attract you. I want to enjoy myself as a human being, and why not? As for copying you, certainly you thought of trousers first and to that extent we must copy you. But we are not such abandoned copy-cats as to attach these useful garments to our bodies with braces. There we draw the line. These machines of leather and elastic are unnecessary and unsuited to the female form. They are, moreover, hideous beyond description. And as for indecency—of which you sometimes accuse the trousers—we at least can take our coats off without becoming the half-undressed, bedroom spectacle that a man presents in his shirt and braces "

So that when we hear that women have once more laid hands upon something which was previously a man's sole privilege, I think we have to ask ourselves: is this trousers or is it braces? Is it something useful, convenient and suitable to a human being as such? Or is it merely something unnecessary to us, ugly, and adopted merely for the sake of collaring the other fellow's property? These jobs and professions, now. It is ridiculous to take on a man's job just in order to be able to say that "a woman has done it—yah!" The only decent reason for tackling any job is that it is *your* job, and *you* want to do it.

At this point, somebody is likely to say: "Yes, that is all very well. But it *is* the woman who is always trying to ape the man. She *is* the inferior being. You don't as a rule find the men trying to take the women's jobs away from them. They don't force their way into the household and turn women out of their rightful occupations."

Of course they do not. They have done it already.

Let us accept the idea that women should stick to their own jobs —the jobs they did so well in the good old days before they started talking about votes and women's rights. Let us return to the Middle Ages and ask what we should get then in return for certain political and educational privileges which we should have to abandon.

It is a formidable list of jobs: the whole of the spinning industry, the whole of the dyeing industry, the whole of the weaving industry. The whole catering industry and—which would not please Lady Astor, perhaps—the whole of the nation's brewing and distilling. All the preserving, pickling and bottling industry, all the bacon-curing. And (since in those days a man was often absent from home for months together on war or business) a very large share in the management of landed estates. Here are the women's jobs—and what has become of them? They are all being handled by men. It is all very well to say that woman's place is the home—but modern civilisation has taken all these pleasant and profitable activities out of the home, where the women looked after them, and handed them over to big industry, to be directed and organised by men at the head of large factories. Even the dairy-maid in her simple bonnet has gone, to be replaced by a male mechanic in charge of a mechanical milking plant.

Now, it is very likely that men in big industries do these jobs better than the women did them at home. The fact remains that the home contains much less of interesting activity than it used to contain. What is more, the home has so shrunk to the size of a small flat that—even if we restrict woman's job to the bearing and rearing of families—there is no room for her to do even that. It is useless to urge the modern woman to have twelve children, like her grand-mother. Where is she to put them when she has got them? And what modern man wants to be bothered with them? It is perfectly idiotic to take away women's traditional occupations and then complain because she looks for new ones. Every woman is a human being—one cannot repeat that too often—and a human being *must* have occupation, if he or she is not to become a nuisance to the world.

I am not complaining that the brewing and baking were taken over by the men. If they can brew and bake as well as women or better, then by all means let them do it. But they cannot have it both ways. If they are going to adopt the very sound principle that the job should be done by the person who does it best, then that rule must be applied universally. If the women make better office-workers than men, they must have the office work. If any indi-vidual woman is able to make a first-class lawyer, doctor, architect or engineer, then she must be allowed to try her hand at it. Once lay down the rule that the job comes first and you throw that job open to every individual, man or woman, fat or thin, tall or short, ugly or beautiful, who is able to do that job better than the rest of the world.

Now, it is frequently asserted that, with women, the job does not come first. What (people cry) are women doing with this liberty of theirs? What woman really prefers a job to a home and family? Very few, I admit. It is unfortunate that they should so often have to make the choice. A man does not, as a rule, have to choose. He gets both. In fact, if he wants the home and family, he usually has to take the job as well, if he can get it. Nevertheless, there have been women, such as Queen Elizabeth and Florence Nightingale, who had the choice, and chose the job and made a success of it. And there have been and are many men who have sacrificed their careers for women—sometimes, like Antony or Parnell, very disastrously. When it comes to a *choice*, then every man or woman has to choose as an individual human being, and, like a human being, take the consequences.

As human beings! I am always entertained—and also irritated—by the newsmongers who inform us, with a bright air of discovery, that they have questioned a number of female workers and been told by one and all that they are "sick of the office and would love to get out of it." In the name of God, what human being is *not*, from time to time, heartily sick of the office and would *not* love to get out of it? The time of female office-workers is daily wasted in sympathising with disgruntled male colleagues who yearn to get out of the office. No human being likes work—not day in and day out. Work is notoriously a curse—and if women *liked* everlasting work they would not be human beings at all. *Being* human beings, they like work just as much and just as little as anybody else. They dislike perpetual washing and cooking just as much as perpetual typing and standing behind shop counters. Some of them prefer typing to scrubbing—but that does not mean that they are not, as human beings, entitled to damn and blast the typewriter when they feel that way. The number of men who daily damn and blast type-writers is incalculable; but that does not mean that they would be happier doing a little plain sewing. Nor would the women.

I have admitted that there are very few women who would put their job before every earthly consideration. I will go further and assert that there are very few men who would do it either. In fact, there is perhaps only one human being in a thousand who is pas-sionately interested in his job for the job's sake. The difference is that if that one person in a thousand is a man, we say, simply, that he is passionately keen on his job; if she is a woman, we say she is a freak. It is extraordinarily entertaining to watch the historians of the past, for instance, entangling themselves in what they were pleased to call the "problem" of Queen Elizabeth. They invented the most complicated and astonishing reasons both for her success as a sovereign and for her tortuous matrimonial policy. She was the tool of Burleigh, she was the tool of Leicester, she was the fool of Essex; she was diseased, she was deformed, she was a man in disguise. She was a mystery, and must have some extraordinary solution. Only recently has it occurred to a few enlightened people that the solution might be quite simple after all. She might be one of the rare people who were born into the right job and put that job first. Whereupon a whole series of riddles cleared themselves up by magic. She was in love with Leicester—why didn't she marry him? Well, for the very same reason that numberless kings have not married their lovers—because it would have thrown a spanner into the wheels of the State machine. Why was she so bloodthirsty and unfeminine as to sign the death-warrant of Mary Queen of Scots? For much the same reasons that induced King George V to say that if the House of Lords did not pass the Parliament Bill he would create enough new peers to force it through—because she was, in the measure of her time, a constitutional sovereign, and knew that there was a point beyond which a sovereign could not defy Parliament. Being a rare human being with her eye to the job, she did what was necessary; being an ordinary human being, she hesitated a good deal before embarking on unsavoury measures —but as to feminine mystery, there is no such thing about it, and nobody, had she been a man, would have thought either her statesmanship or her humanity in any way mysterious. Remarkable they were—but she was a very remarkable person. Among her most remarkable achievements was that of showing that sovereignty was one of the jobs for which the right kind of woman was particularly well fitted.

Which brings us back to this question of what jobs, if any, are women's jobs. Few people would go so far as to say that all women are well fitted for all men's jobs. When people do say this, it is particularly exasperating. It is stupid to insist that there are as many female musicians and mathematicians as male—the facts are otherwise, and the most we can ask is that if a Dame Ethel Smyth or a Mary Somerville turns up, she shall be allowed to do her work without having aspersions cast either on her sex or her ability. What we ask is to be human individuals, however peculiar and unexpected. It is no good saying: "You are a little girl and therefore you ought to like dolls"; if the answer is, "But I don't," there is no more to be said. Few women happen to be natural born mechanics; but if there is one, it is useless to try and argue her into being something different. What we must *not* do is to argue that the occasional appearance of a female mechanical genius proves that all women would be mechanical geniuses if they were educated. They would not.

Where, I think, a great deal of confusion has arisen is in a failure to distinguish between special *knowledge* and special *ability*. There are certain questions on which what is called "the woman's point of view" is valuable, because they involve special *knowledge*. Women should be consulted about such things as housing and domestic architecture because, under present circumstances, they have still to wrestle a good deal with houses and kitchen sinks and can bring special knowledge to the problem. Similarly, some of them (though not all) know more about children than the majority of men, and their opinion, *as women*, is of value. In the same way, the opinion of colliers is of value about coal-mining, and the opinion of doctors is valuable about disease. But there are other questions—as for example, about literature or finance—on which the "woman's point of view" has no value at all. In fact, it does not exist. No special knowledge is involved, and a woman's opinion on literature or finance is valuable only as the judgment of an individual. I am occasionally desired by congenital imbeciles and the editors of magazines to say something about the writing of detective fiction "from the woman's point of view." To such demands, one can only say, "Go away and don't be silly. You might as well ask what is the female angle on an equilateral triangle."

In the old days it used to be said that women were unsuited to sit in Parliament, because they "would not be able to think imperially." That, if it meant anything, meant that their views would be cramped and domestic—in short, "the woman's point of view." Now that they *are* in Parliament, people complain that they are a disappointment: they vote like other people with their party and have contributed nothing to speak of from "the woman's point of view"—except on a few purely domestic questions, and even then they are not all agreed. It looks as though somebody was trying to have things both ways at once. Even critics must remember that women are human beings and obliged to think and behave as such. I can imagine a "woman's point of view" about town-planning, or the education of children, or divorce, or the employment of female shop-assistants, for here they have some special knowledge. But what in thunder is the "woman's point of view" about the devaluation of the franc or the abolition of the Danzig Corridor? Even where women have special knowledge, they may disagree among themselves like other specialists. Do doctors never quarrel or scientists disagree? Are women really *not human*, that they should be expected to toddle along all in a flock like sheep? I think that people should be allowed to drink as much wine and beer as they can afford and is good for them; Lady Astor thinks nobody should be allowed to drink anything of the sort. Where is the "woman's point of view"? Or is one or the other of us unsexed? If the unsexed one is myself, then I am unsexed in very good company. But I prefer to think that women are human and differ in opinion like other human beings. This does not mean that their opinions, as individual opinions, are valueless; on the contrary, the more able they are the more violently their opinions will be likely to differ. It only means that you cannot ask for "the woman's point of view," but only for the woman's special knowledge—and this, like all special knowledge, is valuable, though it is no guarantee of agreement.

"What," men have asked distractedly from the beginning of time, "what on earth do women want?" I do not know that women, *as* women, want anything in particular, but as human beings they want, my good men, exactly what you want yourselves: interesting occupation, reasonable freedom for their pleasures, and a sufficient emotional outlet. What form the occupation, the pleasures and the emotion may take, depends entirely upon the individual. You know that this is so with yourselves—why will you not believe that it is so with us. The late D. H. Lawrence, who certainly cannot be accused of underrating the importance of sex and talked a good deal of nonsense upon the subject, was yet occasionally visited with shattering glimpses of the obvious. He said in one of his *Assorted Articles*:

> "Man is willing to accept woman as an equal, as a man in skirts, as an angel, a devil, a baby-face, a machine, an instrument, a bosom, a womb, a pair of legs, a servant, an encyclopædia, an ideal or an obscenity; the one thing he won't accept her as is a human being, a real human being of the feminine sex."

"Accepted as a human being!"—yes; not as an inferior class and not, I beg and pray all feminists, as a superior class—not, in fact, as a class at all, except in a useful context. We are much too much inclined in these days to divide people into permanent categories, forgetting that a category only exists for its special purpose and must be forgotten as soon as that purpose is served. There is a fundamental difference between men and women, but it is not the only fundamental difference in the world. There is a sense in which my charwoman and I have more in common than either of us has with, say, Mr. Bernard Shaw; on the other hand, in a discussion about art and literature, Mr. Shaw and I should probably find we had more fundamental interests in common than either of us had with my charwoman. I grant that, even so, he and I should disagree ferociously about the eating of meat—but that is not a difference between the sexes—on that point, that late Mr. G. K. Chesterton would have sided with me against the representative of his own sex. Then there are points on which I, and many of my own generation of both sexes, should find ourselves heartily in agreement; but on which the rising generation of young men and women would find us too incomprehensibly stupid for words. A difference of age is as fundamental as a difference of sex; and so is a difference of nationality. *All* categories, if they are insisted upon beyond the immediate purpose which they serve, breed class antagonism and disruption in the state, and that is why they are dangerous.

The other day, in the "Heart-to-Heart" column of one of our popular newspapers, there appeared a letter from a pathetic gentleman about a little disruption threatening his married state. He wrote:

"I have been married eleven years and think a great deal of the wedding anniversary. I remind my wife a month in advance and plan to make the evening a success. But she does not share my keenness, and, if I did not remind her, would let the day go by without a thought of its significance. I thought a wedding anniversary meant a lot to a woman. Can you explain this indifference?"

Poor little married gentleman, nourished upon generalisations—and convinced that if his wife does not fit into the category of "a woman" there must be something wrong! Perhaps she resents being dumped into the same category as all the typical women of the comic stories. If so, she has my sympathy. "A" woman—not an individual person, disliking perhaps to be reminded of the remorseless flowing-by of the years and the advance of old age—but "a" woman, displaying the conventional sentimentalities attributed to her unfortunate and ridiculous sex.

A man once asked me—it is true that it was at the end of a very good dinner, and the compliment conveyed may have been due to that circumstance—how I managed in my books to write such natural conversation between men when they were by themselves. Was I, by any chance, a member of a large, mixed family with a lot of male friends? I replied that, on the contrary, I was an only child and had practically never seen or spoken to any men of my own age till I was about twenty-five. "Well," said the man, "I shouldn't have expected a woman [meaning me] to have been able to make it so convincing." I replied that I had coped with this difficult problem by making my men talk, as far as possible, like ordinary human beings. This aspect of the matter seemed to surprise the other speaker; he said no more, but took it away to chew it over. One of these days it may quite likely occur to him that women, as well as men, when left to themselves, talk very much like human beings also.

Indeed, it is my experience that both men and women are fundamentally human, and that there is very little mystery about either sex, except the exasperating mysteriousness of human beings in general. And though for certain purposes it may still be necessary, as it undoubtedly was in the immediate past, for women to band themselves together, as women, to secure recognition of their requirements as a sex, I am sure that the time has now come to insist more strongly on each woman's—and indeed each man's—requirements as an individual person. It used to be said that women had no *esprit de corps*; we have proved that we have—do not let us run into the opposite error of insisting that there is an aggressively feminist "point of view" about everything. To oppose one class perpetually to another—young against old, manual labour against brain-worker, rich against poor, woman against man—is to split the foundations of the State; and if the cleavage runs too deep, there remains no remedy but force and dictatorship. If you wish to preserve a free democracy, you must base it—not on classes and categories, for this will land you in the totalitarian State, where no one may act or think except as the member of a category. You must base it upon the individual Tom, Dick and Harry, on the individual Jack and Jill—in fact, upon you and me.

THE HUMAN-NOT-QUITE-HUMAN

THE FIRST TASK, WHEN UNDERTAKING the study of any phenomenon, is to observe its most obvious feature; and it is here that most students fail. It is here that most students of the "Woman Question" have failed, and the Church more lamentably than most, and with less excuse. That is why it is necessary, from time to time, to speak plainly, and perhaps even brutally, to the Church.

The first thing that strikes the careless observer is that women are unlike men. They are "the opposite sex"—(though why "opposite" I do not know; what is the "neighbouring sex"?). But the fundamental thing is that women are more like men than anything else in the world. They are human beings. *Vir* is male and *Femina* is female: but *Homo* is male and female.

This is the equality claimed and the fact that is persistently evaded and denied. No matter what arguments are used, the discussion is vitiated from the start, because Man is always dealt with as both *Homo* and *Vir*, but Woman only as *Femina*.

I have seen it solemnly stated in a newspaper that the seats on the near side of a bus are always filled before those on the off side, because, "men find them more comfortable on account of the camber of the road, and women find they get a better view of the shop windows." As though the camber of the road did not affect male and female bodies equally. Men, you observe, are given a *Homo* reason; but Women, a *Femina* reason, because they are not fully human.

Or take the sniggering dishonesty that accompanies every mention of trousers. The fact is that, for *Homo*, the garment is warm, convenient and decent. But in the West (though not in Mohammedan countries or in China) *Vir* has made the trouser his prerogative, and has invested it and the skirt with a sexual significance for physiological reasons which are a little too plain for gentility to admit. (Note: that the objection is always to the closed knicker or trouser; never to open drawers, which have a music-hall significance of a different kind.) It is this obscure male resentment against interference with function that complicates the simple *Homo* issue of whether warmth, safety, and freedom of movement are desirable qualities in a garment for any creature with two legs. Naturally, under the circumstances, the trouser is *also* taken up into the whole *Femina* business of attraction, since *Vir* demands that a woman shall be *Femina* all the time, whether she is engaged in *Homo* activities or not. If, of course, *Vir* should take a fancy to the skirt, he will appropriate it without a scruple; he will wear the houppelande or the cassock if it suits him; he will stake out his claim to the kilt in Scotland or in Greece. If he chooses (as he once chose) to deck himself like a peacock in the mating season, that is *Vir's* right; if he prefers (as he does to-day) to affront the eye with drab colour and ridiculous outline, that is *Homo's* convenience. Man dresses as he chooses, and Woman to please him; and if Woman says she ever does otherwise, he knows better, for she is not human, and may not give evidence on her own behalf.

Probably no man has ever troubled to imagine how strange his life would appear to himself if it were unrelentingly assessed in terms of his maleness; if everything he wore, said, or did had to be justified by reference to female approval; if he were compelled to regard himself, day in day out, not as a member of society, but merely (*salvâ reverentiâ*) as a virile member of society. If the centre of his dress-consciousness were the cod-piece, his education directed to making him a spirited lover and meek paterfamilias; his interests held to be natural only in so far as they were sexual. If from school and lecture-room, Press and pulpit, he heard the persistent outpouring of a shrill and scolding voice, bidding him remember his biological function. If he were vexed by continual advice how to add a rough male touch to his typing, how to be learned without losing his masculine appeal, how to combine chemical research with seduction, how to play bridge without incurring the suspicion of impotence. If, instead of allowing with a smile that "women prefer cave-men," he felt the unrelenting pressure of a whole social structure forcing him to order all his goings in conformity with that pronouncement.

He would hear (and would he like hearing?) the female counterpart of Dr. Peck[1] informing him: "I am no supporter of the Horseback Hall doctrine of 'gun-tail, plough-tail and stud' as the only spheres for masculine action; but we do need a more definite conception of the nature and scope of man's life." In any book on sociology he would find, after the main portion dealing with human needs and rights, a supplementary chapter devoted to "The Position of the Male in the Perfect State." His newspaper would assist him with a "Men's Corner," telling him how, by the expenditure of a good deal of money and a couple of hours a day, he could attract the girls and retain his wife's affection; and when he had succeeded in capturing a mate, his name would be taken from him, and society would present him with a special title to proclaim his achievement. People would write books called, "History of the Male," or "Males of the Bible," or "The Psychology of the Male," and he would be regaled daily with headlines, such as "Gentleman-Doctor's Discovery," "Male-Secretary Wins Calcutta Sweep," "Men-Artists at the Academy." If he gave an interview to a reporter, or performed any unusual exploit, he would find it recorded in such terms as these: "Professor Bract, although a distinguished botanist, is not in any way an unmanly man. He has, in fact, a wife and seven children. Tall and burly, the hands with which he handles his delicate specimens are as gnarled and powerful as those of a Canadian lumberjack, and when I swilled beer with him in his laboratory, he bawled his conclusions at me in a strong, gruff voice that implemented the promise of his swaggering moustache." Or: "There is nothing in the least feminine about the home surroundings of Mr. Focus, the famous children's photographer. His 'den' is panelled in teak and decorated with rude sculptures from Easter Island; over his austere iron bedstead hangs a fine reproduction of the Rape of the Sabines." Or: "I asked M. Sapristi, the renowned chef, whether kitchen-cult was not a rather unusual occupation for a man. 'Not a bit of it!' he replied, bluffly. 'It is the genius that counts, not the sex. As they say in *la belle Ecosse*, a man's a man for

[1] Dr. Peck had disclaimed adherence to the *Kinder, Kirche, Küche* school of thought.

a' that'—and his gusty, manly guffaw blew three small patty pans from the dresser."

He would be edified by solemn discussions about "Should Men serve in Drapery Establishments?" and acrimonious ones about "Tea-Drinking Men"; by cross-shots of public affairs "from the masculine angle," and by irritable correspondence about men who expose their anatomy on beaches (so masculine of them), conceal it in dressing-gowns (too feminine of them), think about nothing but women, pretend an unnatural indifference to women, exploit their sex to get jobs, lower the tone of the office by their sexless appearance, and generally fail to please a public opinion which demands the incompatible. And at dinner-parties he would hear the wheedling, unctuous, predatory female voice demand: "And why should you trouble your handsome little head about politics?"

If, after a few centuries of this kind of treatment, the male was a little self-conscious, a little on the defensive, and a little bewildered about what was required of him, I should not blame him. If he traded a little upon his sex, I could forgive him. If he presented the world with a major social problem, I should scarcely be surprised. It would be more surprising if he retained any rag of sanity and self-respect.

"The rights of woman," says Dr. Peck, "considered in the economic sphere, seem to involve her in competition with men in the struggle for jobs." It does seem so indeed, and this is hardly to be wondered at; for the competition began to appear when the men took over the women's jobs by transferring them from the home to the factory. The mediæval woman had effective power and a measure of real (though not political) equality, for she had control of many industries—spinning, weaving, baking, brewing, distilling, perfumery, preserving, pickling—in which she worked with head as well as hands, in command of her own domestic staff. But now the control and direction—all the intelligent part—of those industries have gone to the men, and the women have been left, not with their "proper" *work* but with *employment* in those occupations. And at the same time, they are exhorted to be feminine and return to the home from which all intelligent occupation has been steadily removed.

There has never been any question but that the women of the poor should toil alongside their men. No angry, and no compassionate, voice has been raised to say that women should not break their backs with harvest work, or soil their hands with blacking grates and peeling potatoes. The objection is only to work that is pleasant, exciting or profitable—the work that any human being might think it worth while to do. The boast, "My wife doesn't need to soil her hands with work," first became general when the commercial middle classes acquired the plutocratic and aristocratic notion that the keeping of an idle woman was a badge of superior social status. Man must work, and woman must exploit his labour. What else are they there for? And if the woman submits, she can be cursed for her exploitation; and if she rebels, she can be cursed for competing with the male: whatever she does will be wrong, and that is a great satisfaction.

The men who attribute all the ills of *Homo* to the industrial age, yet accept it as the norm for the relations of the sexes. But the brain, that great and sole true Androgyne, that can mate indifferently with male or female and beget offspring upon itself, the cold brain laughs at their perversions of history. The period from which we are emerging was like no other: a period when empty head and idle hands were qualities for which a man prized his woman and despised her. When, by an odd, sadistic twist of morality, sexual intercourse was deemed to be a marital right to be religiously enforced upon a meek reluctance—as though the insatiable appetite of wives were not one of the oldest jokes in the world, older than mothers-in-law, and far more venerable than kippers. When to think about sex was considered indelicate in a woman, and to think about anything else unfeminine. When to "manage" a husband by lying and the exploitation of sex was held to be honesty and virtue. When the education that Thomas More gave his daughters was denounced as a devilish indulgence, and could only be wrung from the outraged holder of the purse-strings by tears and martyrdom and desperate revolt, in the teeth of the world's mockery and the reprobation of a scandalised Church.

What is all this tenderness about women herded into factories? Is it much more than an excuse for acquiescing in the profitable herding of men? The wrong is inflicted upon *Homo*. There are temperaments suited to herding and temperaments that are not; but the dividing lines do not lie exactly along the sexual boundary. The Russians, it seems, have begun to realise this; but are revolution and blood the sole educational means for getting this plain fact into our heads? Is it only under stress of war that we are ready to admit that the person who does the job best is the person best fitted to do it? Must we always treat women like Kipling's common soldier?

> *It's vamp and slut and gold-digger, and "Polly, you're a liar!"*
> *But it's "Thank-you, Mary Atkins" when the guns begin to fire.*

We will use women's work in wartime (though we will pay less for it, and take it away from them when the war is over). But it is an unnatural business, undertaken for no admissible feminine reason—such as to ape the men, to sublimate a sexual repression, to provide a hobby for leisure, or to make the worker more bedworthy—but simply because, without it all *Homo* (including *Vir*) will be in the soup. But to find satisfaction in doing good work and knowing that it is wanted is human nature; therefore it cannot be feminine nature, for women are not human. It is true that they die in bombardments, much like real human beings: but that we will forgive, since they clearly cannot enjoy it; and we can salve our consciences by rating their battered carcases at less than a man's compensation.[1]

Women are not human. They lie when they say they have human needs: warm and decent clothing; comfort in the bus; interests directed immediately to God and His universe, not intermediately through any child of man. They are far above man to inspire him, far beneath him to corrupt him; they have feminine minds and feminine natures, but their mind is not one with their nature like the minds of men; they have no human mind and no human nature. "Blessed be God," says the Jew, "that hath not made me a woman."

God, of course, may have His own opinion, but the Church is reluctant to endorse it. I think I have never heard a sermon preached on the story of Martha and Mary that did not attempt, somehow, somewhere, to explain away its text. Mary's, of course, was the better part—the Lord said so, and we must not precisely contradict Him. But we will be careful not to despise Martha. No doubt, He approved of her too. We could not get on without her, and indeed (having paid lip-service to God's opinion) we must admit that we greatly prefer her. For Martha was doing a really feminine job, whereas Mary was just behaving like any other disciple, male or female; and that is a hard pill to swallow.

Perhaps it is no wonder that the women were first at the Cradle and last at the Cross. They had never known a man like this Man—there never has been such another. A prophet and teacher who never nagged at them, never flattered or coaxed or patronised; who never made arch jokes about them, never treated them either as "The women, God help us!" or "The ladies, God bless them!"; who rebuked without querulousness and praised without condescension; who took their questions and arguments seriously; who never mapped out their sphere for them, never urged them to be

[1] This last scandal did in the end outrage public opinion and was abolished.

feminine or jeered at them for being female; who had no axe to grind and no uneasy male dignity to defend; who took them as he found them and was completely unself-conscious. There is no act, no sermon, no parable in the whole Gospel that borrows its pungency from female perversity; nobody could possibly guess from the words and deeds of Jesus that there was anything "funny" about woman's nature.

But we might easily deduce it from His contemporaries, and from His prophets before Him, and from His Church to this day. Women are not human; nobody shall persuade that they are human; let them say what they like, we will not believe it, though One rose from the dead.

LIVING TO WORK

(*Written for Broadcasting*)

WHEN I LOOK AT THE WORLD—not particularly at the world at war, but at our Western civilisation generally—I find myself dividing people into two main groups according to the way they think about work. And I feel sure that the new world after the war will be satisfactory or not according to the view we are all prepared to take about the work of the world. So let us look for a moment at these two groups of people.

One group—probably the larger and certainly the more discontented—look upon work as a hateful necessity, whose only use is to make money for them, so that they can escape from work and do something else. They feel that only when the day's labour is over can they really begin to live and be themselves. The other group—smaller nowadays, but on the whole far happier—look on their work as an opportunity for enjoyment and self-fulfilment. They only want to make money so that they may be free to devote themselves more single-mindedly to their work. Their work and their life are one thing; if they were to be cut off from their work, they would feel that they were cut off from life. You will realise that we have here a really fundamental difference of outlook, which is bound to influence all schemes about work, leisure and wages.

Now the first group—that of the work-haters—is not made up solely of people doing very hard, uninteresting and ill-paid work.

It includes a great many well-off people who do practically no work at all. The rich man who lives idly on his income, the man who gambles or speculates in the hope of getting money without working for it, the woman who marries for the mere sake of being comfortably established for life—all these people look on money in the same way: as something that saves them from the curse of work. Except that they have had better luck, their outlook is exactly the same as that of the sweated factory hand whose daily work is one long round of soul-and-body-destroying toil. For all of them, work is something hateful, only to be endured because it makes money; and money is desirable because it represents a way of escape from work. The only difference is that the rich have already made their escape, and the poor have not.

The second group is equally mixed. It includes the artists, scholars and scientists—the people really devoured with the passion for making and discovering things. It includes also the rapidly-diminishing band of old-fashioned craftsmen, taking a real pride and pleasure in turning out a good job of work. It includes also—and this is very important—those skilled mechanics and engineers who are genuinely in love with the complicated beauty of the machines they use and look after. Then there are those professional people in whom we recognise a clear, spiritual vocation—a call to what is sometimes very hard and exacting work—those doctors, nurses, priests, actors, teachers, whose work is something more to them than a mere means of livelihood; seamen who, for all they may grumble at the hardships of the sea, return to it again and again and are restless and unhappy on dry land; farmers and farm-workers who devotedly serve the land and the beasts they tend; airmen; explorers; and those comparatively rare women to whom the nurture of children is not merely a natural function but also a full-time and absorbing intellectual and emotional interest. A very mixed bag, you will notice, and not exclusively confined to the "possessing classes," or even to those who, individually or collectively, "own the means of production."

But we must also admit that, of late, the second group of workers has become more and more infected with the outlook of the first group. Agriculture—especially in those countries where farming is prosperous—has been directed, not to serving the land, but to bleeding it white in the interests of money-making. Certain members of the medical profession—as you may read in Dr. Cronin's book, *The Citadel*—are less interested in preserving their patients' health than in exploiting their weaknesses for profit. Some writers openly admit that their sole aim is the manufacture of best-sellers. And if we are inclined to exclaim indignantly that this kind of conduct is bad for the work, bad for the individual, and bad for the community, we must also confess that we ourselves—the ordinary public —have been only too ready to acquiesce in these commercial standards, not only in trade and manufacture, but in the professions and public services as well.

For us, a "successful" author is one whose sales run into millions; any other standard of criticism is dismissed as "highbrow." We judge the skill of a physician or surgeon, not by his hospital record, but by whether or not he has many wealthy patients and an address in Harley Street. The announcement that a new film has cost many thousands of pounds to make convinces us that it must be a good film; though very often these excessive production costs are evidence of nothing more than graft, incompetence and bad organisation in the studios. Also, it is useless to pretend that we do not admire and encourage the vices of the idle rich so long as our cinemas are crowded with young men and women gaping at film-stars in plutocratic surroundings and imbecile situations and wishing with all their hearts that they too could live like the heroes and heroines of these witless million-dollar screen stories. Just as it is idle to demand selfless devotion to duty in public servants, so long as we respect roguery in business, or so long as we say, with an admiring chuckle, about some fellow citizen who has pulled off some shady deal with our local borough authorities, that "Old So-and-so is hot stuff, and anybody would have to get up early to find any flies on *him*."

We have *all* become accustomed to rate the value of work by a purely money standard. The people who still cling to the old idea that work should be served and enjoyed for its own sake are diminishing and—what is worse—are being steadily pushed out of the control of public affairs and out of contact with the public. We find them odd and alien—and a subservient journalism (which we encourage by buying and reading it) persuades us to consider them absurd and contemptible. It is only in times of emergency and national disaster that we realise how much we depend upon the man who puts the integrity of his job before money, before success, before self—before all those standards by which we have come to assess the value of work.

Consequently, in planning out our post-war economic paradise, we are apt to concentrate exclusively on questions of hours, wages and conditions, and to neglect the really fundamental question whether, in fact, we want work to be something in which a man can enjoy the exercise of his full natural powers; or merely a disagreeable task, with its hours as short as possible and its returns as high as possible, so that the worker may be released as quickly as possible to enjoy his life in his leisure. Mind, I do not say for a moment that hours, wages and conditions ought not to be dealt with; but we shall deal with them along different lines, according as we believe it right and natural that men should work to live or live to work.

At this point, many of you will be thinking: "Before we can do anything about this, we must get rid of the capitalist system." But the much-abused "system" is precisely the system that arises when we think of work in terms of money-returns. The capitalist is faithfully carrying to its logical conclusion the opinion that work is an evil, that individual liberty means liberty to emancipate one's self from work, and that whatever pays best is right. And I see no chance of getting rid of "the system," or of the people who thrive on it, so long in our hearts we accept the standards of that system, envy the very vices we condemn, build up with one hand what we pull down with the other, and treat with ridicule and neglect the people who acknowledge a less commercial—if you like, a more religious— conception of what work ought to be.

But now we are faced with a big difficulty. Suppose we decide that we want work to provide our natural fulfilment and satisfaction, how are we to manage this in an age of industrial machinery? You will have noticed that all the workers in my second group possess three privileges. (1) Their work provides opportunity for individual initiative. (2) It is of a kind that, however laborious it may be in detail, allows them to view with satisfaction the final results of their labour. (3) It is of a kind that fits in with the natural rhythm of the human mind and body, since it involves periods of swift, exacting energy, followed by periods of repose and recuperation, and does not bind the worker to the monotonous, relentless, deadly pace of an inhuman machine.

The factory hand has none of these advantages. He is not required to show initiative, but only to perform one unimaginative operation over and over again. He usually sees no step in the process of manufacture except that one operation, and so can take no interest in watching the thing he is making grow to its final perfection; often, indeed, it is some useless thing that only exists to create profits and wages, and which no worker could admire or desire for its own sake. Thirdly, it is the pace that kills—the subjection of the human frame to the unresting, unchanging, automatic movement of the machine. The other day, a journalist was talking to some miners. He says: "With one voice they told me that they think the machines are becoming monsters, draining their life-blood, and how they longed for the old days when they worked longer shifts, but with their hands, and the process of procuring the coal was less exhausting."

This last statement is very interesting, since it shows that the regulation of hours and wages cannot by itself do away with the difficulty about certain kinds of work. The economic solution will not solve this problem, because it is not really an economic problem at all, but a problem about human nature and the nature of work.

Some people are so greatly depressed by these considerations that they can see no way out of the difficulty except to do away with machines altogether, as things evil in themselves and destructive of all good living. But this is a counsel of despair. For one thing, it is not a practical proposition in the present state of things. Also, this suggestion takes no account of the real delight and satisfaction that the machines are capable of giving. It throws on the scrap-heap the skill and creative enthusiasm of the designer, the engineer's pride in his craft, the flying man's ecstasy in being air-borne, all the positive achievements of mechanical invention, and all those products—and they are many—which are actually *better* made by machinery than by hand. To renounce the machines means, at this time of day, to renounce the world and to retire to a kind of hermitage of the spirit. But society cannot be exclusively made of saints and solitaries; the average good citizen, like the average Christian, has to live *in* the world; his task is not to run away from the machines but to learn to use them so that they work in harmony with human nature instead of injuring or oppressing it.

Now, I will not attempt, in the last few minutes of a short broadcast, to produce a cut-and-dried scheme for taming machinery to the service of man. I will only say that I believe it can be done, and (since my opinion would not carry very much weight) that there are many people, with personal experience of factory conditions, who have already worked out practical proposals for doing it. But it can only be done if we ourselves—all of us—know what we want and are united in wanting the same thing; if we are all prepared to revise our ideas about what work ought to be, and about what we mean by "having a good time."

For there is one fact we must face. Victory is the only possible condition upon which we can look forward to a "good time" of any kind; but victory will not leave us in a position where we can just relax all effort and enjoy ourselves in leisure and prosperity. We shall be living in a confused, exhausted and impoverished world, and there will be a great deal of work to do. Our best chance of having a good time will be to arrange our ideas, and our society, in such a way that everybody will have an opportunity to work hard and find happiness in doing *well* the work that will so desperately need to be done.

HOW FREE IS THE PRESS?

(1941)

THAT WITHOUT A FREE PRESS there can be no free people is a thing that all free peoples take for granted; we need not discuss it. Nor will we at this moment discuss the restrictions placed upon the Press in time of war. At such times all liberties have to be restricted; a free people must see to it that when peace comes full freedom is restored. In the meantime, it may be wholesome to consider what that freedom is, and how far it is truly desirable. It may turn out to be no freedom at all, or even a mere freedom to tyrannise; for tyranny is, in fact, the uncontrolled freedom of one man, or one gang, to impose its will on the world.

When we speak of "the freedom of the Press," we usually mean freedom in a very technical and restricted sense—namely, freedom from direction or censorship by the Government. In this respect, the British Press is, under ordinary conditions, singularly free. It can attack the policy and political character of ministers, interfere in the delicate machinery of foreign diplomacy, conduct campaigns to subvert the Constitution, incite citizens to discontent and rebellion, expose scandals and foment grievances, and generally harry and belabour the servants of the State, with almost perfect liberty. On occasion, it can become a weapon to coerce the Government to conform to what it asserts to be the will of the people.

So far, this is all to the good. Occasionally, this freedom may produce disastrous hesitations and inconsistencies in public policy, or tend to hamper the swift execution of emergency measures; but, generally speaking, it works to secure and sustain that central doctrine of Democracy as we understand it—that the State is not the master but the servant of the people.

The Press, *as a whole*, and in this technical and restricted sense, is thus pretty free in a peaceful Britain. There is no shade of political opinion that does not somehow contrive to express itself. But if we go on to imagine that *any particular organ* of the Press enjoys the larger liberty of being a "forum of public opinion," we are gravely mistaken. Every newspaper is shackled to its own set of overlords and, in its turn, like the Unmerciful Servant, exercises a powerful bondage upon its readers and on the public generally. Indeed, we may say that the heaviest restriction upon the freedom of public opinion is not the official censorship *of* the Press, but the unofficial censorship *by* a Press which exists not so much to express opinion as to manufacture it.

The editorial policy of a popular daily is controlled by two chief factors. The first is the interest of the advertisers from whom it gets the money which enables it to keep up its large circulation. No widely circulated newspaper dare support a public policy, however much in the national interest, that might conflict with the vested interests of its advertisers. Thus, any proposal to control the marketing of branded goods (as, for example, of margarine in 1939) will be violently opposed, on the loftiest hygienic grounds, by the papers that carry the branded advertising. On the other hand, any product that refuses to pay the high advertising rates of a powerful national organ will be (again on the highest moral and hygienic grounds) denounced, smashed, and driven off the market; you are not allowed to use any product that dissociates itself from the advertising ring. All this is understandable, since a big circulation spells bankruptcy if the paper has to depend on its sales for its revenue. Every newspaper lives in a perpetual precarious balance: it *must* increase its sales to justify its advertising rates, and to increase its sales, it *must* sell itself far below the cost of production; but if it sells more copies than its advertising will pay for, it faces financial disaster. Consequently, the more widespread and powerful the organ, the more closely it has to subserve vested interests.

This means that the cheap daily paper, which goes everywhere and has most influence, is far less free than the more expensive weekly or monthly, which draws a higher proportion of its revenue from sales. Therefore it is only the comparatively rich who can afford to read independent expressions of opinion.

The second chief source of a newspaper's revenue is the wealth of the man or company that owns it; accordingly, its policy is largely determined by the personal spites and political ambitions of its proprietor. The failure, for example, of a great newspaper magnate to secure a government appointment may be the signal for the unleashing of a virulent campaign, in every organ which he controls, against the minister or the party which has disappointed his ambitions. The public, knowing nothing of the personal bias behind the attack and little of the vast network of control which ties up whole groups of the London and Provincial Press in the hands of a single man or combine, sees only that great numbers of (what appear to him to be) independent organs are united in a single, savage and persistent condemnation. Unless he is exceptionally shrewd, exceptionally cynical, or of exceptionally resolute and independent mind, he can scarcely help being influenced, and having his vote influenced; and it is odds that he will never realise the nature of the pressure brought to bear upon him.

But still more serious, because more subtle, than the control applied to individual papers by various kinds of interest is the control and censorship exercised by the Press upon the news and opinions which it disseminates. This control rests upon and exploits two basic assumptions about the public—(a) that they have not the wit to distinguish truth from falsehood; (b) that they do not care at all that a statement is false, provided it is titillating. Neither assumption is flattering; and indeed, between the language used privately by the late Lord Northcliffe about his British readers and the language used publicly by Hitler about his German readers there is very little to choose. Both assume that readers can be made to believe anything. The result is that accurate reporting, which used to be the pride of the old-fashioned independent newspaper, has largely given place to reporting which is at best slipshod and at worst tendentious.

I should like to illustrate, with quite trivial examples drawn from personal experience, the various ways by which both fact and opinion can be distorted, so that a kind of smear of unreality is spread over the whole newspaper page, from reports of public affairs down to the most casual items of daily gossip.

1. *Sensational Headline: False Emphasis: and Suppression of Context.* This year[1] at the Malvern Conference, I read a paper dealing with the theological grounds for the Church's concern with politics and sociology, with the complementary dangers of pietism and Cæsarism, and with the importance of Incarnation doctrine in this connection. Out of 8,000 words, some 250 dealt with the connection between Cæsarism and an undue emphasis placed on sexual, as contrasted with financial, morality. This quite subsidiary paragraph was reported everywhere, under sensational headlines, in such a manner as to convey that this passing allusion formed the whole subject-matter of my address. Out of the 8,000 words about theology, the reporters picked the only one which they presumed their readers capable of understanding—to wit, "fornication." You,

[1] 1941.

the reader, will appreciate the compliment. I will, however, add for your comfort that this report was not made (as you might well suppose) by a Pressman from your favourite paper, specially selected for his understanding of ecclesiastical affairs. All the distorted reports emanated from a News Agency; and the individual editors, when remonstrated with, were for the most part content to disavow responsibility. This is how you learn what happens at public meetings.

2. *Garbling*. This is the special accomplishment of the Press interviewer. During the production of my latest play, I was asked, "What were my plans for the future?" I replied that I never made plans; that I preferred writing plays to novels, though novels paid better; and that, financial considerations notwithstanding, if the opportunity to write a play were to present itself—for example, another commission for the Canterbury Festival—I should undoubtedly write it. This reply duly appeared in the Press, in the form: "Miss Sayers said she would write no more plays, except on commission."

Bland perversions of this kind, together with the interviewer's playful habit of making statements himself and attributing them to his victim, make reported interviews singularly unreliable reading. (One must allow for the Pressman's vivid imagination. I remember reading with interest that my eyes "glittered behind my glasses" when making some remark or other; since that particular interview was given by telephone, I could only conclude that the interviewer's own eyes must have been "double-magnifying gas microscopes of extra power.") But the last, best word on Press interviews has been written by "Q" in *From a Cornish Window*; those who believe that public characters say everything they are reported as saying should read it and take warning.

3. *Inaccurate Reporting of Facts*. Some time ago a daily paper reported that my flat had been broken into the previous day, and that I had returned from (I think they said) Oxford, in time to disturb the thieves. This was true enough, *except* that every detail was wrong. The date was three days earlier than alleged, I was not at Oxford but at the King's Garden Party, and the intruders had been disturbed, not by me, but most likely by the newspaper boy. The interest here lies in the probable reasons for the misstatements. The date had to be changed to conceal the fact that the news was already "cold"; and I was substituted for the boy, presumably for my greater snob-value. The altered date was a bad blunder—Buckingham Palace would have adorned the tale to so much better advantage.

4. *Plain Reversal of the Facts*. On a summons for unshaded lights,

a letter of mine was read to the Bench explaining that my servant had carefully drawn the curtains, but that there had proved, unfortunately, to be a defect in the curtains themselves. The local paper duly reported: "Miss Sayers said that a servant had forgotten to draw the curtains." (This was calculated to cause pain and distress to my servant—but why should anybody care?)

5. *Random and Gratuitous Invention.* Without consulting me at all, a small and gossipy paper recently informed its readers that two of my favourite hobbies were "gardening and keeping cats." I do not see why anybody should want to know my hobbies—but if they do it would surely be better to mention the right ones. This choice was peculiarly unfortunate. If there is anything I detest, it is gardening; and although my household always includes a necessary cat, which lives in the kitchen and is supposed to catch mice, I have little to do with it, except to remove it and its hairs from the chairs and cushions, and open the door for it from time to time under protest.[1]

6. *Deliberate Miracle-mongering.* It was recently reported in various local papers that, in a public address, I had delivered some 20,000 words in the space of an hour and a quarter. This would in any case have been impossible. Actually, the reporter *had had the full text of my speech in his hands*, and could have seen for himself that it consisted of almost exactly 8,000 words. The error was thus precisely 150 per cent., a useful figure on which to base one's estimate of truth in reporting.

Of these six main forms of misrepresentation, the first two are the most dangerous. There is no remedy against them. They do not come within the narrow range of the law of libel; for to misrepresent a man's attitude and opinions is no offence. Nor could one readily persuade a jury that a lie had been told about one, since a sort of formal veracity *in detail* is used to convey a totally false impression of the speaker's words *as a whole.* Consequently, it is next door to impossible to secure either correction or apology. Which brings us to:

7. *Flat Suppression.* Letters of protest may be written. These may be (*a*) ignored; (*b*) printed in full or in part, accompanied by an editorial comment to the effect that the words reported were actually said, and that the speaker must not expect to monopolise the whole of the paper's valuable space; (*c*) answered privately by the editor—a manœuvre that does nothing to correct the false impression left in the public mind. Only occasionally, and usually from a provincial

---

[1] Shortage of domestic staff has since constrained me to live on more intimate terms with the cat. But if he is a "hobby," then so are the handy-man and the "daily woman."

paper, does one receive full apology and correction. Let me quote, *honoris causâ*, a note written to me from an editor of the older school: "Thank you for your letter, which we thought it our duty to print . . . we try to preserve our reputation for balanced news." Here are three old-fashioned words, *duty, balance, reputation*: do they still represent what the reader demands, or expects, from Fleet Street?

To get misleading statements corrected entails, in any case, a heavy and exhausting effort of correspondence—for the falsehood may be syndicated all over the world overnight and appear simultaneously in several hundred papers. In addition, if one makes a fuss, or ventures to accuse the newspapers of lack of veracity, there always lurks in the background the shadow of a genteel blackmail. Any public person—writer, speaker, actor, politician—is subtly made to feel that if he offends the Press he will suffer for it.

No threat, of course, is openly uttered; but books and plays may be unfavourably noticed or silently ignored—allusions sneering, though not actually libellous, may crop up in the gossip columns—a thousand hints will be quietly conveyed that the Press can make or break reputations. Books which venture to criticise the Press are therefore rare; nor is it easy to find a paper honest enough to print an article on the subject.

Speeches may be made, of course, but they will not reach the wider public, for they will not be reported in full; only a carefully isolated sentence or so will find its way into the papers, under some such headline as: "Bishop Seeks to Muzzle Press," or "M.P. Attacks Press Liberty." Indeed, the slightest effort to hinder the irresponsible dissemination of nonsense is greeted by a concerted howl: "This is a threat to the Freedom of the Press!"

No wonder that within three days lately the Archbishop of York and a Minister of the Crown were heard to utter the same despairing cry in face of journalistic misrepresentation and indiscretion: "We cannot control the Press!"

The particular examples I have given are, you will say, of very small importance. True: that is what makes them so symptomatic and so disquieting. They do not show any direct wresting of the truth towards a propagandist end—against such attempts the reader may, with a little mental effort, efficiently arm himself. What they do clearly show is an all-pervading carelessness about veracity, penetrating every column, creeping into the most trifling item of news, smudging and blurring the boundary lines between fact and fancy, creating a general atmosphere of cynicism and mistrust.

He that is unfaithful in little is unfaithful also in much; if a common court case cannot be correctly reported, how are we to believe the reports of world-events? If an interviewer misinterprets the novelist whom we have all seen, what does he do with the foreign statesman whom we have never seen? If the papers can be convicted of False Emphasis, Garbling, Inaccuracy, Reversal of the Fact, Random Invention, Miracle-Mongering and Flat Suppression in cases where such distortions are of advantage to nobody, what are we to suppose about those cases in which vested interests are closely concerned? And, above all, what are we to make of the assumptions on which all this is based—that the reader is too stupid to detect falsehood and too frivolous even to resent it?

Decent journalists do not like the present state of affairs. Nor do the more responsible editors. But the number of editors and journalists who can maintain a high standard of "duty, balance, and reputation" in the face of pressure grows less day by day. It is difficult for any paper that presents its news soberly to maintain its circulation: perhaps it is true that every nation gets the Press it deserves.

But supposing the reader *does* care about accuracy, *does* resent contempt for his intelligence, *does* want the truth about what is said and done—what steps is he to take? How is he to get at the facts which are withheld; or smothered under these mountains of distortion and absurdity? How is he to make his will felt? Is he to write angry letters, or transfer his daily penny from one organ to another? Will anybody care if he does? They will care if he protests in sufficient numbers. But his penny is a small weapon to oppose against the vested interests and the pooled money of the great combines. His helplessness is a measure of the freedom which the Press enjoys—but is the reader free?

The common man has a vote in Parliament. He has a Parliamentary representative whom he can badger and heckle and whose tenure of office rests upon his consent. If he likes to make use of the machinery of a democracy, he can have questions asked in the House; in the last resort, he can destroy one government and make another. But there is no machinery by which he can control the organs which mould opinion. For that, his sole resource is a penny a day and his native wit and will. In time of crisis, the newspapers are first with the cry: "Let the people know the facts!" But perhaps Fact is a deity invoked by the people only in the last emergency when the easy gods of peace have failed them.

Studies in Sherlock Holmes

(*References to the Sherlock Holmes canon are to the two-volume edition published by John Murray.*)

HOLMES' COLLEGE CAREER

THE EVIDENCE AS TO HOLMES' COLLEGE career rests upon two short passages, occurring in the adventures of *The Gloria Scott* and *The Musgrave Ritual* respectively. Brief as they are, these passages contain more than one apparent contradiction, and present a curious and interesting series of problems to the critic.

The passage in *The Gloria Scott* is as follows:

"(Victor Trevor) was the only friend I made during the two years I was at college. I was never a very sociable fellow, Watson, always rather fond of moping in my rooms and working out my own little methods of thought, so that I never mixed much with the men of my year. Bar fencing and boxing, I had few athletic tastes, and then my line of study was quite distinct from that of the other fellows, so that we had no points of contact at all. Trevor was the only man I knew, and that only through the accident of his bull-terrier freezing on to my ankle one morning as I went down to chapel" (p. 375).

The passage in *The Musgrave Ritual* also purports to be Holmes' *ipse dixit*. It runs:

"When I first came up to London I had rooms in Montague Street . . . and there I waited, filling in my too abundant leisure time by studying all those branches of science which might make me more efficient. Now and again cases came in my way, principally through the introduction of old fellow students, for during my last years at the university there was a good deal of talk there about myself and my methods. The third of these cases[1] was that

[1] It is not clear whether Holmes means actually "my third case" or, more specifically, "the third case obtained by means of these introductions." The former interpretation has found greater favour with the critics, but the latter is at least possible, and offers more elbow-room to the student of Holmes chronology. See below, p. 137.

of the Musgrave Ritual. . . . Reginald Musgrave had been in the same college as myself, and I had some slight acquaintance with him. . . . In appearance he was a man of an exceedingly aristocratic type. . . . He was indeed a scion of one of the very oldest families in the kingdom. . . . Now and again we drifted into talk, and I can remember that more than once he expressed a keen interest in my methods. . . . For four years I had seen nothing of him, until one morning he walked into my room in Montague Street."

Tantalisingly meagre though they are, these two passages are of the utmost importance, since they are almost all that we have to go upon in establishing, not merely the educative and formative influences which presided over our greatest detective's youth, but also the actual date of his birth. It will, therefore, not be wasted labour if we examine them with particular attention, in the hope of answering these questions, viz:

- (A) Which was Holmes' university?
- (B) How long did his academic career last?
- (C) When did he matriculate?
- (D) In what year was he born?
- (E) What subject or subjects did he study?
- (F) Which was his college?
- (G) What did he do immediately after leaving college?

(A) Considering first that simple dichotomy which forms so complete and satisfying a disjunction of the academic universe, we have to ask ourselves: Was Holmes at (*a*) Oxford or Cambridge or (*b*) one of the others? Here, at least, we can speak with some measure of certainty. There is no doubt whatever that he passed a portion at any rate of his time at one of the older universities. It is not for one moment conceivable that Reginald Musgrave (whom Holmes could never even look at without connecting him with grey archways and mullioned windows) could, in the 'seventies, have been connected with any provincial place of learning. On this point, all the commentators are agreed.

Blakeney, however, in his thoughtful little work, *Sherlock Holmes: Fact or Fiction?* makes the interesting suggestion that, after two years at Cambridge, Holmes "preferred to gravitate to London," which thus "has claims to Holmes's student days." He bases this suggestion on the following facts: (1) that Holmes was "only two years at college," (2) that at the time of the *Gloria Scott* case he already had rooms in Town, (3) that during the (Cambridge) Long Vacation he was doing chemical research in London, (4) that as late as 1881 he was utilising the laboratories at Bart's, (5) that London was better suited to his "desultory studies" than one of the older universities, and (6) that Holmes speaks of "coming up" to London at some time before the affair of the Musgrave Ritual.

This theory, attractive as it is at first sight, will not, I think, hold water. Let us take Blakeney's points in order. Point (1) raises at once the great question of the discrepancy between Holmes' own two statements—namely, that whereas in the *Gloria Scott* account he declares that he was only two years at college, in the *Musgrave Ritual* account he speaks of his "last years" at the university. Blakeney's theory is apparently designed to reconcile these two conflicting statements, but, as we shall see, it does not do this and, in failing to do so, loses much of its reason for existence. Point (2) implies that Holmes' affiliation to London University began in the October of the same year that saw the adventure of the *Gloria Scott* (for if it does not mean this, it has no bearing on the matter). We shall find that to assume this involves us in some serious chronological difficulties. For the moment, however, it is enough to say that there is nothing to prevent a Cambridge undergraduate from taking rooms in London in order to pursue a course of reading in the long vacation, and that Holmes' narrative implies, on the whole, that at the end of his vacation he intended to return to the university from which he had come. This observation contains in itself the reply to Point (3). Point (4) seems to have little bearing on the question, since permission to use the laboratories could be obtained by a qualified research student from another university. Point (5) has some force, and it is by no means impossible that Holmes undertook some kind of post-graduate course in London in 1876 or 1877, but not (I think) at the early date which Blakeney suggests. Point (6) contains in itself its own best refutation. Blakeney admits that Holmes "came up" to London "seemingly after leaving the 'Varsity" and "settled down to a career," and he adds: "this surely indicates that hitherto he had dwelt mainly elsewhere." Now this means that Holmes' coming to London and his settling down to a career were synchronous, and that therefore they took place in the *Gloria Scott* year, which Blakeney himself places "not *less* than four years previous to *The Musgrave Ritual*" and more probably five years earlier. His own date (p. 47) is 1874, and this agrees with H. W. Bell's calculation that *The Musgrave Ritual* is to be placed in September, 1878. We thus find that Holmes (being at the same time *in statu pupillari*) "waited" in Montague Street for work to come his way, and filled in his "too abundant leisure time" with tudies, for *four years*, during which time he handled only two cases.[1] To this lengthy period he afterwards refers as "all those months of inaction." This is meiosis indeed! Twelve months, even eighteen months, might be so referred to, but surely, if he had really waited four solid years, he would have said so. No; we cannot possibly admit this hypothesis; Holmes cannot have come to London before 1876 at the earliest, and thus the theory of an undergraduate course in London falls to the ground, the phrase "came up" to London acquires only a metropolitan, not an academic significance, and the problem of the length of Holmes' university career remains unsolved.

And the problem is a very real one. It is not only that Holmes' own reported statements are ambiguous. There is also an awkward chronological difficulty, which will be better appreciated when we come to deal with a later part of the problem.

Setting, therefore, the question of Holmes' residence in London aside for the moment, we must consider the rival claims of Oxford and Cambridge. It is, I think, evident from the text that the friendship with Victor Trevor was made at one of the older universities, and not in London: the bulldog, the attendance at chapel and the reference to athletics as a major interest of university life all point to this conclusion; moreover, Mr. Trevor, "now in late life a J.P. and a landed proprietor," would doubtless wish to secure for his son just those social and educational advantages which he himself had missed and which, in those days, Oxford and Cambridge were alone considered to bestow.

It also appears likely that the friendship with Trevor preceded the acquaintanceship with Musgrave, since, in the one connection, Holmes is shown almost entirely friendless, whereas, in the other, he has so far imposed his personality on his surroundings as to occasion talk among the men about his methods.

The crucial point of the *Gloria Scott* paragraph is now clearly seen to be the bulldog. Father Knox has pointed out, with the unanswerable cogency which belongs to inside knowledge, that the animal would not have been allowed inside the college gates. Blakeney replies that this objection is not insuperable, since Holmes was probably living "out" at the time, and may have been bitten in the town. Now, if the university had been Oxford, and if Holmes had resided there for two years only, or if in any case the acquaintance with Trevor is to be placed in the *first two years* of Holmes' residence there, then this situation would have been altogether

[1] But see note, p. 134. In any case, it is evident that the cases were few and far between.

impossible. At Oxford, freshmen are at once allotted rooms in college; they reside there for two years, and only move out into lodgings in the town at the beginning of their third year of residence. At Oxford, therefore, the biting of Holmes while on his way to chapel through the streets of the town could not possibly have occurred before his third year—unless, indeed, we are to suppose that the word "morning" is a slip of Watson's, and that Holmes was so piously minded as to attend voluntary evening chapels, which from his habits of mind and thought appears unlikely.

At Cambridge, however, the system is different.[1] There, the freshman is usually accommodated with lodgings in the town during his first year and even (if the college lists are full) during his second year also. It is at once obvious that this system makes it very much more difficult for a man of solitary habits and reserved disposition to make friends among the men of his own year than the Oxford system. It would therefore be quite in accordance with probability that Holmes should have remained friendless during his first two years at Cambridge, and it seems possible that what he actually said to Watson was something like this: "He was the only friend I made in my first two years at Cambridge, when I was living out of college." Watson, either misunderstanding this at the time, or noting with hasty abbreviation, "Only friend—2 yrs. out college," and subsequently misreading "out" as "at," may have introduced here the complication which has proved so puzzling to commentators. The possibility that "at" is a mistake for "in"— referring to a friendless two years spent in residence inside the college—is tempting, but must, I think, be discounted. It is the first two years that would be friendless, not the last two; and a *first* two years within the college walls would imply residence at Oxford: a hypothesis which we have already been obliged to set aside on account of the bulldog episode.

But even if we allow the expression to have been correctly reported, it is quite within the bounds of possibility that the contradiction between Holmes' statement here and his further statement in *The Musgrave Ritual* is only apparent. We shall consider

[1] "The Student's first business on arriving at Cambridge will be to procure himself rooms. The Tutor will inform him whether any sets of rooms within the College itself are vacant, and if not, which of the licensed houses in the town can admit him. . . . At some of the Colleges room is made within the walls for the freshmen, by expelling the questionists, i.e. undergraduates of the fourth year, into lodgings; but in the majority the freshmen are served last as being the last arrived, and in many cases have to wait more than one term for admittance. . . . Nor . . . does the student in lodgings taste the genuine flavour of College-life; besides, he will generally be at a greater distance from Chapel, Hall, and the Lecture-rooms" (*Student's Guide to Cambridge*, 1874).

this point more carefully when we come to examine the question of Holmes' academic studies. The really important matter is that Holmes was more friendless during the period of his acquaintance with Trevor than during his "last years," and that this friendless period coincided with his residence outside the college; this state of things necessarily indicates that he was at Cambridge and not at Oxford.

(B) We now come to the important question of the length of Holmes' residence at Cambridge. The theory that he was only there for two years, adopted by Blakeney on the strength of the *Gloria Scott* passage, seems to be contradicted by the expression "my last years at the University" in *The Musgrave Ritual*. We must now see whether these two statements[1] can be reconciled.

Now, from various considerations,[1] it appears practically certain that the date 1878 for the adventure of *The Musgrave Ritual* is correct. At this period, Holmes had seen nothing of Reginald Musgrave for four years, i.e. since 1874. Since their acquaintance was but slight, it is improbable that they had met since leaving the University; therefore both Holmes and Musgrave were still at Cambridge in 1874. When and at what age did Musgrave go down? Certainly not later than 1876, for he himself states that since his father's death in that year he had been managing his own estates, which he could scarcely have done had he still been an undergraduate. In addition to this, he is "member for his district." Bearing this in mind, we shall be inclined to assign the earliest possible date and the latest probable age for his leaving college. If he had gone up to Cambridge in the usual way at about eighteen, remained for the usual period of three years and visited Holmes four years later, he would be at most twenty-five or twenty-six at the date of the *Musgrave Ritual*, and it seems unlikely that he would be a Member of Parliament at a much earlier age than that. We will therefore suppose that he went down not later than June, 1874.

We must now consider to what extent his college career overlapped that of Sherlock Holmes. From the description given of him (his aristocratic appearance, dandified dress, grave, quiet manner and so forth), we shall not be disposed to conclude that he was the kind of person who would have "drifted into talk" with a freshman of his own college, still less have "sucked up" (as the expression goes) to senior men in his own first year. The same thing may be said of Holmes himself. "Distrust the fresher who goes about with third-year men" is a commonplace of university philosophy. It appears highly probable that between these two students

[1] Admirably set forth by H. W. Bell, *Sherlock Holmes and Dr. Watson*, p. 12.

there was not more than a year or so either way: and in fact, Holmes' own remarks in the *Gloria Scott* story (p. 375) rather imply that if he could not mix much with the men of his own year he would not and did not mix with any others. For these reasons, I find it impossible to accept Bell's suggestion that Holmes went up in 1873, while Musgrave went down in 1874. It seems more likely that at this time both were senior men, Holmes in his third year and Musgrave in his third or fourth.

It is implied that Musgrave visited Holmes in consequence of the "talk" at the University about his detective methods. This talk took place during Holmes' "last years," and, had he not gone up till 1873, would have to be dated forward to 1875 or 1876, that is, one or two years after Holmes' last meeting with Musgrave. Although it is possible that Musgrave had heard about them from men who left college later than himself, it seems more likely that he had personally taken part in these discussions; this statement therefore affords additional proof that Musgrave and Holmes were contemporaries.

(C, D). We thus find ourselves obliged to put back Holmes' matriculation to October 1871,[1] in order to make him a third-year man in June 1874. Since he cannot well have been less than eighteen at the former date, this gives us either 1853 or late 1852 as the year of his birth, at latest. That it cannot have been very much earlier is suggested by the fact that in August, 1914, he is described as being sixty years of age (p. 1,076). This calculation agrees sufficiently well with that of Blakeney (*op. cit.*, p. 3), who offers 1852–3, with a slight preference for 1852;[2] Bell's date of 1854 (*op. cit.*, p. xx) is probably a trifle too late. We may adopt 1853 as a *via media*.

The extraordinary internal chronology of the adventure of *The Gloria Scott* prevents us from placing any great reliance upon it for the actual dating of Holmes' career. The dates given by Holmes[3] are clearly impossible. We are, therefore, again thrown back upon the external indications given in the introduction to that story and to *The Musgrave Ritual*. If we are correct in concluding that the "two years" mentioned in *The Gloria Scott* refer to Holmes' first two years at college, we must suppose that his acquaintance with Victor Trevor was formed between October, 1871, and June, 1873. The visit to Trevor's home took place in the first month of the Long Vacation, so that we have the choice between July, 1872, and July, 1873. There is but little to guide us, since Holmes does not say in

---

[1] See below, pp. 143 *sqq.*   [2] But see below, p. 144.
[3] As contained in Old Trevor's MS. and apparently accepted by Holmes.

140

what year of his residence the bulldog attacked him, nor how long it was before his friendship with Trevor ripened sufficiently to permit of an invitation. The fact that Holmes was engaged during the Vacation in chemical researches in London, together with the reticence placed by Trevor upon his advice and assistance, make the later date perhaps preferable. Bell gives 1875, but this is too late, based as his calculation is on the assumption that Holmes did not matriculate till 1873; he thinks, however, that the Long Vacation at the end of Holmes' second year is the likeliest; this brings it to 1873, the date selected by Blakeney.

(E) Some further light on the subject may be gained by a consideration of Holmes' probable course of studies at the University.

We know little of Holmes' parentage and early history. That he was of gentle birth is clear, and that his financial position was somewhat straitened is proved by the fact that at the time of his first meeting with Watson in 1881 he was unable to afford the full rent of the rooms in Baker Street. We may therefore conclude that his father was not a rich man, and it is quite possible that he came up to Cambridge with a scholarship at one of the smaller and less expensive colleges. If he was a Scholar, he would naturally be expected to aim at an Honours Degree, and, indeed, it would be surprising if a man of his exceptional ability were to content himself with a Pass.

At that date, the Triposes open to him were: Moral Sciences; Natural Sciences; Law and History; Theology; Mathematics; and Classics. Classics and Theology we may eliminate at once; nothing could be further from his line of thought. Nor can his occasional allusions to the ancient philosophers be taken to show that he had worked for his Tripos in the Moral Sciences. They suggest rather a desultory acquaintance than any profound study, while (as Father Knox has pointed out)[1] a certain looseness in his terminology suggests that, although possessing a powerful logical faculty, he was not altogether perfectly familiar with the processes of formal Logic.[2]

Mathematics may be excluded with equal certainty—not so much on account of the bent of his mind, which seems admirably adapted to the study, but because of his statement that his "line of study was quite distinct from that of the other fellows." At that period, as subsequently, the Mathematical Tripos at Cambridge was the largest and most famous of all. In 1874 the students taking Honours in Mathematics numbered 111 as against 71 in the next largest Tripos (Classics), and it would be absurd to suppose that Holmes

[1] *Essays in Satire*, p. 169.
[2] The Moral Sciences Tripos comprised three papers each in Moral and Political Philosophy, Mental Philosophy, Logic, and Political Economy.

would not have found mathematical fellow students in any one of the seventeen Cambridge colleges.

We are thus restricted to a choice between (*a*) Law and History, (*b*) Natural Sciences.

Law would, no doubt, have had considerable attractions for him. The old Law and History Tripos, abolished after 1874, comprised one paper each on Roman Law, Criminal Law, International Law, Legal "Problems," Jurisprudence and Real Property, and one on set books. The Law side was thus much stronger than the History side, which consisted only of one paper on Political History of Europe, and two on English History. It might be natural to ask: Could a student of history have been so ignorant of the period succeeding the Crimean War as to accept the ludicrous errors of date incident to Old Trevor's account of his mis-spent youth? The answer is, that it is perfectly possible. Owing to the singular academic theory that no historical event is of the slightest importance until it has well-nigh passed from living memory, the periods covered by the 1874 Tripos syllabus are confined to the years 1814–30 for Political History of Europe, and those between the Norman Conquest and the death of King John for English History, while the Special Period of English History is 1647–88. There is no general paper on either English or European History; so that it is more than likely that a man taking this Tripos would remain in abysmal ignorance of every historical event subsequent to 1830. The Law and History Tripos was not a very popular one, numbering thirty-four candidates in 1874, so that we cannot altogether exclude it from consideration.

But when we come to the Natural Sciences Tripos, the probability becomes so very much stronger that it almost amounts to a violent presumption of fact. This is, *a priori*, the Tripos which we should expect Holmes to take, having regard to his habit of mind and his known attainments. The scope of the Tripos was exceedingly wide, covering (1) Chemistry, (2) Mineralogy, including Crystallography, (3) Geology and Palæontology, (4) Botany, including Vegetable Anatomy and Physiology, (5) Comparative Anatomy and Physiology. Students were not, of course, expected to familiarise themselves with the whole of this monstrous syllabus; it was sufficient to show intimate knowledge of two, or even one, of the subjects in order to obtain Honours, while the scope of each subject was to some extent restricted by the syllabus. The twelve general papers set for the Tripos were framed to contain, each, one or more questions on each of the five subjects, so that on each and every day of the Examination a student seeking Honours might

142

devote himself to those branches of study with which he was best acquainted. From what we know of Holmes' interests, we should consider it likely that he would select Subjects 1 and 5. These subjects, moreover, carried the highest number of marks, being rated at 2,000 marks apiece; whereas only 1,200 marks were allotted to Geology, Botany and Mineralogy respectively.[1]

When we come to look at the numbers of students taking the Natural Sciences Tripos, probability becomes almost certainty. In 1874, only seventeen students faced this gargantuan set of examination papers (comprising in all 168 questions, exclusive of the practical papers in Anatomy and Physiology, and Physics, Chemistry and Mineralogy), and these students were divided among six colleges only, eight being from St. John's, four from Trinity, two from Caius and one each from Clare, Sidney Sussex and Pembroke. An undergraduate from any other college who took this Tripos might well observe that his "line of study was distinct from that of the other fellows."

The examination for the Natural Sciences Tripos[2] was at that time held in the Michaelmas Term and might be taken by any student who had already passed the Previous, not earlier than his eighth and not later than his tenth term after entering college, supposing that he had kept his statutory terms of residence. If, therefore, Holmes had matriculated in the Lent or Easter Term of 1871, he would have become eligible to take his Tripos in the Michaelmas Term of 1873. Since, however, we know that Holmes and Musgrave were together in 1874, it seems more reasonable to suppose that Holmes came up in the usual course at Michaelmas, 1871, and proceeded to his Tripos in his tenth term, viz. Michaelmas, 1874. Alternatively, it is possible that he came up in Lent or Easter, 1872,[3] and took his Tripos at Michaelmas, 1874, in his eighth term. In the latter case, his acquaintance with Victor Trevor would still date from 1872 or 1873, the affair of the *Gloria Scott* (1873) occurring when he had been four or five terms in residence. If we accept this hypothesis, we are able to reconcile the conflicting statements of the *Gloria Scott* and *Musgrave Ritual*, by reckoning eight terms (spread over the three years 1872, 1873, 1874) in the one case as "roughly" two years, and in the other as "roughly" three years.

[1] Geology and Palæontology may be definitely excluded from Holmes' studies. It would be difficult to take a Tripos in these subjects without being aware that the earth went round the sun (*Study in Scarlet*, p. 16).

[2] As also for Law and History.

[3] This practice of coming up in the middle of the Academic year, though unusual, and discouraged by the University authorities, was occasionally adopted from motives of economy.

This would also enable us to accept Bell's birth-year of 1854. See, further, the conclusion reached in (b) below.

We are now in a position to attempt a more precise chronology of Holmes' academic career. Possible alternative dates are inserted within brackets:

1853 (late 1852 or early 1854)	Birth of Sherlock Holmes.
1871, October (1872, January or April)	Holmes goes up to Cambridge.
1872 (1873)	Holmes, while still living "out," makes the acquaintance of Victor Trevor.
1873 (1872), early July . .	Holmes visits the Trevors.
1873 (1872), late September or early October . . .	Death of Old Trevor; conclusion of the *Gloria Scott* adventure. Trevor goes down.
1873 (1872), October . .	Holmes moves into rooms in College and becomes acquainted with Reginald Musgrave. (See below (a).)
1874, December (March)[1] .	Musgrave takes his Tripos and goes down.
1874, November–December .	Holmes takes his Tripos, either going down immediately or remaining up to complete a second course of studies. (See below (b).)
1875–6	Holmes engages in other studies. (See below (G).)
1876	Holmes takes up residence in London in Montague Street.
1878, September . . .	*The Musgrave Ritual.*

(a) It is not perfectly clear whether or not Victor Trevor belonged to the same college as Holmes.[2] It is probable that he was a man of Holmes' own year or of the year immediately above him. In the latter case, Trevor would, in the ordinary course of events, be going down in 1873, and, if they both belonged to the same college, Holmes may have succeeded to Trevor's rooms. If, on the other hand, Trevor still had another year at the University, we may ask ourselves whether it was his account of Holmes' "methods" that started "talk" among the undergraduates. Attractive as this

[1] See below: Note on Reginald Musgrave.
[2] If so, he must have been cutting Chapel on the morning of his fateful meeting with Holmes, since the bulldog could not have formed part of the congregation.

theory is, it seems improbable that either Holmes or Trevor would have entered into public discussion of events so painful as those attending the decease of Trevor senior. It seems more likely that Trevor went down after his father's death, and that the "methods" were demonstrated in some other, and more trivial, connection.

(b) Having reached this point, our next step is obviously to examine the published lists of Cambridge Honours men for the period under review, to see how far they support our contentions. Unhappily, the name of Sherlock Holmes does not appear in the *Cambridge History of Triposes* for 1874, or for any other year; and we are forced to conclude, either that some accident prevented him from actually sitting for his Tripos or that the lists were compiled with a lack of accuracy very far from consonant with the dignity of an academic body. When we turn, however, to the *Book of Matriculations and Degrees*, we find that a T. S. Holmes, who matriculated at Sidney Sussex in the Michaelmas Term of 1871, was admitted to the Degree of Bachelor of Arts in the Michaelmas Term of 1875. It is true that the Christian names are given as "Thomas Scott," but the "Scott" may be an error, due possibly to transcription from the Tripos Class list, where the habit of translating Christian names, where possible, into Latin occasionally gives rise to confusion.[1] The date 1875 obviously refers to the actual date of taking the degree and not to the date of taking the Tripos, the thirteenth term after Matriculation being too late for the latter activity. If this entry refers to Sherlock Holmes, he must have allowed a year to elapse between taking the examination and presenting himself for the degree—a course which is not unusual.

(F) It is tempting to identify Holmes with the Sidney Sussex man who obtained a First Class in Natural Sciences in 1874. Unfortunately, the name differs, so that we have here either another error of nomenclature or a regrettable omission.

In this connection, we may examine the claims of Sidney Sussex to be Holmes' college. It is one of the smaller colleges, having only fifty undergraduates on its books in 1874, the only colleges with a smaller membership at that date being Magdalene (49), St. Catherine's (46), St. Peter's (45), Downing (40) and Queens' (37). Its room-rents were moderate, ranging from £7 to £16 p.a., as compared, on the one hand, with Clare (£3 to £15) and on the other, with Caius (£12 10s. to £25). It possessed a Laboratory, and offered, in addition to its Foundation Scholarships, twelve Junior Scholarships, on the Taylor Foundation, of £40 p.a., several

---

[1] As when Mr. G. (Giles) Brown appears as Mr. E. (Egidius) Brown, and the like.

of which were given in Natural Sciences. It also offered a Special Course in Natural Sciences, and in connection with this, an Annual Examination was held in Chemistry, Electricity and General Physics, carrying with it a prize to the value of £20, which was awarded each year if any candidate attained a high enough standard to merit it. It thus appears that, of all the Cambridge colleges, Sidney Sussex perhaps offered the greatest number of advantages to a man in Holmes' position, and, in default of more exact information, we may tentatively place him there. Even if Holmes is not actually to be identified with the Sidney Sussex man mentioned in the 1874 Tripos list, the fact that there was one other student in his year and college reading for the same Tripos does not necessarily conflict with his statement that his line of study was distinct from that of the other fellows; the "other fellow" may have specialised in Botany or Mineralogy, and may, in addition, have been a disagreeable or rumbustious person with whom Holmes would not care to associate. Apart from the special facilities in Nat: Sci:, the chief interests of the College appear to have been mathematical, while a large number of its scholars and exhibitioners were drawn from the sons of the clergy and from certain specified schools. These men would undoubtedly have interests in common, from which Holmes might find himself excluded.

(G) The last question that remains to be decided is: What did Holmes do between taking his Tripos in November–December, 1874, and coming up to London in 1876? It is barely possible that he remained for another year at Cambridge to complete a second course of study—possibly in medicine. The fact (if it is a fact) that he did not take his B.A. till 1875 rather suggests, however, that he was elsewhere, and it seems exceedingly probable that he spent some time abroad. We know that he was able to quote German (*Sign of Four*, pp. 192, 271) and that at sundry periods in his career he undertook investigations in France (*French Government Case*, etc.) and Italy (*The Vatican Cameos*, etc.) and conducted negotiations with various foreign agents; and it seems impossible that he should have transacted all this delicate and important business with the aid of interpreters. The suggestion that he learnt to speak modern languages with the requisite fluency either at his public school or at the University will not hold water for a moment. In all probability he passed the year 1875 studying chemistry and languages at a German university, with vacation trips to France and Italy, returning to England in December to take his B.A. and then proceeding (perhaps after a short holiday at home) to London to wait for clients in Montague Street.

BIBLIOGRAPHY

Cambridge History of Triposes, 1854–88; *Cambridge Book of Matriculations and Degrees, 1850–1900*; *The Students' Guide to the University of Cambridge*, 1866 and 1874 edns.

NOTE ON REGINALD MUSGRAVE

To the observations already made about this young man, we may add the following:

Although of the highest social position, there is no mention of his ever having been at a public school, and he states that he learnt trigonometry with his "old tutor." The trigonometry would be required for his "Little-Go" if he aspired to Honours in any Tripos, and was no doubt studied for this purpose, so that he probably went straight to College from a course of private tuition at home. This exclusiveness would account sufficiently for his choice of a small college, where he could work hard and be free from the social pressure of public-school coteries. The choice of Oliver Cromwell's college is perhaps curious in a man of such Royalist tendencies, but this objection is of minor importance.

Since he was destined for a political career, he very possibly read the Law and History Tripos. In this case, he would go up in October, 1871, and take his Tripos at the same time as Holmes, viz. December, 1874. This fits the other data very well. In October, 1878, Holmes would not have seen him for three years and ten months —roughly "four years." The theory receives some support from Musgrave's acquaintance with seventeenth-century spelling and his interest in the period of the Great Rebellion, which was, as we have seen, the Special Period for the Law and History Tripos, 1874.

On the other hand, these interests may be referred to his family traditions, and his Tripos may have been Classical or Mathematical. The examinations for these were held in the Lent Term and could be taken not earlier than the ninth term of residence. In that case, Musgrave probably matriculated some time between October, 1870, and April, 1871, and would thus be about one year senior to Holmes, going down in March, 1874, nine months before him.

147

DR. WATSON'S CHRISTIAN NAME

A Brief Contribution to the Exegetical Literature of Sherlock Holmes

It has always been a matter of astonishment to Dr. Watson's friends, and perhaps of a little malicious amusement to his detractors, to observe that his wife[1] apparently did not know her own husband's name. There can be no possible doubt that Watson's first Christian name was John. The name "John H. Watson" appears, conspicuously and in capital letters, on the title-page of *A Study in Scarlet*,[2] and it is not for one moment to be supposed that Watson, proudly contemplating the proofs of his first literary venture, would have allowed it to go forth into the world under a name that was not his. Yet in 1891 we find Watson publishing the story of *The Man with the Twisted Lip*, in the course of which Mrs. Watson addresses him as "James."

Mr. H. W. Bell (*Sherlock Holmes and Dr. Watson*, p. 66, n. 2) has been unable to account for this, and despairingly suggests that it is a mere printer's error. "Watson," he remarks, with much truth, "was a very careless reader of proof." But if he had read the proofs *at all*, this particular error could not have failed to catch his eye. A man's own name is a subject on which he is sensitive; nothing is more exasperating than to be "called out of one's name." Moreover, in December, 1891, Mary Watson was still alive. Tenderly devoted as she was to her husband, she could not have failed to read his stories attentively on publication in the *Strand Magazine*, and she would have undoubtedly drawn his attention to an error so ridiculous and immediately reflecting on herself. In the month immediately preceding, the Doctor had made another trivial slip in connection with his wife's affairs; he said that during the period of the adventure of *The Five Orange Pips* Mrs. Watson was visiting her mother. Mrs. Watson, who was, of course, an orphan (*Sign of Four*), evidently took pains to point out this error and see that the careless author made a note of it; for on the publication of the

[1] His first wife, and only true love, Mary, *née* Morstan. There is a conspiracy afoot to provide Watson with as many wives as Henry VIII, but, however this may be, only one is ever mentioned by him and only one left any abiding memory in his heart.

[2] It also appears, plainly marked in capitals, at the foot of the sketch-plan illustrating *The Priory School*.

collected *Adventures* in 1892 the word "mother" is duly corrected to "aunt."[1] On such dull matters as dates and historical facts the dear woman would offer no comment, but on any detail affecting her domestic life she would pounce like a tigress. Yet the name "James" was left unaltered in all succeeding editions of the story.

How are we to explain this?

The solution is probably to be sought in a direction which has been too little explored by the commentators. In fact, the whole subject of Dr. Watson's second Christian name has been treated with a levity and carelessness which are a positive disgrace to scholarship.

Mr. S. C. Roberts (*Dr. Watson*, p. 9) suggests, without an atom of evidence, that Watson's mother was "a devout woman with Tractarian leanings," merely in order to presume that her son was named "John Henry" after the great Newman himself. If there were, in Dr. Watson's character, the slightest trace of Tractarian sympathies, or even of strong anti-Tractarian sympathies, the suggestion might carry some weight, for no one could be brought up in an atmosphere of Tractarian fervour without reacting to it in one way or another. But Watson's religious views remain completely colourless. Of Holmes' beliefs we know little, but of Dr. Watson's, nothing. The hypothesis is purely frivolous.

Mr. H. W. Bell, with his wonted scholarly caution, rejects the Newman theory. "It must be objected," he says (*Sherlock Holmes and Dr. Watson, loc. cit.*), "that Newman had become a Catholic in 1845, seven years before the date which Mr. Roberts proposes for Watson's birth. If Mrs. Watson had indeed had . . . Tractarian leanings . . . she would hardly have named her son after the illustrious convert." But Mr. Bell makes no effort to solve the problem himself, although this observation actually forms part of his note about the name "James." The true solution was staring him in the face, and if he had given the matter proper attention he must have seen it. But he dismissed "James" as a typographical error and went on his way, leaving the Watsons still enveloped in a cloud of ridicule.

Mr. T. S. Blakeney behaves still more absurdly. Postulating a composite James-John authorship, he calls for a J. M. Robertson to "sift the accretions of the pseudo-Watson from the core of matter deriving solely from the hand of the veritable John Henry"—forgetting that John *Henry* Watson is even more conjectural than *Jesus*

[1] It appears from this that Watson, with a shyness not uncommon in authors, did not show his wife either his manuscript or his proofs. After publication he would probably leave the *Strand* carelessly lying about the house to be dutifully perused by Mary, to his deprecatory astonishment.

Barabbas,[1] and thus making the fabulous name into a guarantee of the genuine identity. Illogicality could go no further.[2]

There is only one plain conclusion to be drawn from the facts. Only one name will reconcile the appellation James with the initial letter H. The doctor's full name was John Hamish Watson.

Hamish is, of course, the Scottish form of James. There is no reason to feel any surprise that Dr. Watson should bear a Scottish name. Sturdily and essentially English as he was, he may well, like most English people, have had a Scottish ancestor in his family tree. The English are probably the only people in the world who actually make a boast of mongrel ancestry. The words "hundred per cent. English" are never heard on true English lips, for the English know well enough that their cross-breeding is their strength. Scotsmen, Welshmen, Irishmen, Jews cling to the purity of their descent, realising that to blend their nationality is to lose it. But English blood is so strong that one drop of it will make the whole blend English. A hundred Scottish ancestors, nay, even a Scottish mother, would in no way affect the indomitable Englishry of Dr. Watson.

In fact, there is some slight evidence for a Scots strain in Watson. It may not be mere coincidence that led Holmes (a shrewd student of national character) to select the adjective "pawky" for the vein of humour which Watson displayed during the adventure of *The Valley of Fear* and which took his distinguished friend a little aback. Watson's mother may have been a Scot—not, I think, a Highland woman, but a native of Eastern Scotland[3]—and it may have pleased her to give a Scottish name to her son.

But there is no real need to assume Scottish descent to explain a Scottish name. The English, with their romantic love of the outlandish, their tendency to concoct a mixed genealogy for themselves, and their incurable disdain for other people's racial sensitiveness, are notorious for their habit of annexing foreign names, merely because they think them pretty or poetical. The suburbs of London swarm with Douglases and Donalds, Malcolms and Ians, whose ancestors never crossed the border, with Patricks and Brians and

[1] For the complicated structure of deduction built by Drews and others upon this highly disputable reading, see Thorburn, *Mythical Interpretation of the Gospels*, pp. 264 *sqq.*

[2] It is only justice to add that Mr. S. C. Roberts lost no time in pointing out this lamentable confusion between "objective data and legitimate surmise" and deprecating it with equal firmness and courtesy (*Observer*, October 30th, 1932).

[3] The true Highlander is a Celt—quick-tempered, poetical, and humourless—everything that Watson was not. Dourness and pawkiness belong to the Aberdeen side of the country.

Sheilas who owe nothing to Erin, with Gwladyses whose names are spelled according to fancy and not to inheritance, and with other exotics still more remote. The combination John Hamish Watson has nothing about it that need disconcert us.

Nor is it at all unusual for a wife to call her husband by his second name, in preference to his first. It is a pretty thought that he should be known to her by a name which is not the common property of the outside world. Possibly Mrs. Watson did not care for the name John. It was painfully connected in her mind with Major John Sholto, who had helped to ruin her father and bring about his death. "Johnnie" would be open to the same objection; besides, no one with any sense of the fitting would call Dr. Watson "Johnnie." There seems to be nothing specially objectionable about "Jack," but it may have seemed to her too flippant and jaunty. The probability, however, is that she preferred to cut out all association with "John." There remained the choice between "Hamish" and a pet-name. "Hamish" seemed to her perhaps a little highfalutin. By playfully re-Englishing it to "James" she found for her husband a pet-name which was his own name as well; a name by which no one else would think of calling him, a name free from the tiresome skittishness of the ordinary pet-name, and a name eminently suitable to his solid and sober character.[1]

It would be natural enough that Dr. Watson, accustomed for over three years to being called "James" by his wife, should automatically incorporate the name into his story when reproducing the dialogue between his Mary and himself—forgetting that, to the uninstructed reader, it might present an odd appearance. Nor would Mrs. Watson correct it. To her, the doctor was "her James"; that she should be supposed to call him by any other name would seem to her unnatural, almost improper. Smilingly she perused the pages of the *Strand*, delighted to recognise herself and her home life accurately portrayed in all the glory of print.

[1] An interesting parallel case of the interchangeability of "James" and "Hamish" occurs in Mrs. Wood's novel, *The Channings*: "The eldest son of the family, James; or, as he was invariably styled, Hamish." This book was extremely popular in the 'nineties, achieving its hundred-and-fortieth thousand in 1895, and may actually have suggested the idea to Mrs. Watson.

DR. WATSON, WIDOWER

Startling revelations about the private lives of the
great have always found the ear of the public pricked and twitch-
ing, and when, in 1931, Mr. S. C. Roberts first promulgated the
theory of Dr. Watson's second marriage, he created a literary
sensation only equalled in recent times by the exposure of Words-
worth's lapse into frailty and the publication of Charlotte Brontë's
love-letters to M. Héger. The first reaction was one of shocked
incredulity. Though there is nothing in itself irregular or repre-
hensible about the remarriage of a widower, we had for so long
been accustomed to look on the good doctor as indissolubly wedded
to the memory of Mary Morstan that the suggestion appeared in-
congruous and distasteful, as though we had detected him in a
breach of faith, or, at the very least, of decorum.

But the human mind is elastic. The first movement of repugnance
was of short duration. Within a year, the critics had accepted the
second marriage, and one of them—a prey to that fury of iconoclasm
which urges us to dance upon the fragments of a fallen idol and
grind them, if possible, to powder—had come forward with the
hypothesis of yet a third Watson marriage.

Quousque tandem . . .? Are a fourth and a fifth Mrs. Watson to be
disinterred from nameless graves in obscure paragraphs in order
that each fresh commentator may show himself a more avid ghoul
than his predecessors? Is every blank page in Watson's notebook
to be filled with a conjectural marriage certificate? Or is it possible
to check this itch of match-making and forbid, in the words of a
poet who owes his sole fame to the brutality of his critic, the "red
and raging eye" of imagination to pry further?

The evidence for *one* marriage after the death of Mary Watson
(*née* Morstan) in 1891–4 is, so far as it goes, substantial. It comes to
us under the hand of Sherlock Holmes himself, and is comprised
in the notorious passage in *The Blanched Soldier*: "I find from my
notebook that it was in January, 1903, just after the conclusion of
the Boer War. . . . The good Watson had at that time deserted me
for a wife, the only selfish action which I can recall in our association." The statement is categorical; the date is adduced from
Holmes' written notes and does not depend upon his memory;
moreover, it is confirmed by the internal testimony of the story

itself, which is concerned with events that could only have taken place during and after the Boer War. The one puzzling thing about the passage is Holmes' remark, "the only selfish action . . . in our association." The remark, which, in its sub-acid flavour, is characteristic of Holmes and bears every mark of authenticity, implies that the desertion of a friend in favour of any wife at all was a selfish action. If so, then the marriage of 1887 was selfish too, and the marriage of 1902 did not stand alone in its egotism. Some commentators have gone so far as to reject *The Blanched Soldier* altogether from the canon on the strength of this anomaly, while Mr. H. W. Bell, rushing to the opposite extreme, says: "This argument might be advanced . . . in denial of Watson's undoubted first marriage, in 1887. If Holmes' words do not imply that the marriage in 1902 was Watson's only marriage, there can be no reason to deny the possibility of a third."[1]

There may, however, have been special reasons which made the 1902 marriage peculiarly obnoxious to Holmes. What was excusable in the man of thirty-five[2] may have seemed merely wanton in the man of fifty. The breaking-up of the Baker Street household may have come as a heavier blow after twenty years of fellowship than it had done when that fellowship was only six years old. Holmes himself was not getting younger, and with increasing fame and increasing burdens may have felt the loneliness of genius more keenly than in his younger days. Always sensitive to any slight, he may have become querulous and crabbed when, in 1926, and at the advanced age of seventy-three,[3] he wrote the story of *The Blanched Soldier*. To the aged detective, looking back over the years, the long-distant 'eighties appeared as a remote and golden age when all was well with the world. He had forgiven the earlier desertion—had he not, after all, helped to bring the lovers together? —but the betrayal of twenty-three years back still irked him with a sense of loss and estrangement. It is quite possible that this desertion was the final blow that broke the back of Holmes' energy, for in the year 1903, he retired from practice, and the old connection with Baker Street was severed completely and for good.

For these reasons, I shall make no attempt to upset the 1902 marriage. If any one wishes to do so, he may perhaps take the line that the words "for a wife" are an error or an interpolation, and that what Holmes really wrote or dictated was "for a while" or

[1] *Sherlock Holmes and Dr. Watson*, p. 94.
[2] I accept Mr. S. C. Roberts' date of 1852 for the birth of Dr. Watson.
[3] It appears likely that Holmes was born between 1852 and 1854. On grounds given elsewhere (see my paper on "Holmes' College Career," p. 134), I am inclined to give my preference to 1853.

"for a whim" or "for his work," or some such phrase. It is note-worthy that, while Holmes always assumed an attitude of kindly tolerance towards Watson's early matrimonial preoccupations, and remained on a very friendly footing with the first Mrs. Watson,[1] he did, on one occasion, display a certain jealousy, not of Watson's wife, but of his work. " 'My practice——' I began. 'Oh, if you find your cases more interesting than mine——' said Holmes, with some asperity. 'I was going to say that my practice could get along very well for a day or two, since it is the slackest time in the year.' 'Excellent,' said he, recovering his good humour" (*Naval Treaty*, p. 515). And it is possible that the jealous feelings were not all on the one side. Watson remarks: "The relations between us in those latter days were peculiar. He was a man of habits, narrow and concentrated habits, and I had become one of them. As an institu-tion, I was like the violin, the shag tobacco, the old black pipe, the index books, and others perhaps less excusable. . . . I had uses. . . . His remarks could hardly be said to be made to me—many of them would have been as appropriately addressed to his bedstead—but none the less, having formed the habit, it had become in some way useful that I should register and interject. . . . Such was my humble rôle." The passage[2] should be studied carefully *in extenso*. It carries a suggestion that Watson, for all his loyalty, was suffering under a sense of grievance which was rather more than a passing pique. He found himself treated as a mere convenience, like the fiddle and the old pipe, to be picked up or cast aside as Holmes' fancy took him. His faithful heart was really wounded. He withdrew him-self and occupied his mind with his practice.[3] When the call comes, he answers it, but not quite with the old alacrity. "Was it for so trivial a question as this that I had been summoned from my work?" he asks himself, with a touch of bitterness.[4] Never before had he resented an intrusion on his "work." This was in 1903. His final departure from Baker Street had occurred in the previous year,

[1] "Holmes, for his part, maintained his respect for Mrs. Watson, and Mrs. Watson never failed to encourage her husband to collaborate with his old friend. . . . Holmes would descend upon Watson near midnight, ask for a bed, and carry off his friend by the eleven o'clock train; if an old friend of Watson was in trouble, his wife would acquiesce at once in his rushing off to Holmes," etc. (Roberts, *Dr. Watson*, p. 22). Holmes was also "occasionally persuaded" to pay the Watsons a friendly visit in their house near Paddington (*Engineer's Thumb*). If he "gave a most dismal groan" when Watson announced his engagement (*Sign of Four*, p. 270), he followed it up with a handsome compliment to the lady, and it is evident that his protest was made, and received, with the utmost good humour.

[2] *The Creeping Man*, p. 1,244.

[3] In *The Mazarin Stone*, dated in the same year as *The Creeping Man* (1903), he bears "every sign of the busy medical man."

[4] *The Creeping Man*, p. 1,245.

before the adventure of *The Illustrious Client*,[1] and on p. 1,095 there is a very significant juxtaposition of paragraphs.

> "I have not had occasion to mention Shinwell Johnson in these memoirs because I have seldom drawn my cases from the latter phases of my friend's career. During the first years of the century he became a valuable assistant. . . . It was to him that Sherlock Holmes now proposed to turn.
>
> "It was not possible for me to follow the immediate steps taken by my friend, for I had some pressing professional business of my own."

Was it perhaps Shinwell Johnson, that man of dubious antecedents, who caused a little friction between the two friends? Watson pointedly refrains from selecting many cases from those "latter phases" when Johnson was the chosen partner. When Holmes announces that "Shinwell Johnson might be a help," Watson suddenly remembers "pressing professional business" of his own. If he is not wanted, he will go away.

It is melancholy to find these traces of coldness and jealousy marring the perfection of such a friendship. Both men had reached a difficult period of middle age, when the emotional make-up tends to become unstable.[2] That there was no real change in Watson's affection is abundantly shown by his instant rush to his friend's side after the murderous attack by Baron Gruner's hirelings, and by his readiness to co-operate even with the detested Shinwell Johnson in order to set Holmes' mind at rest (*Illustrious Client*, p. 1,107). But the little rift within the lute had made its presence felt. Watson, in a final effort at self-assertion, left Holmes; left him for his own work, certainly, and for a second wife, not improbably. Holmes, the man of iron, lost heart and set *finis* to his life's work. The autumn of life had breathed its chilling influence on both of them.

So much for the 1902 marriage. But the marriage of 1896, proposed by Mr. H. W. Bell, rests on a very different basis of evidence, a basis almost as slender as that iota which split Christendom asunder.

Mr. Bell, with great frankness, admits as much. Let us quote his own words:

---

[1] September, 1902.

[2] Holmes, about this time, exhibits an unprecedented liability to bursts of almost hysterical eloquence. See his description of Violet de Merville and his report of his conversation with her (*Illustrious Client*, pp. 1,102 *sq.*).

"The evidence for Dr. Watson's second marriage[1] is contained in a few brief sentences in *The Veiled Lodger*: 'One forenoon—it was late in 1896—I received a hurried note from Holmes asking for my attendance'; and 'Two days later, when I called upon my friend . . .' That is all."

From this, Mr. Bell proceeds to build up his theory. His arguments are:

(1) Why had Watson left Baker Street? He had not gone away for his health, for he was close at hand when summoned and got round to Baker Street before the new client had finished her story. He was not in practice, for in the following year (February, 1897)[2] he refers to "the degree to which I had lost touch with my profession" (*Missing Three-Quarter*, p. 821). The only conceivable motive for his desertion is marriage.

(2) Holmes often twits Watson with being a "ladies' man," and there is some evidence that, at the time of the Lady Frances Carfax affair,[3] Watson had shared a hansom-cab with a lady and resented being questioned about it.

(3) Apart from *The Veiled Lodger*, we have no record of any case for the year 1896, evidence pointing to a dissolution of partnership in that year.

(4) At the time of *The Sussex Vampire*,[4] Holmes was obliged to explain to Watson that *Matilda Briggs* was the name of a ship and not of a woman, evidence pointing in the same direction.

(5) Without assuming some such temporary dissolution of partnership, we cannot account for the statement that Holmes and Watson were associated for "seventeen years" only (*The Veiled Lodger*).

Let us examine these points.

(1) is the most urgent, and forms, in fact, the foundation of the whole superstructure. Without, at the moment, discussing other possible reasons for Watson's absence, I will say definitely and at once that I believe the date of *The Veiled Lodger* to be wrong and that, in my opinion, this error has caused the whole misunderstanding.

[1] Second, that is, in point of time.

[2] All dates are taken from Mr. Bell's own chronology, as being essential to his theory; that of *The Missing Three-Quarter* is well supported by the text.

[3] Mr. Bell's date (1895) depends upon the theory of the 1896 marriage. See note below.

[4] Mr. Bell's date again depends on the 1896 marriage, but there is collateral evidence to support it. See note below.

156

(2) It is true that Holmes does continually twit Watson about his admiration for the fair sex. This was a time-honoured jest which had begun when Watson fell in love with Mary Morstan, but there is nothing to show that it was anything more than a pleasantry depending for its point upon its absurdity. It is to be classed with Holmes' determination to look upon Watson as "a man of letters."[1] And no doubt Watson laid himself open to the charge, by pretending to an *histoire galante* to which he had no proper claim. We know that Watson was apt to exaggerate his own prowess, and that the smaller his experience, the more he boasted of it. He is always, to himself, the "old campaigner"—whereas his actual experience of military service was limited to a period of about twelve months, of which six, at least, were spent in hospital.[2] So in *The Sign of Four*, written in 1890, he refers to "an experience of women which extends over many nations and three separate continents." Now, Mr. S. C. Roberts, in his *Dr. Watson* (p. 15), has made it fairly clear that these continents were Australia, Asia (India) and Europe. "In all probability," he says, "the period of Watson's Australian residence was before he reached the age of 13."[3] This is not an age at which "experience of women" can be taken in any very man-of-the-world sense—not, at any rate, in the case of a man so normally constituted as Watson. India also, thanks to Mr. Roberts, we know all about. Watson embarked for Bombay in the spring of 1880, joined his regiment in Kandahar, fought in the Battle of Maiwand on July 27th, was wounded and was removed to the Base Hospital at Peshawar. There, when his convalescence had only so far advanced as to enable him to "walk about the wards and bask a little upon the verandah," he was struck down by enteric and "despaired of" for months, being left at last in a weak and emaciated state unsuited for amorous adventure. He was then shipped straight back to London. Thus his "experience of women" was confined, as regards Asia, to such opportunities as he may have found in his few weeks with his regiment at Kandahar, or, as Mr. Roberts suggests, among the staff-nurses at Peshawar.[4]

The European experiences (covering "many nations") are relegated by Mr. Roberts to such conjectural visits as he may have

[1] *Wisteria Lodge*, p. 891.

[2] Roberts, *Dr. Watson*, pp. 12 *sq.*

[3] *Op. cit.*, p. 9. He considers it "conceivable, though not likely," that Watson revisited Australia between 1881 and 1883 (p. 15).

[4] Watson was never in civil practice before 1887–8, so that we cannot count on any unprofessional interest in female patients, unless, indeed, we fall back on the melancholy specimens of humanity he may have encountered in his student days in the hospitals.

paid to Continental gambling resorts at intervals between 1881 and 1883.[1] No wonder that Holmes' eyes twinkled when he chaffed Watson about his Don Juan propensities. Watson was a good soul, but he had his weaknesses, and a tendency to pose as a connoisseur of female charms was one of them.

But there can be no doubt whatever about Watson's pure and single-minded devotion to Mary Morstan. From the moment of meeting her, he was completely bowled over, and his reactions are certainly not those of a hardened womaniser, but of a man who, at the mature age of thirty-five, tumbles unprepared into all the absurdities of calf-love. Men whose "experience of women" extends over continents and nations do not sit babbling in cabs about double-barrelled tiger cubs,[2] nor, if they hold hands with a lady in a garden at night, do they do so in any childlike spirit.[3] No; Mary Morstan was the object of Watson's first serious attachment; his admiring affection breathes in every word he writes about her; their home life was serenely happy until it was cut short by her death; he was deeply and sincerely moved by her loss. So we have always believed; so Holmes himself believed, if we may judge him by his speech and actions; so Watson evidently intended us to believe, and if it was not so, then he was a hypocrite indeed.

Mrs. Watson died some time between 1891 and 1894, and Mr. Bell, noting that in April of 1890[4] Watson is living in Baker Street over a period of at least a fortnight, and that, further, her name is not mentioned in either *The Greek Interpreter* (summer, 1890) or *The Red-Headed League* (October, 1890), concludes that about this time her health began to fail and that she had gone away to a sanatorium. "What more natural," asks Mr. Bell, "than that Watson, in his loneliness and sorrow, should have returned for a while to Baker Street . . . until he had recovered some measure of self-control?"[5]

Mr. Bell then proceeds: "There is an indication that he was not long in regaining it. Watson was always a ladies' man; and even his grief did not prevent him from taking favourable notice of Miss Violet Hunter, in whom 'rather to my disappointment,' as he himself faithfully records, Holmes 'manifested no further interest' once the case was ended. Watson, however, kept himself informed, and may even have maintained a correspondence with her."[6]

This passage shows to what strange lengths a man may be carried in pursuit of a favourite theory. In order to prove that Watson was

[1] *Op. cit.*, p. 15.
[2] *Sign of Four*, p. 162.
[3] *Ibid.*, p. 178.
[4] *The Copper Beeches.*
[5] *Sherlock Holmes and Dr. Watson*, p. 68.
[6] *Loc. cit.*

the kind of man who might have had three wives, Mr. Bell permits himself the heartless and abominable suggestion that, at the very moment when his wife lay stricken with a mortal illness, Watson was endeavouring to get up an intrigue with another woman—for in 1890 a married man did not maintain a correspondence with a young unmarried woman for prunes and prisms.

Let us see what Watson actually says about Miss Violet Hunter. He describes her as being "plainly but neatly dressed, with a bright, quick face, freckled like a plover's egg, and with the brisk manner of a woman who has had her own way to make in the world."[1] This is not exactly a lover-like beginning; Watson's first impressions of Mary Morstan had been very different.[2] When the client takes her leave, Watson observes to Holmes: "At least she seems to be a young lady who is very well able to take care of herself." Self-reliance is the last feminine quality to appeal to a man of Watson's temperament, who invariably "likes 'em clinging."[3] When he arrives at the Copper Beeches with Holmes and Miss Hunter, Watson goes in with Holmes, leaving the lady outside; there is no holding childlike hands in the garden on this occasion. In the dreadful incidents which follow, Watson leaves Miss Hunter to look after herself while he (very properly) concentrates on rendering first aid to the mangled Rucastle and dispatching the butler to break the news to Mrs. Rucastle. Then, at Holmes' suggestion, the two friends together escort the lady home. Watson's last word on Miss Hunter is that "she is now [1892] the head of a private school at Walsall, where I believe that she has met with considerable success."

If Mr. Bell can make a sentimental attachment out of this, he can do anything. Granted, that if there had been such an attachment, Watson would not have said so in so many words, yet some kind of positive evidence is needed with which to construct a theory.

[1] This and the following quotations are from *The Copper Beeches*.

[2] "Her face had neither regularity of feature nor beauty of complexion, but her expression was sweet and amiable, and her large blue eyes were singularly spiritual and sympathetic. . . . I have never looked upon a face which gave a clearer promise of a refined and sensitive nature" (*Sign of Four*, p. 152). "My mind ran upon our late visitor—her smiles, the deep, rich tones of her voice. . . . If she were seventeen at the time of her father's disappearance she must be seven-and-twenty now—a sweet age," etc. (*op. cit.*, p. 158). Later, there is a picture of her, dressed in "some sort of diaphanous material," with the shaded lamplight "playing over her sweet, grave face, and tinting with a dull, metallic sparkle the rich coils of her luxuriant hair" (*op. cit.*, p. 240). A perfect little oleograph of the romantic 'nineties.

[3] "There was in her [Mary Morstan] also the instinct to turn to me for comfort and protection" (*Sign of Four*, p. 178). " 'But would he come?' she asked, with something appealing in her voice and expression. 'I shall be proud and happy,' said I, fervently" (*ibid.*, p. 156).

The "correspondence" probably boils down to the receipt at Baker Street of a prospectus of Miss Hunter's school (Watson was married, and, for all she knew, might have had some use for the document). They may have received accounts of her from persons who knew the school—Watson's "I believe" need imply nothing more intimate.[1]

In fact, if the story is read in an unprejudiced spirit, it is perfectly plain that it was Holmes himself who (to Watson's malicious amusement, no doubt) was suspected of feeling a personal interest in his client, and that Watson was "disappointed" at being deprived of the pleasure of welcoming Holmes to the Benedictine fold. (For it is well known that, like the fox who lost his tail, a married man is commonly eager to persuade his friends into his own situation.) Here are the relevant phrases:

"I could see that Holmes was favourably impressed by the manner and speech of his new client." (Mr. Bell, by annexing the word "favourable," endeavours to delude us into thinking that the impression was made upon Watson; this is disingenuous.) When Miss Hunter has told her story, Holmes says, with a touch of human feeling rare, at that date, in his dealings with women clients,[2] "I confess that it is not the situation which I should like to see a sister of mine apply for," and, not content with that, continues to mutter the same expression at intervals for a fortnight on end, while Watson is idly wondering, in an academic sort of way, whether the lonely woman has fallen into the hands of a philanthropist or a villain. At the conclusion of the interview with Miss Hunter at Winchester, Holmes praises her in words that bespeak a very sincere admiration: "You seem to have acted all through this matter like a brave and sensible girl, Miss Hunter. Do you think that you could perform one more feat? I should not ask it of you if I did not think you a quite exceptional woman." And when she has succeeded in locking up Mrs. Toller in the cellar, he cries with enthusiasm, "You have done well indeed!"[3]

Watson might well imagine that his friend's armour of indifference had been pierced at last, and feel disappointment when nothing

[1] Watson likewise made a "short note" at the end of his "manuscripts" dealing with *The Solitary Cyclist*, giving particulars of the subsequent career of Miss Violet Smith (who married Cyril Morton, the electrical engineer) and of her abductors. No doubt it was usual to keep tabs on clients.

[2] With Miss Morstan, highly as he esteemed her, he was more brusque. "She put her hand to her throat, and a choking sob cut short the sentence. 'The date?' asked Holmes, opening his notebook" (*Sign of Four*, p. 154). This was more characteristic of his early manner with women.

[3] It is noteworthy that Holmes, though he "disliked and distrusted" the female sex as a whole, had no petty, masculine jealousy. He admired self-dependence and initiative and, while extending his chivalrous protection to the Mrs. St. Clairs of this world, reserved his homage for the Violet Hunters and Irene Adlers.

came of so promising a start; but he himself never utters a single word expressive of particular admiration for Violet Hunter, and to pretend that her bright, quick, freckled face could for one moment have displaced the sweet image of Mary Morstan in his heart is a libel upon an honest gentleman. Had not the suggestion been put forward in so peculiarly insidious and misleading a manner, it would scarcely seem necessary to refute it at so much length. It affects the question of the 1896 marriage only as showing from what untrustworthy materials the fable of Watson's amativeness has been fabricated.

The affair of the hansom cab in *Lady Frances Carfax* will not carry very much weight either. The assumption is that Watson was sharing it with a lady because he sat on the left-hand side. But even when the occupants of a hansom are two men, one of them must necessarily sit there. If the date of the adventure could be proved by internal evidence to have been 1895, there might be some significance in the incident; unhappily, Mr. Bell relies on the marriage to prove the date and not vice versa. Nor is Watson's "asperity" on being convicted of cab-sharing necessarily referable to embarrassment about his companion. It is sufficiently accounted for as he himself accounts for it: namely, by Holmes' irritating behaviour in first deducing his Turkish bath from his boots and then (in reply to a courteously-phrased request to explain his reasoning) producing no explanation, but only a fresh illustration of his own powers.[1] It is just as likely as not that Watson had merely given a male fellow bather a lift home from the Turkish baths.

(3) The year 1896 is not the only year for which we have only one published account of a case. For the year 1899, there is not merely no written account, but actually no mention of any case at all; the years 1883, 1884 and 1885 have one apiece (*The Speckled Band, Charles Augustus Milverton* and *The Cardboard Box*); during all these years[2] Watson was admittedly in close association with Holmes.

(4) Mr. Bell's point about the "Matilda Briggs" involves exactly the same sort of subtle misrepresentation as the assertion that Watson took "favourable notice" of Violet Hunter. Holmes was not "obliged," so far as we can see, to explain the identity of "Matilda Briggs" at all, for Watson asked no question and expressed no opinion on the point. The letter from Morrison, Morrison and Dodd "*re* vampires" ends thus:

[1] This was one of Holmes' favourite tricks. He played it on Watson in the prologue to *A Scandal in Bohemia* (1888). Watson then exclaimed that it was "too much!" and that in the Middle Ages Holmes would have been burnt for a wizard. By the time the Carfax case came on, the jest had begun to pall.

[2] Mr. Bell's own dates.

"We have not forgotten your successful action in the case of Matilda Briggs."

Holmes' comment "in a reminiscent voice" is volunteered immediately upon Watson's reading of the letter:

"Matilda Briggs was not the name of a young woman, Watson. It was a ship."[1] The remark was called for, since Messrs. Morrison, Morrison and Dodd's representative had fallen into the solecism (common to-day among journalists) of writing the name of the ship without the definite article. Neither Holmes nor Watson suggests that there was any reason why the latter should ever have heard of the *Matilda Briggs*. But Mr. Bell goes on to say that, since Watson had no knowledge of the episode, it is probably to be ascribed to 1896, the year of Watson's second marriage; and he seems to think that he can somehow use this to prove that the marriage took place. There is a name for this kind of reasoning. It is called *petitio principii*, and it is not the sort of thing one cares to see in any work with pretensions to scholarship. As a matter of fact, there is not the smallest reason for supposing that the episode of the *Matilda Briggs* took place in the year immediately preceding *The Sussex Vampire*;[2] it may belong to the period of Watson's first marriage or to the years before he had ever heard of Sherlock Holmes. Indeed, Holmes' "reminiscent voice" and the solicitors' assurance that they "have not forgotten" it, rather point to some earlier date than the preceding year.

(5) Mr. Bell's fifth point has more reason behind it. It is clear that an interruption of one year did occur at some point in the partnership. It seems as though we had to choose between the blank year 1899 and the year 1896, blank but for the affair of *The Veiled Lodger*.

The time has now come to examine *The Veiled Lodger* more closely with a view to determining this crucial question of date.

The date as we have it is supplied by Watson himself. "It was late in 1896" when he hurried round to Baker Street at an urgent summons from Holmes and found Mrs. Merrilow relating her story about Mrs. Ronder, who had been her lodger for the last seven years. The name "Abbas Parva" is mentioned, and when Mrs. Merrilow has gone, Holmes asks Watson: "Have you no recollection of the Abbas Parva tragedy?" "None, Holmes." "And yet you were with me then." And that the tragedy at Abbas Parva actually took place in the same year in which Mrs. Ronder went to lodge with

[1] *The Sussex Vampire*, p. 1,178.
[2] See note below on the date of this adventure.

Mrs. Merrilow[1] is made clear when Holmes goes on to describe it: "On this particular night, seven years ago."

Now, seven years subtracted from 1896 brings us to 1889, and at once a doubt arises in our minds. In 1889 Watson certainly was "with" Holmes in the sense that they were friends and to some extent still fellow workers. On the other hand, this was a year in which Watson was living at home with his wife, and was particularly busy with his practice, as is shown by his accounts of the three cases belonging to that year. In *The Boscombe Valley Mystery* (June, 1889) Watson receives Holmes' telegram at breakfast and says to his wife: "I really don't know what to say. I have a fairly long list at present." She replies that he has "been looking a little pale lately" (no doubt from overwork) and that "the change" will do him good. In *The Man with the Twisted Lip* (same date), Watson is visiting the opium den in search of one of his own patients and encounters Holmes by accident. It is only the "definiteness" and the "air of mastery" with which Holmes puts his request that lead him to accompany his friend on the adventure. At the time of *The Blue Carbuncle*, Watson was so busy that, as Mr. S. C. Roberts points out,[2] "he did not call upon Holmes to wish him the compliments of the season until the 27th of December, and a case delayed him on that day until nearly half-past six." Watson was, therefore, only in a very limited sense "with" Holmes in 1889, and it would not be surprising if he should altogether fail to recall an incident of which Holmes' own impression was "very superficial, for there was nothing to go by, and none of the parties had engaged (his) services."[3] Yet the cuttings relative to the affair were in the commonplace books, it had worried Holmes at the time, and he says, "it will probably come back to your memory as I talk."[4] In the course of the conversation, it comes out that Watson *was* there at the time and *did* remember it, for when Holmes mentions how young Edmunds of the Berkshire Constabulary had dropped in and smoked a pipe or two over it, Watson identifies him at once as "a thin, yellow-haired man," and Holmes replies, "Exactly. I was sure you would pick up the trail presently."[5]

[1] The "tragedy" must, therefore, have occurred early in the year, for it was six months before Mrs. Ronder was sufficiently recovered to give evidence at the adjourned inquest, let alone go out to look for lodgings. Mrs. Merrilow "reckons" that she had already tried other rooms, but it is evident that the trials can only have been short ones. It is odd that, if "Ronder was a household word," Mrs. Merrilow should not have associated her lodger's name with the accident at the circus some months earlier, but possibly she was one of those people who "keep themselves to themselves" and never read the papers.

[2] *Dr. Watson*, p. 23. [3] *Veiled Lodger*, p. 1,291. [4] *Loc. cit.*

[5] *Ibid.*, p. 1,293. It is not clear whether Edmunds' visit took place at the time of the tragedy or of the inquest six months later. In either case the date would still be 1889. See note above.

Thus the difficulty of assigning the date of the "tragedy" to 1889 links itself on to the difficulty of accounting for Watson's absence from Baker Street in 1896 and raises a certain amount of doubt about the episode.

Now, all doubts and difficulties would vanish from the case immediately if it were possible to suppose that 1896 was a mistake for 1890. No two figures are so easily mistaken for one another as a "6" and a "0," and there is nothing in the story of *The Veiled Lodger* to make 1890 an improbable date *per se* for the adventure. In October of 1890, Watson was living at home, for he "called upon" Holmes on the fourth[1] of that month, and it is probable that "late in the year"[2] he was still at his own address. Seven years subtracted from 1890 gives us 1883 as the date of the Abbas Parva tragedy—a date before Watson's marriage, when he was most certainly "with" Holmes and associated with him in the matter of *The Speckled Band*.

There is, however, one very weighty objection to the year 1890, and that is Watson's categorical statement, made in 1893,[3] that "in the year 1890 there were only three cases of which I retain any record," and these three cases must be *The Copper Beeches*, *The Greek Interpreter* and *The Red-Headed League*.[4] If Watson was literally exact about this, 1890 must be abandoned.

There are, however, certain reasons which might plausibly be advanced to explain why Watson should have deliberately omitted *The Veiled Lodger* from his 1890 records. To begin with, it was not, strictly speaking, a "case" at all. Holmes made no investigations in connection with it, and was only called in by Mrs. Ronder as "a man of judgment" to whom she could "tell her terrible story." In the second place, it was not until 1927 that Watson felt himself at liberty to make the facts public, and then only with a "change of name and place." At the time, he probably expunged the affair from his note-books and, as far as possible, from his memory. Not until more than thirty years later[5] did he think it safe to disinter it from oblivion, and it is exceedingly possible that, in so doing, he intentionally altered the date as well as the other indications.

[1] The text has "9th," but see Bell, p. 70, and my own study on the dates in *The Red-Headed League*, p. 168

[2] November is the likeliest month of 1890. During the winter, Watson did not see Holmes, but only read of his doings in the papers. *Final Problem*.

[3] *The Final Problem*, p. 537.

[4] For all these three cases, Mr. Bell's dates appear to me to be established without possibility of contradiction.

[5] Whether we take 1890 or 1896.

This reasoning may appear a little forced. Are we then thrust back on 1896 as the only possible alternative to 1890? If so, the question would still remain whether some hypothesis less drastic than that of a marriage may not be advanced to explain Watson's absence from Baker Street. The simplest and most obvious solution is that he was staying with friends—very likely with the Percy Phelpses. Phelps had no doubt been married for some time to Miss Harrison, and may easily have taken a house in Town, situated perhaps in the neighbourhood of Lancaster Gate. The house at Woking belonged, of course, to Percy's parents, and it is in any case probable that he would prefer to live in Town during the winter.

But are we, in fact, obliged to choose between 1890 and 1896? Whichever of these dates we select, it is curious that Watson should have waited quite so long as he did before publication. Mrs. Ronder's intention in taking Holmes into her confidence was to set herself right with the world before she died. She considered herself justified in doing so, since Leonardo, the only other person who could have been injured by the truth, was dead. She herself did not commit suicide as she had meant to do, but, according to Mrs. Merrilow, her health was failing fast and she was "wasting away." If it was her death that Watson waited for, when did it occur? To explain the long silence and the extreme precautions taken in writing the story, it would seem as though she could not have died very much before 1927, so that, if the adventure took place in 1896, she must have lived for nearly thirty years afterwards. It is not, of course, impossible. She was married in the first years of her womanhood and was perhaps only about thirty years old when Holmes visited her. Perhaps she died in the early nineteen-twenties, and Watson —who may have received a suggestion from Holmes to this effect —then thought it right to make her story known, with precautions which would baffle idle curiosity, but which could, in the nature of the case, present no obstacle to those who had been concerned in the tragedy at the circus and might have some claim to learn the true facts.

There remains, however, one other possibility—namely, that 1896 is (by error or intentional mystification on Watson's part, probably the former) the date, not of the case, but of the Abbas Parva tragedy itself. Seven years added to that bring the case to the end of 1903, when Watson had left Holmes, and just before the time of Holmes' own retirement from practice.[1] In 1896, Watson

[1] Watson tells us that *The Creeping Man* (September, 1903) was "one of the very last cases handled by Holmes before his retirement," p. 1,244.

would be "with" Holmes in Baker Street,[1] and all the conditions of the problem would be fulfilled. This theory reduces the long gap between the case and its publication, and brings it into line with the other 1902–3 cases, all of which were made public at intervals during the nineteen-twenties.

In that case, nothing remains to be accounted for but the one year's interruption of the partnership, which must now be placed some time between July-August, 1898 (*The Dancing Men*), and May, 1901 (*The Priory School*), and most likely between July–August, 1898, and July, 1900.[2] And this is, indeed, the most probable period for it. It seems almost incredible that, if Watson really was at Baker Street during the whole of those two years, no case of any kind should have presented itself worthy of record. It was during this period (October, 1899) that the War broke out in the Transvaal, and it would be only natural that Watson (that spirited old war-horse) should hear his country's call and hasten to place his services, in some capacity, at the disposal of the Government. Whether he actually went to South Africa or not is uncertain; his health would not stand prolonged strain in arduous conditions. It is, however, quite on the cards that he took up hospital work at home in order to release younger medical men for service abroad during Lord Roberts' campaign. Possibly (if he did marry again in 1902) he made the acquaintance of his future wife at this time—she may have been a hospital nurse—and wedded her at the conclusion of the War. He was once more busily in practice in 1903 (*Mazarin Stone*), so it is evident that, in spite of "the degree to which he had lost touch with his profession," his interest in medicine had been somehow stimulated and a fresh connection secured during the first years of the century.

The foregoing suggestions are put forward somewhat tentatively, not in order to discredit Mr. Bell's careful and exhaustive research work, which is invaluable, but rather as a plea for more evidence before accepting his pronouncement that no other solution is possible. Mr. Bell's emphasis of assertion is understandable; for him the 1896 marriage is *vital*, since he depends upon it for the precise chronology of many cases.[3] But any theory, if sound, must be able to face criticism, particularly a theory so startling in itself and based

[1] Since this theory disposes of any necessity to postulate a marriage in that year.

[2] Mr. Bell's dates for *The Six Napoleons* (July, 1900) and *Thor Bridge* (October, 1900) are partly dependent on the theory of the 1896 marriage, but have nothing inherently improbable about them. During all but one year of this period Watson *must* have been in close association with Holmes, and probably in Baker Street.

[3] e.g. *The Six Napoleons*, *The Conk-Singleton Forgery*, *Thor Bridge*, *The Matilda Briggs*, *The Sussex Vampire*, *Lady Frances Carfax*, *The Coiner*.

upon so slender a foundation. Reluctant as any commentator must be to tamper with the established text, we cannot help asking ourselves: Is it not perhaps less extravagant to suppose a trifling *lapsus calami* on the part of a man like Watson, who in so many instances has been proved guilty of similar inaccuracies, than to drag in a wholly hypothetical marriage, unrecorded, and lasting less than twelve months,[1] with the sole purpose of explaining Watson's temporary absence from Baker Street?

NOTE ON THE DATE OF "THE SUSSEX VAMPIRE"

Mr. Bell's date, November 19th, 1897, for this rests on the theory of the 1896 marriage. But it will be enough for him if we can place it later than 1896. In any case, it cannot have occurred between 1891 and 1894, when Holmes was abroad, and any earlier date than 1891 is quite clearly impossible. Ferguson had played Rugger as three-quarter for Richmond and had encountered Watson on the field. This cannot have happened before 1870, when Watson was eighteen, and may more plausibly be placed a few years later. Watson distinctly states that he had known Ferguson "in his [Ferguson's] prime." Now, the "prime" of a Rugger-player is a comparatively short period, and it is unlikely that Ferguson would be playing for a crack club after the age of twenty-five or so. Even if we allow that he was as much as twenty-five as early as 1870, then, *before* 1891, he would have been forty-five at the outside. But Watson's description of him at the time of *The Sussex Vampire* suggests a man considerably older than this. He is the wreck of a fine athlete, his great frame has fallen, his hair is scanty, his shoulders are bowed. Unless he had "crocked" in an exceptional manner, we should expect him to be between fifty and sixty. By placing the adventure as late as possible—1897—we can contrive to make him as much as fifty-two, thus reaching something more like probability, and attaining Mr. Bell's conclusion by a different route. The later the date the better for our purpose (since he would probably be in reality rather under twenty-five than over in 1870). Since Mr. Bell has excluded all dates *after* 1897 on other grounds, 1897 achieves its place on its own merits. Ferguson had been married at least sixteen years at the time, and probably wedded his first wife when he was about thirty-five.

[1] "Before twelve months had passed, his wife, it appears, was dead, since at the beginning of 1897 we find him back again in the rooms at Baker Street," Bell, p. 94. Watson would seem to have been rather a perilous marriage-partner, and Mr. Bell's theory suggests that it might have been advisable to check up the contents of his poison cupboard!

At the date of this adventure, Lady Frances was "not more than forty," and it seems clear that the Hon. Philip Green was not a great deal older. His father (Admiral Philip Green, later elevated to the peerage) had been made an Admiral before the time of the Crimean War (1854) and was still alive (otherwise the Hon. Philip would have succeeded to the title). The Admiral would scarcely be an Admiral at a very much less age than forty-five, and is not likely to have been much more than eighty-five at the date of the adventure. Adding forty years to 1854, we get 1894. If we take Mr. Bell's date of 1895 as being approximately correct, we get a plausible age, both for the Admiral and his son. It cannot be earlier than 1894, since it is after the Return; it cannot be very much later, since that would tend to make the Admiral and his son rather too old. Without the suggested marriage, however, it is difficult to date it more closely. Our alternative theory, placing the "interruption of partnership" in 1899–1900, would set a limit of 1894–9. The case is not included in Watson's list of cases for that "memorable year, 1895."

THE DATES IN *THE RED-HEADED LEAGUE*

Among the curious chronological problems encountered by the Sherlock Holmes student, one of the most delicate and fascinating is that of the dates in *The Red-Headed League*. Its difficulties have been most ably set forth by Mr. H. W. Bell in his scholarly and comprehensive study, *Sherlock Holmes and Dr. Watson*. This work—the first and only attempt to place *all* the cases in chronological order—must inevitably form the basis of all future Holmes-Watson exegesis, and the following statement of the problem is summarised from its pages:

1. Watson says that Jabez Wilson's visit to Baker Street took place on a Saturday in the autumn of 1890. Later on, the day is fixed, by the notice on the door of the League's premises, as October 9th. But October 9th, 1890, was a Thursday.

2. The advertisement shown to Holmes on this occasion is stated by Watson to have appeared in the *Morning Chronicle* of April 27th, "just two months ago." This is incompatible with all the other dates.

3. Jabez Wilson says that the advertisement appeared "this day eight weeks," which, reckoning back from October 9th, would bring it to Thursday, August 14th.

4. Wilson also says that the League paid him £4 every Saturday for eight weeks, and that this "cost them two-and-thirty pounds." It is hardly conceivable that Wilson should be mistaken about the money he received. But on the last Saturday ("October 9th") the office of the League was closed, and he got no pay. If, therefore, he only worked for eight weeks, he should have received only £28 in all.

Let us now see what we can make of these contradictions. The year 1890 is determined by the original date of publication in the *Strand Magazine* for August, 1891 ("One day in the autumn of last year") and by the notice on the League door ("The Red-Headed League is dissolved, Oct. 9, 1890"). The day of the week on which Wilson visited Holmes is also fixed, not merely by Holmes' own statements ("to-day is Saturday"—"to-day being Saturday rather complicates matters"), but also by the fact that, as Mr. Bell points out, "the choice of Saturday was an essential part of the bank-robbers' plot." The visit to Baker Street, the investigation at Wilson's establishment, and the final capture of the criminals all take place within twenty-four hours (Saturday morning[1] to the early hours of Sunday), so that we are restricted to a Saturday in the autumn of 1890. Since the date "April 27th" is an obvious error, which could not by any stretch of the imagination be called "a day in the autumn," there is no reason to reject the month of October mentioned in the notice. We are therefore obliged to choose between the four Saturdays in October, 1890, which fell on the 4th, 11th, 18th and 25th respectively.

Mr. Bell, thinking that Dr. Watson may have misread his own figure "4" as a "9," selects October 4th. I emphatically agree that this is the correct date, though I differ from Mr. Bell as to the precise way in which the mistake came about. In my opinion, the crucial points of the problem are (*a*) the surprising error "April 27th," and (*b*) the discrepancy about the money, neither of which anomalies is accounted for in Mr. Bell's commentary. In the following notes I shall hope to show exactly how (*a*) occurred, and to prove that (*b*) was no error at all, and thus to establish the date by two independent and mutually supporting lines of reasoning.

[1] Mr. Bell says "early afternoon"; but Wilson's visit, Holmes' fifty minutes of reflection, and the journey to the City all took place before lunch. Wilson probably arrived about eleven o'clock, coming immediately from Pope's Court, which he had reached at 10 a.m.

1. The date October 4th for Wilson's visit to Holmes is *a priori* the most likely, since, as Mr. Bell remarks, Watson is hardly likely to have mistaken any one of the double figures 11, 18, or 25 for the single figure 9.

2. The advertisement in the *Morning Chronicle* directed the applicants to attend at 7 Pope's Court "on Monday." It was evidently on the very Monday specified in the advertisement that Vincent Spaulding showed the paper to Wilson, since they "put the shutters up" and started for Pope's Court immediately.

3. The wording of the advertisement at first sight suggests that it appeared in the previous Saturday's issue, and this suggestion is supported by Wilson's remark that it appeared "this day *eight weeks*." On examination, however, this will not hold water. If the advertisement appeared on the Saturday, why did Spaulding (who lived on the premises) not show it to Wilson at once? Why should he be reading Saturday's paper on Monday morning? The inference is that the advertisement actually appeared on the Monday. The wording may have been due to carelessness; or the advertisement may have been intended to appear on the Saturday and have been crowded out or arrived too late for insertion on that day.

4. This view is strongly supported by Watson's remark that the advertisement appeared "just *two months* ago." This, if accurate, brings us back to Monday, August 4th. Wilson, no doubt, made the common error of reckoning a month as four weeks, whereas Watson was going correctly by the calendar.

5. Duncan Ross asked Wilson if he could "be ready to-morrow," and he accordingly started work the day following the interview, viz. Tuesday, August 5th. On the Saturday immediately succeeding, he was paid £4 "for my week's work." Actually, he had only worked five days, but the salary would, no doubt, be reckoned as from the time of his engagement on the Monday, and, in fact, it is clear from the text that this was so.

6. Wilson thus received in all eight payments of £4, viz. on August 9th, 16th, 23rd and 30th, and September 6th, 13th, 20th and 27th, before the League was dissolved on the morning of the *ninth* Saturday, October 4th; these payments making up the correct total of £32.

7. The only difficulties which now remain are the two incorrect dates given in the text: (*a*) April 27th as the date of the advertisement, and (*b*) October 9th as the date of the dissolution of the League.

(*a*) This is patently absurd, and suggests the error of a not-too-intelligent compositor at work upon a crabbed manuscript. Watson was a doctor, and his writing was therefore probably illegible at the best of times; moreover, he may have written his dates in a contracted form and used, in addition, a J pen in a poor state of repair. The adjoined pair of figures show how easily "Augst 4" might be mistaken, under these conditions, for "April 27." In this way, the very error itself provides independent testimony that August 4th was the actual date of

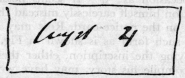

Fig. 1. *Dr. Watson's writing of August 4th* (*Augst. 4*). Note the formation of the "g" (loopless), the ill-shaped "s" and the uncrossed "t"; also the preliminary flourish to the left-hand stroke of the "4."

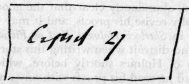

Fig. 2. *Dr. Watson's writing of April 27th.* Note the "pr" without loop and the undotted "i."

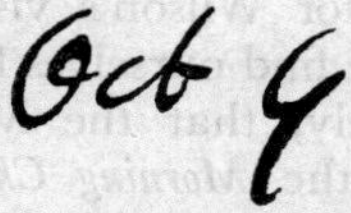

Fig. 3. *Ross's suggested method of writing "October 4th."*

the advertisement, since it is difficult to see how any of the other dates in August (11, 18, 25)[1] could have been mistaken for 27, while the Saturday dates have already been shown to be impossible. But if August 4th was the date of the advertisement, then October 4th must have been the date of Wilson's visit to Holmes; thus the two conclusions are mutually checked and

[1] Any one of these dates would throw the date of the dissolution of the League forward to a double-figure date (October 11th, 18th, 25th), which could not readily be mistaken for a "9." August 25th is open to the further objection that Watson (as is clearly proved by Mr. Bell in an interesting study of *The Sign of Four*) wrote his "5" rather like a "6," without the cross-bar, so that it certainly could not have resembled a "7."

confirmed. No other system of dating accounts *either* for the error "April 27th" *or* for the £32, whereas the present hypothesis accounts reasonably for *both* and is the only one that will do so.

(*b*) If we accept this explanation of "April 27th," we are confronted with a slight difficulty about the second error: "Oct. 9th" for "Oct. 4th" in the notice pinned on the League door. Could Watson write the figure "4" in two such dissimilar ways that it could be misread, on the one occasion as "27" and on another occasion as "9"? It seems possible that, in this instance, Watson himself carelessly misread the handwriting of Duncan Ross on the notice-card. Ross may have written his "4" in some such form as is shown in Fig. 3, and Watson, hurriedly espying the inscription, either then or later, when he came to compile his story, may have written down what he thought he saw, without troubling to verify the date by the calendar.

It is, in any case, abundantly clear that the good doctor did not at any time carefully revise his proofs, and it may be (as Mr. T. S. Blakeney suggests in *Sherlock Holmes: Fact or Fiction?*) that he was especially vague and distrait when writing this story, owing to "the (presumed) death of Holmes shortly before, which evidently hit Watson hard." Had he read his proofs with any attention, he could not possibly have passed the blatant absurdity of "April 27th."[1]

Having now shown that October 4th and August 4th are almost certainly the correct dates for Wilson's visits to Holmes and to Pope's Court respectively, we find ourselves face to face with a very remarkable corollary—namely, that the Monday on which the advertisement appeared in the *Morning Chronicle*, and on which Wilson entered upon his engagement with the Red-Headed League, was August Bank Holiday. This appears, at a first glance, to be most improbable. However, in Holmes' own words, "I ought to know by this time that when a fact appears to be opposed to a long train of deductions it invariably proves to be capable of bearing some other interpretation." And, in fact, when we examine the text in detail, we shall find the strongest corroborative evidence in favour of Bank Holiday.

Let us begin by examining the nature of Jabez Wilson's business

[1] Students may object that Mr. Bell has discovered another occasion (*The Man with the Twisted Lip*) on which Watson read his own "4" as a "9" (Bell, p. 66). But I am inclined to think that here Mr. Bell's second suggestion may be the correct one, and that Watson simply wrote "Ju. 19th," forgetting that this abbreviation might stand either for June or for July.

and the geography of Saxe-Coburg Square (or Coburg Square; there seems to be some doubt as to the precise title, due also, no doubt, to Watson's slip-shod method of jotting down his notes).

The first thing we observe is that Wilson describes his establishment as "a small pawnbroker's business." Now, pawnbroking is usually carried on in connection with a shop of some kind, having a window in which unredeemed pledges are displayed for sale. But there is no mention of either shop or window[1] in connection with Jabez Wilson's pawnbroking, and it is, in fact, quite evident from the text that nothing of the kind existed. On p. 42 Holmes says, "To-day is Saturday," and, after a brief interval of contemplation, turns to Watson with the words, "Put on your hat and come." It is before lunch (p. 43), and therefore all the shops would be open, and certainly were open, for we read on p. 44 of "the immense stream of commerce" and the footpaths "black with the hurrying swarm of pedestrians." This was *after* the visit to Wilson's, so that we may conclude that, if Wilson had had a shop, it should have been open when Holmes and Watson called.

This being so, if Holmes wanted to see the shop-assistant, Vincent Spaulding, in a casual way, without arousing suspicion, what should we expect him to do? Surely to walk straight in and enquire the price of some object in the window. (True, in such a case, the knees of Spaulding's trousers, which Holmes particularly wanted to examine, might have been concealed by the counter, but that difficulty could readily have been overcome by requesting him to bring the object forward into the light of the doorway.) But it seems clear that no such opportunity presented itself. The place was only "announced" by "three gilt balls and a brown board." There was no shop and no window, and Holmes was thus obliged to fall back upon knocking at the door of the house and, on having it opened to him, putting forward an unconvincing enquiry about the way to the Strand, which could have been put with far more propriety at the tobacconist's, the little newspaper shop or the Vegetarian Restaurant.

So far, so good. There was no shop; and we must suppose that the business was a moneylending business and nothing more, unredeemed pledges being presumably disposed of by private arrangement with other second-hand establishments.

Let us now go back to the events of Monday, August 4th, the day on which Wilson and Spaulding answered the advertisement.

[1] It is true that the *Strand Magazine* artist depicts the establishment with a window which appears to be intended for a shop window, but no goods are displayed there. In any case, the evidence of the illustrations is only to be accepted with caution. See Mr. Bell's section on *The Musgrave Ritual* (p. 14).

We are told that, on this occasion, Vincent Spaulding "came down into the office." This, to begin with, supports the conclusion that the business was carried on in an office and not in a shop. Where, then, did Spaulding come "down" from? Certainly not from the shop, if such had existed (for any shop or place of public business would be on the ground floor), unless we suppose the "office" to have been in the basement, which seems scarcely reasonable. If, then, Spaulding came "down" to the office, it was either from a bedroom or living-room on an upper floor, or else from some upper room used for the storage of goods. If he came from a living-room or (*a fortiori*) from a bedroom, then he was idling while his employer worked, and, with so exceptionally diligent a young man, how could that have happened at any other time than a public holiday? (I shall come presently to the nature of Jabez Wilson's work in the office.) If, on the other hand, Spaulding came "down" from a store-room, it is quite possible that he was engaged in putting away and inventorying the goods deposited there—a very suitable occupation for a day on which no regular business was being transacted. Actually, I am inclined to think that he was thus employed,[1] since on p. 35 Wilson states that Spaulding "was very glad to have a holiday," thus suggesting that he would, in the ordinary course of events, have expected to work on that particular day.

Jabez Wilson, in the office, was undoubtedly at work—and upon what? It appears very likely that both he and Spaulding were engaged in storing, valuing and otherwise dealing with pledges deposited on the previous Saturday, and booking up the various transactions completed on that day. Thursday and Friday, as we know, were normally Wilson's busiest days, but Saturday, being pay-day, is the day on which pledges are most frequently redeemed, and pawnbrokers always keep open to a late hour on Saturdays. This means that a good deal of business would be left to be carried over, on Monday, from the day-book to the ledger. In addition, if the Monday was a Bank Holiday, there would also be a number of thriftless people who had actually pawned goods on the Saturday so as to get extra money for their week-end pleasuring. Thus we get a mental picture of Spaulding engaged (or supposed to be engaged) in stocktaking upstairs, while his employer is at work on the books in the office, both taking advantage of the public holiday to set their house in order. It is also quite conceivable that they

[1] At the moment when he came down he was presumed to have been reading the paper, but this need only mean that he had knocked off work for a few minutes. Perhaps it was the regular time for his "elevenses." He would not, of course, get the paper till Wilson had finished with it.

174

would not be averse from doing a little moneylending even on a Bank Holiday morning. What was there to prevent the man who had squandered his wages in the public-house on the Saturday and Sunday from sending his wife round to knock discreetly at the front door on Monday, bringing the Family Bible or the flat-irons in a modest paper parcel?

But now we come to a very important point. When Spaulding had shown Jabez Wilson the paper, he was instructed to "put up the shutters for the day and come right away"; after which Wilson adds, "so we shut the business up." Immediately we ask ourselves: If there was no shop-window, to what shutters does this refer? Why should any shutters be put up at all? If this was an ordinary week-day, with the "girl of fourteen" at home and working about the house, what imaginable reason could there be for putting up the shutters, which (in the absence of a shop), could only be the shutters of the "office" or the dwelling rooms? The point is puzzling, in any case; but the most reasonable answer seems to be this: That it was Bank Holiday, that the girl had been given the day off, and that the shutters were put up on the ground floor, first, to indicate to any caller that there was nobody to answer the door and secondly, as a measure of protection for the money in the office safe, which could not, of course, have been paid in to the Bank either on the Saturday evening, the Sunday or the Bank Holiday morning. In short, the shutters were put up because the house was empty, and the expression "we shut the business up" probably merely means that the work upon the books, etc., was discontinued.

The next passage to be considered is the description of the journey to Pope's Court. It is noticeable that no mention is made anywhere of open shops or of the ordinary City traffic. On the contrary, it is distinctly asserted that "Fleet Street was choked" with red-headed folk, and that Pope's Court was packed "like a coster's orange-barrow." This was in 1890, not in 1934. Even to-day, it would be difficult to find enough permanently unemployed red-headed men in London[1] to "choke" Fleet Street on a working day; in 1890, it would have been impossible. Therefore, if all these men were able to leave their work to answer an advertisement, it must have been because Bank Holiday had already released them. And can we suppose that so serious a dislocation of the traffic as the "choking" of Fleet Street would imply could have been permitted on a working day without police interference? Evidently there was no attempt at the formation of an orderly queue outside the League premises,

[1] The advertisement had only appeared that morning, and there was no time for applicants to come in from the provinces.

since Spaulding was permitted to "push, pull and butt" his way through the crowd; yet we hear of no protest from the occupiers of other premises in Pope's Court. It is evident that no business was being carried on that day in the City; the day was a Monday; therefore the day was Bank Holiday Monday. This unusual date was, doubtless, expressly chosen so that neither Wilson nor Spaulding should have any pressing reason for staying in Saxe-Coburg Square. We must remember that it was important, from the conspirators' point of view, that *both* men should be free to attend at Pope's Court, not merely so as to avoid delay and error in getting hold of the right Jabez Wilson, but also so that Spaulding[1] should be at hand to influence his employer's decision by offering to attend to the business in his absence.

It is, no doubt, odd that Wilson should not have mentioned to Holmes that the interview took place on Bank Holiday; but in his flustered state of mind the fact had probably slipped his memory, nor was there any reason why he should attach special importance to it. It may, perhaps, be a small corroborative point that he waited until the morning following the interview before effecting the purchase of a penny bottle of ink, a quill pen and seven sheets o foolscap. True, he was in low spirits on the Monday evening, but, on the other hand, he had returned from Pope's Court in a state of joyful excitement, and Spaulding might well have suggested the immediate purchase of the stationery, had any shops been open at the time. I do not, however, insist upon this. The most interesting and suggestive point in the narrative is, I submit, the absence of a shop-window combined with the putting-up of the shutters. It will be noticed, by the way, that the shutters were "put up for the day," although (until he saw the crowds) Wilson could have had no reason to suppose that the interview would occupy more than a couple of hours at most. Evidently he had determined to make a day of it in any case; and this adds further weight to the argument for Bank Holiday.

NOTE ON DR. WATSON'S HANDWRITING

The only document we possess, purporting to be in the handwriting of Dr. Watson, is the sketch-map which illustrates the adventure of *The Priory School*.[2] It bears his name in block letters

---

[1] Spaulding would, indeed, miss a few hours of valuable time from his tunnelling work under the empty Bank, but this would be considered of minor importance, compared with the necessity of carrying through the plot to get Wilson out of the way.

[2] *Strand Magazine*, February, 1904.

at the right-hand bottom corner, and presents at first sight an aspect of authenticity. The wording is clear, and the letters, on the whole, neatly formed, though five out of the ten small "i's" are undotted, the small "r" is loopless and tends to degenerate into a single stroke, the capital "E" resembles a "C," and there are variations in the forms of the capitals "R" and "T." In any case, whoever executed this wording would, of course, be taking particular pains to make it legible and suitable for reproduction as a line-block, and it probably is very unlike the same person's hand when writing ordinary MS. or notes.

But is the writing necessarily that of Dr. Watson? In *The Naval Treaty* we find a sketch-plan in exactly the same handwriting, purporting to have been drawn by Percy Phelps. In *The Golden Pince-nez* the identical handwriting again makes its appearance, masquerading this time as that of Stanley Hopkins.

It is possible, of course, that Watson himself re-drew the two last-mentioned sketches for the blockmaker, though, since he evidently had access to Holmes' collection of original documents, (e.g. the letter reproduced in *The Reigate Squires*) there is no obvious reason why he should have done so. It may be urged that at the time of *The Naval Treaty* (1888) he was married and not living in Baker Street; but this does not apply to *The Golden Pince-nez*, which belongs to 1894, the year of Holmes' return.

The probability is that all three of the plans—hurriedly executed on scraps of paper—reached the blockmaker in a crumpled and dirty condition unsuitable for reproduction, and were re-drawn by him from the originals. Or, since the same artist illustrated the whole series of stories, from the *Adventures* to the *Return*, he may have done the re-drawing.

The letter in *The Reigate Squires* is in a different category. The exact reproduction of the original handwritings was essential, and, although we know that it was badly crumpled during Holmes' struggle with Alec Cunningham, it was, of course, carefully ironed out and preserved as an important piece of evidence in the case; the blockmaker had to do his best with it.

It is a very curious thing that the handwriting on the blotting-paper in *The Missing Three-Quarter* should also bear a suspicious resemblance to that of this ubiquitous calligrapher. It is supposed, on this occasion, to be the autograph of Godfrey Staunton, written on a telegraph form with "a broad-pointed quill pen," and blotted with "thin" post-office blotting-paper. For a document produced under these conditions, it is remarkably legible, and the ink has spread very little.

Finally, in the definitive ("Omnibus") edition of 1928, the signature "John H. Watson" has been omitted from the map of the Priory School. This cannot be without significance. Watson doubtless felt its presence to be misleading, and had it excised from the block as a tacit admission that neither sketch nor writing was from his own hand.

ARISTOTLE ON DETECTIVE FICTION[1]

Lecture delivered at Oxford, March 5th, 1935

SOME TWENTY-FIVE YEARS AGO, it was rather the fashion among commentators to deplore that Aristotle should have so much inclined to admire a kind of tragedy that was not, in their opinion, "the best." All this stress laid upon the plot, all this hankering after melodrama and surprise—was it not rather unbecoming—rather inartistic? Psychology for its own sake was just then coming to the fore, and it seemed almost blasphemous to assert that "they do not act in order to portray the characters; they include the characters for the sake of the action." Indeed, we are not yet free from the influence of that school of thought for which the best kind of play or story is that in which nothing particular happens from beginning to end.

Now, to anyone who reads the *Poetics* with an unbiased mind, it is evident that Aristotle was not so much a student of his own literature as a prophet of the future. He criticised the contemporary Greek theatre because it was, at that time, the most readily available, widespread and democratic form of popular entertainment presented for his attention. But what, in his heart of hearts, he desired was a good detective story; and it was not his fault, poor man, that he lived some twenty centuries too early to revel in the Peripeties of *Trent's Last Case* or the Discoveries of *The Hound of the Baskervilles*. He had a stout appetite for the gruesome. "Though the objects themselves may be painful," says he, "we delight to view the most realistic representations of them in art, the forms, for example, of the lowest animals and of dead bodies." The crawling horror of *The Speckled Band* would, we infer, have pleased him no less than *The Corpse in the Car*, *The Corpse in Cold Storage* or *The*

---

[1] The translation of *The Poetics* used throughout this lecture is that of Professor Ingram Bywater, published by the Clarendon Press.

Body in the Silo. Yet he was no thriller fan. "Of simple plots and actions," he rightly observes, "the episodic are the worst. I call a plot episodic when there is neither probability nor necessity in the sequence of the episodes." He would not have approved of a certain recent book which includes among its incidents a machine-gun attack in Park Lane, an aeroplane dropping bombs on Barnes Common,[1] a gas attack by the C.I.D. on a West-End flat and a pitched battle with assorted artillery on a yacht in the Solent. He maintained that dreadful and alarming events produced their best effect when they occurred, "unexpectedly," indeed, but also "in consequence of one another." In one phrase he sums up the whole essence of the detective story proper. Speaking of the dénouement of the work, he says: "It is also possible to discover whether some one has done or not done something." Yes, indeed.

Now, it is well known that a man of transcendent genius, though working under difficulties and with inadequate tools, will do more useful and inspiring work than a man of mediocre intellect with all the resources of the laboratory at his disposal. Thus Aristotle, with no better mysteries for his study than the sordid complications of the Agamemnon family, no more scientific murder-methods than the poisoned arrow of Philoctetes or the somewhat improbable medical properties of Medea's cauldron; above all, with detective heroes so painfully stereotyped and unsympathetic as the inhuman array of gods from the machine, yet contrived to hammer out from these unpromising elements a theory of detective fiction so shrewd, all-embracing and practical that the *Poetics* remains the finest guide to the writing of such fiction that could be put, at this day, into the hands of an aspiring author.

In what, then, does this guidance consist? From the start Aristotle accepts the Detective Story as a worthy subject for serious treatment. "Tragedy," he observes (tragedy being the literary form which the detective story took in his day), "also acquired magnitude"—that is, it became important both in form and substance. "Discarding short stories and a ludicrous diction, it assumed, though only at a late point in its progress, a tone of dignity." I am afraid that "short stories and a ludicrous diction" have characterised some varieties of the *genre* up to a very late point indeed; it is true, however, that there have recently been great efforts at reform. Aristotle then goes on to define tragedy in terms excellently applicable to our subject; "The imitation" (or presentment, or representation—

---

[1] It is perhaps necessary to remind readers that this kind of incident, though it has since become quite commonplace, was unusual at the date (1935) when this paper was first written.

we will not quarrel over the word) "of an action that is serious"—
it will be admitted that murder is an action of a tolerably serious
nature—"and also complete in itself"—that is highly important,
since a detective story that leaves any loose ends is no proper
detective story at all—"with incidents arousing pity and fear,
wherewith to accomplish its catharsis of such emotions."

Too much has already been said and written on the vexed subject
of the catharsis. Is it true, as magistrates sometimes assert, that
little boys go to the bad through reading detective stories? Or is it,
as detective writers prefer to think with Aristotle, that in a nerve-
ridden age the study of crime stories provides a safety valve for the
bloodthirsty passions that might otherwise lead us to murder our
spouses? Of all forms of modern fiction, the detective story alone
makes virtue *ex hypothesi* more interesting than vice, the detective
more beloved than the criminal. But there is a dangerous error
going about—namely that "if . . . detective fiction leads to an
increase in crime, then the greater the literary merit, the greater
will be the corresponding increase in crime."[1] Now, this is simply
not true: few people can have been inspired to murder their uncles
by the literary merits of *Hamlet*. On the contrary, where there is
no beauty there can be no catharsis; an ill-written book, like an
ill-compounded drug, only irritates the system without purging.
Let us then see to it that, if we excite evil passions, it is so done
as to sublimate them at the same time by the contemplation of
emotional or intellectual beauty. Thus far, then, concerning the
catharsis.

Aristotle next discusses Plot and Character. "A detective story,"
we gather, "is impossible without action, but there may be one
without character." A few years ago, the tendency was for all
detective stories to be of the characterless or "draught-board"
variety; to-day, we get many examples exhibiting a rather slender
plot and a good deal of morbid psychology. Aristotle's warning,
however, still holds good:

> "One may string together a series of characteristic speeches of
> the utmost finish as regards diction and thought, and yet fail
> to produce the true dramatic effect; but one will have much
> better success with a story which, however inferior in these
> respects, has a plot."

And again:

> "The first essential, the life and soul, so to speak, of the detective
> story, is the plot, and the characters come second."

[1] Editorial in *The Author*, spring, 1935.

180

As regards the make-up of the plot, Aristotle is again very helpful. He says firmly that it should have a beginning, a middle and an end. Herein the detective story is sharply distinguished from the kind of modern novel which, beginning at the end, rambles backwards and forwards without particular direction and ends on an indeterminate note, and for no ascertainable reason except the publisher's refusal to provide more printing and paper for seven-and-sixpence. The detective story commonly begins with the murder; the middle is occupied with the detection of the crime and the various peripeties or reversals of fortune arising out of this; the end is the discovery and execution of the murderer—than which nothing can very well be more final. Our critic adds that the work should be of a convenient length. If it is too short, he says, our perception of it becomes indistinct. (This is meiosis; he might have said that it will not be perceived at all, since the library subscriber will flatly refuse to take it out, on the ground that "there isn't enough reading in it.") He objects, still more strongly, to the work that is of vast size or "one thousand miles long." "A story or plot," he reminds us, "must be of some length, but of a length to be taken in by the memory." A man *might* write a detective story of the length of *Ulysses*,[1] but, if he did, the reader would not be able to bear all the scattered clues in mind from the first chapter to the last, and the effect of the final discovery would be lost. In practice, a length of from 80,000 to 120,000 words is desirable, if the book is to sell; and this is enough to allow, in Aristotle's general formula, of "the hero's passing by a series of probable or necessary stages from misfortune to happiness or from happiness to misfortune." Later, however, he conveys a very necessary warning: "A writer often stretches out a plot beyond its capabilities, and is thus obliged to twist the sequence of incident." It is unwise to "write-up" a short-story type of plot to novel length, even to fulfil a publisher's contract.

The next section of the *Poetics* gives advice about the unity of the plot. It is not necessary to tell us everything that ever befel the hero. For example, says Aristotle, "in writing about Sherlock Holmes" (I have slightly adapted the instance he gives)—

"the author does not trouble to say where the hero was born, or whether he was educated at Oxford or Cambridge, nor does he enter into details about incidents which—though we know they occurred—are not relevant to the matter in hand, such as the cases of Vamberry the Wine Merchant, the Aluminium

[1] I refer, of course, to Mr. James Joyce's novel; not to Homer's poetical treatment of the subject.

Crutch, Wilson the Notorious Canary-Trainer or Isadora Persano and the Remarkable Worm."

The story, he says—

> "must represent one action, a complete whole, with its several
> incidents so closely connected that the transposal or withdrawal
> of any one of them will disjoin and dislocate the whole."

In other words, "murder your darlings"—or, if you must write a purple passage, take care to include in it some vital clue to the solution, which cannot be omitted or transposed to any other part of the story. Thus, in *Trent's Last Case*, the description of Marlowe's room conveys the necessary clue that he has been a member of the O.U.D.S. and is therefore to be presumed capable of acting a part; the poker-game in *The Canary Murder Case* throws needful light on the murderer's character; the picture of the Shivering Sands in *The Moonstone* prepares us for the discovery of the paint-stained nightgown in that spot; and so forth.

But now comes the important question: What kind of plot are we to choose? And this raises the great central opposition of the Probable and the Possible. It is *possible* that two Negroes should co-exist, so much alike as not only to deceive the eye, but to possess the same Bertillon measurements; that they should both bear the same Christian and surnames, and that they should both be confined in the same prison at the same time: it is possible, since it actually occurred.[1] But if we are to found a plot upon such a series of coincidences it will have an improbable appearance.

It is open to us to contrive stories based upon such incidents in real life, either giving the characters their real names or otherwise calling upon the witness of history. Thus there have been books founded on the Bravo case, the Crippen murder, the Penge tragedy, the case of W. H. Wallace, and so on. When the facts are well known, the reader will accept the events as narrated. But it often turns out that the stories so written appear less convincing than those that are wholly invented; and it is frequently necessary to add inventions to the known facts, in order to make these true events appear probable. "So that," says Aristotle, "one must not aim at a rigid adherence to the traditional stories," particularly as "even the known stories are known only to a few." Thus, even where the possibility cannot be challenged, probability should be studied.

But where both names and incidents are invented, then, "a likely impossibility is always preferable to an unconvincing possibility."

---

[1] The case of the two Will Wests, U.S. Penitentiary, Leavenworth, Kansas, 1903.

It may be impossible that the leaden bullet buried in a man's body should be chemically recovered from his ashes after cremation; but, by skilful use of scientific language, Dr. Austin Freeman persuades us that it is probable, and indeed inevitable. Whereas, when an author seeks to persuade us that a pleasant young Cambridge man of gentle birth is affronted by being asked to take his place in a queue behind a taxi-driver or some such person, the incident, though physically possible, offends by its improbability, being contrary to the English character, whose eternal patience in arranging itself in orderly queues is well known to amount to genius. "The story," says Aristotle, "should never be made up of improbable incidents; there should be nothing of the sort in it." Lest this seem too severe, he suggests as a practical compromise that "if such incidents are unavoidable, they should be kept outside the action." Thus, in the story of *The Gloria Scott*, while the previous history of Old Trevor is not merely improbable, but, according to the dates given, impossible, we do not notice this in reading, because the episode stands outside the action of the plot. Similarly, as regards the characters, the impossible-probable is better than the improbable-possible; for (says Aristotle again) "if a detective such as Conan Doyle described be impossible, the answer is that it is better he should be like that, since the artist ought to improve on his model."

In the matter of scientific detail, Aristotle is all for accuracy. If, he says in effect, you cannot attain your artistic end without some impossible device (such as the instantaneously fatal and undiscoverable poison), then, at a pinch, you may be justified in using it:

"If, however, the poetic end might have been as well or better attained without sacrifice of technical correctness in such matters, the impossibility is not to be justified, since the description should be, if it can, entirely free from error."

Thus, in Mr. John Rhode's *The Corpse in the Car*, the emission of an undetectable gas from the wireless set is more justifiable, because scientifically feasible, than the same author's release of hydrocyanic acid gas from a rubber hot-water bottle in *Poison for One*, a method which (I am told) would not be effective in practice.

Concerning the three necessary parts of a detective plot—peripety, or reversal of fortune, discovery, and suffering—Aristotle has many very just observations. On suffering, we need not dwell long. Aristotle defines it as "action of a destructive or painful nature, such as murders, tortures, woundings and the like." These are common enough in the detective story, and the only remark to be made is that they ought always to help on the action in some way, and not be put in merely to harrow the feelings, still less to distract attention from a weakness in the plot.

A reversal of fortune may happen to all or any of the characters: the victim—who is frequently a man of vast wealth—may be reduced to the status of a mere dead body; or may, again, turn out not to be dead after all, as we had supposed. The wrongly suspected person, after undergoing great misfortunes, may be saved from the condemned cell and restored to the arms of his betrothed. The detective, after several errors of reasoning, may hit upon the right solution. Such peripeties keep the story moving and arouse alternating emotions of terror, compassion and so forth in the reader. These events are best brought about, not fortuitously, but by some *hamartia* or defect in the sufferer. The defect may be of various kinds. The victim may suffer on account of his unamiable character, or through the error of marrying a wicked person, or through foolishly engaging in dubious finance, or through the mistake of possessing too much money. The innocent suspect may have been fool enough to quarrel with the victim, or to bring suspicion on himself by suppressing evidence with intent to shield somebody. The detective suffers his worries and difficulties through some failure of observation or logic. All these kinds of defect are fruitful in the production of peripety.

Aristotle mentions many varieties of the discovery which forms the dénouement. This is usually the discovery, either of the identity of the murderer, or of the means by which the crime was committed.

(1) The worst kind are *discoveries made by the author himself*. These are, indeed, so inartistic as to be scarcely permissible in the true detective story: they belong to the thriller. It is, however, possible, where the villain's identity is known, to make an agreeable story by showing the moves and counter-moves made successively by villain and detective (Wilkie Collins in *No Name*; Austin Freeman in *The Singing Bone*).

(2) The *discovery by material signs and tokens* is very common: in *The Trial of Mary Dugan* the discovery that a person is left-handed leads to his conviction; in *The Eye of Osiris* the identity of the (supposed) Egyptian mummy with the missing corpse is proved by the discovery of identical tooth-stoppings and a Potts fracture in both.

(3) *Discovery through memory* is also used: thus, in *Unnatural Death*, the murder-method—the production of an air-lock in a main artery—is discovered to the detective by his memory of a similar air-lock in the petrol-feed of a motor-cycle.

(4) *Discovery through reasoning* is perhaps most common of all: the murderer was in the house at such a time, he is an electrician, he is tall and smokes Sobranie cigarettes; only X corresponds to all these indications, therefore X is the murderer.

(5) Aristotle's fifth type of discovery is particularly interesting. He calls it *discovery through bad reasoning by the other party*. The instance he adduces is obscure, the text being apparently mutilated and referring to a play unknown. But I think he really means to describe the *discovery by bluff*. Thus, the detective shows the suspect a weapon saying, "If you are not the murderer, how do you come to be in possession of this weapon?" The suspect replies: "But that is not the weapon with which the crime was committed." "Indeed?" says the detective, "*and how do you know?*"

This brings us to the very remarkable passage in which Aristotle, by one of those blinding flashes of insight which display to the critic of genius the very core and centre of the writer's problem, puts the whole craft of the detective writer into one master-word: *Paralogismos*. That word should be written up in letters of gold on the walls of every mystery-monger's study—at once the guiding star by which he sets his compass and the jack-o'-lantern by which he leads his readers into the bog; paralogism—the art of the false syllogism—for which Aristotle himself has a blunter and more candid phrase. Let us examine the whole paragraph, for it is of the utmost importance.

"Homer," says he—if he had lived in our own day he might have chosen some more apposite example, such as Father Knox or Mrs. Agatha Christie, but, thinking no doubt of *Odysseus*, he says Homer—"Homer more than any other has taught the rest of us the art of *framing lies in the right way*.[1] I mean the use of paralogism. Whenever, if A is or happens, a consequent, B is or happens, men's notion is that, if the B is, the A also is—but that is a false conclusion. Accordingly, if A is untrue, but there is something else, B, that on the assumption of its truth follows as its consequent, then the right thing is to present us[2] with the B. Just because we know the truth of the consequent, we are in our own minds led on to the erroneous inference of the truth of the antecedent."

There you are, then; there is your recipe for detective fiction: the art of framing lies. From beginning to end of your book, it is your whole aim and object to lead the reader up the garden; to

---

[1] ψευδῆ λέγειν ὡς δεῖ.

[2] προσθεῖναι [δεῖ] Bywater: "to add on the B." Wharton: "it is natural to pre-suppose the first" (i.e. the A). Whichever translation is preferred, the general sense is clear: if the author provides the consequent, the reader may be trusted to infer (falsely) the antecedent for himself.

induce him to believe a lie. To believe the real murderer to be innocent, to believe some harmless person to be guilty; to believe the detective to be right where he is wrong and mistaken where he is right; to believe the false alibi to be sound, the present absent, the dead alive and the living dead; to believe, in short, anything and everything but the truth.

The art of framing lies—but mark! of framing lies in *the right way* (ὡς δεῖ). There is the crux. Any fool can tell a lie, and any fool can believe it; but the right method is to tell the *truth* in such a way that the *intelligent* reader is seduced into telling the lie for himself. That the writer himself should tell a flat lie is contrary to all the canons of detective art. Is it not amazing that Aristotle, twenty centuries ahead of his time, should thus have struck out at a blow the great modern theory of fair-play to the reader? A is falsehood; B is truth. The writer must not give us A upon his own authority, for what he says upon his own authority we must be able to believe. But he may tell us B—which *is* true—and leave us to draw the false conclusion that A is true also.

Thus, at the opening of a story, the servant Jones is heard to say to his master, Lord Smith, "Very good, my lord. I will attend to the matter at once." The inference is that, if Jones was speaking to Smith, Smith was also speaking to Jones; and that, therefore, Smith was alive and present at the time. But that is a false conclusion; the author has made no such assertion. Lord Smith may be absent; he may be already dead; Jones may have been addressing the empty air, or some other person. Nor can we draw any safe conclusion about the attitude of Jones. If Jones is indeed present in the flesh, and not represented merely by his voice in the form of a gramophone record or similar device (as may well be the case), then he may be addressing some other party in the belief that he is addressing Smith; he may have murdered Smith and be establishing his own alibi; or Smith may be the murderer and Jones his accomplice engaged in establishing an alibi for Smith. Nor, on the other hand, is it safe to conclude (as some experienced readers will) that *because* Smith is not heard to reply he is *not* therefore present. For this may very well be the Double Bluff, in which the reader's own cunning is exploited to his downfall. The reader may argue thus:

Jones spoke to Smith, but Smith did not speak to Jones.

Many authors employ this device so as to establish the false inference that Smith was alive and present.

I therefore conclude that Smith is absent or dead.

But this syllogism is as false as the other. "Many authors" is not the same thing as "all authors at all times." It does not exclude the possibility that an author may at some time imply the truth in such a manner that it looks like a lie.

A fine example of this double bluff is found in Father Knox's *The Viaduct Murder*. A man is found dead, with his face beaten into unrecognisable pulp. Circumstantial evidence suggests that the dead man was X. The detectives and the reader are invited to reason after the following manner:

> The dead man is thought to be X.
> But he is unrecognisable.
> Therefore he is not X.
> Therefore he is someone else, namely Y.
> And, since X is undoubtedly missing, X is probably the murderer.

But the disfigured corpse turns out to be X after all; so that all the ingenious conclusions founded upon the false premise are false also.

Another variety of the paralogism is found in a syllogism built upon the following lines:

> A is the obvious suspect.
> But in a detective story, the obvious suspect is always innocent.
> Therefore A is innocent.

But for the middle term of this proposition there is no warrant whatever. The statement is neither universally true nor logically necessary. The obvious suspect is innocent more frequently than not, but nothing compels the author to make him so.

Nothing in a detective story need be held to be true unless the author has vouched for it *in his own person*. Thus, if the author says—

> Jones came home at 10 o'clock

then we are entitled to assume that Jones did indeed come home at that time and no other. But if the author says—

> The grandfather clock was striking ten when Jones reached home

then we can feel no certainty as to the time of Jones's arrival, for nothing compels us to accept the testimony of the clock. Nor need we believe the testimony of any character in the story, unless the author himself vouches for that character's integrity.

Thus, let us suppose that the butler gives evidence that Jones returned at ten. The butler's employer asserts that he has always found the butler scrupulously truthful. Are we therefore to believe the butler? By no means; for the employer may be deceived, or may have deceived the butler, or may be backing up the butler's testimony for reasons of his own.

But if the author himself says: "No one could possibly doubt that the butler was speaking the truth"—then, I think, we must believe that the butler is a truthful witness, for the author himself has stated, on his own authority, that doubt was impossible.

Remember, however, that the person telling the story is not necessarily the author. Thus, in *The Murder of Roger Ackroyd*, the story is told by the detective's *fidus Achates* or (to use the modern term) his Watson. Arguing from the particular to the general, we may be seduced into concluding that, because the original Dr. Watson was a good man, all Watsons are good in virtue of their Watsonity. But this is false reasoning, for moral worth and Watsonity are by no means inseparable. Thus, the first man sinned and laid the blame upon his wife; but it would be an error to conclude that all men, when they sin, blame their wives—though in fact they frequently do. There may be found rare men who, having wives, yet refrain from blaming them and are none the less men on that account. So, despite the existence of a first innocent Watson, we may yet admit the possibility of a guilty one; nor, when the Watson in *Roger Ackroyd* turns out to be the murderer, has the reader any right to feel aggrieved against the author—for she has vouched only for the man's Watsonity and not for his moral worth.

This brings us, however, to the consideration of the characters, concerning whom Aristotle takes a very twentieth-century point of view. He says that they must be *good*. This, I suppose, must be taken relatively, to mean that they should, even the meanest and wickedest of them, be not merely monsters and caricatures, like the personages in a low farce, but endued with some sort of human dignity, so that we are enabled to take them seriously. They must also be *appropriate*: a female, he says, must not be represented as clever. This is a delicate point—would he, or would he not, have approved of Miss Gladys Mitchell's diabolically clever Mrs. Bradley? We may take it, however, that the cleverness should only be such as is appropriate to the sex and circumstances of the character—it would be inappropriate that the elderly maiden sister of a country parson should carry out or detect a murder by means of an intricate and clever method knowable only to advanced chemical experts; and so with the other characters. Thirdly, the characters must be *like the reality* (τό ὅμοιον). Scholars differ about what Aristotle means by this word. Some think it means, "conformable to tradition": that the villain should be easily recognisable as villainous by his green eyes, his moustache and his manner of ejaculating "Ha!" and the detective by his eccentricities, his pipe and his dressing-gown, after the more ancient models. But I do not agree with them, and believe that the word means, as we say to-day, "realistic," i.e. with some moderate approximation in speech and behaviour to such men and women as we see about us. For elsewhere, Aristotle takes the modern, realistic view, as when he says, for instance, that the plot ought not to turn on the detection and punishment of a hope-lessly bad man who is villainous in all directions at once—forger, murderer, adulterer, thief—like the bad baron in an Adelphi melo-drama; but rather on that of an intermediate kind of person—a decent man with a bad kink in him—which is the kind of villain most approved by the best modern writers in this kind. For the more the villain resembles an ordinary man, the more shall we feel pity and horror at his crime and the greater will be our surprise at his detection. So, too, as regards the innocent suspects and the police; in treating all such characters, a certain resemblance to real life is on the whole to be desired. Lastly, and most important and difficult of all, the characters must be *consistent* from first to last. Even though at the end we are to feel surprise on discovering the identity of the criminal, we ought not to feel incredulity; we should rather be able to say to ourselves: "Yes, I can see *now* that from the beginning this man had it in him to commit murder, had I only had the wits to interpret the indications furnished by the author." Thus, the villainy of the apparently amiable father in *The Copper Beeches* is betrayed by his participation in his offspring's cruel enjoyment in the slaughter of flies, and the character is seen to be consistent. Inconsistency in the characters destroys the prob-ability of the action, and, indeed, amounts to a breach of the rule of fair play, since we are entitled to believe that a character remains the same person from beginning to end of the story and *nemo repente fuit turpissimus*.

This discourse is already too long. Let me remind myself of Aristotle's own warning: "There are many writers who, after a good complication, fail to bring off the dénouement." This is pain-fully true of detective stories; it has also some application to lectures and speeches upon whatever occasion. But indeed, everything that Aristotle says about writing and composition is pregnant with a fundamental truth, an inner rightness, that makes it applicable to all forms of literary art, from the most trivial to the most exalted. He had, as we say, the root of the matter in him; and any writer who tries to make a detective story a work of art at all will do well if he writes it in such a way that Aristotle could have enjoyed and approved it.